WANDERLUST

WANDERLUST

Real-life Tales *of*
Adventure *and* Romance

Edited by
DON GEORGE

Foreword by Pico Iyer

MACMILLAN

First published 2000 by Villard Books,
a division of Random House, Inc., New York

This edition published 2001 by Macmillan
an imprint of Macmillan Publishers Ltd
25 Eccleston Place, London SW1W 9NF
Basingstoke and Oxford
Associated companies throughout the world
www.macmillan.com

ISBN 0333 90502 4

1 3 5 7 9 8 6 4 2

A CIP catalogue record for this book is available from
the British Library.

Printed and bound in Great Britain by
Mackays of Chatham plc, Chatham, Kent

To Kuniko, Jenny, and Jeremy,

for enriching my journey beyond words,

and to Mom and Dad,

for starting me on the right path

foreword

WHY WE TRAVEL

Pico Iyer

> "Travel is like love: It cracks you open, and so pushes you over all the walls and low horizons that habits and defensiveness set up."

The first time I ever met Don George (then the travel editor for a San Francisco newspaper, though "Wanderlust" was already his motto and his destination), we found ourselves talking just like that, and talking and talking and talking, about the ways in which love quickens a sense of vulnerability and so admits us to states of mind, or areas of knowledge, that we didn't know we had (to that extent travel always moves invisibly). Don in Greece and Paris, I in Thailand and Cuba, and both of us most poignantly and heart-shakingly in Japan, had come to relish the sensation of being spellbound outsiders, wide open to all the beauties of a place, and in a state of excitement for which the only words we could find were those associated with romance and passion. To travel is to trust again, and to believe anew in many of the deeper qualities that get mislaid on the office desk.

As the years went on, Don and I found ourselves crossing paths in all kinds of unlikely places, from Marin County, California, to Melbourne, Australia, from a waiting room in Los Angeles International Airport to a dining room beside the swan-filled gardens of the Bel Air Hotel. And whenever we did, our conversation (with a life of its own, it seemed) would pull us back to what really sent us: the trips that made the soul fly. All the journeys we most deeply cherished and remembered were the ones that threw into question—or rotation—our notions of home and abroad, and reminded us that home is fundamentally something portable that we carry around inside us (and find when we feel an affinity).

"Wanderlust" is in that respect a misnomer: The "lust" part has more to do with surrender than with conquest, and is closer to what I would call gusto; and the "wander" has little to do with crossing borders and getting stamps in one's passport, and everything to do with stretching the boundaries of one's perspective and being drawn constantly to challenge. The person susceptible to "wanderlust" is not so much addicted to movement as committed to transformation.

One day I decided to try to summarize some of the conversations Don and I had had, and to formulate why exactly it is that some of us are moved to travel. The essay that follows is, therefore, like all our conversations, both a collaboration and an exploration.

Nara, Japan
February 2000

We travel, initially, to lose ourselves; and we travel, next, to find ourselves. We travel to open our hearts and eyes and learn more about the world than our newspapers will accommodate. We travel to bring what little we can, in our ignorance and knowledge, to those parts of the globe whose riches are differently dispersed. And we travel, in essence, to become young fools again—to slow time down and be taken in, and fall in love once more. The beauty of this whole process was best described, perhaps, before people even took to frequent flying, by George Santayana in his lapidary essay "The Philosophy of Travel." We "need sometimes," the Harvard philosopher wrote, "to escape into open solitudes, into aimlessness, into the moral holiday of running some pure hazard, in order to sharpen the edge of life, to taste hardship, and to be compelled to work desperately for a moment at no matter what."

I like that stress on work, since never more than on the road are we shown how proportional our blessings are to the difficulty that precedes them; and I like the stress on a holiday that's "moral," since we fall into our ethical habits as easily as into our beds at night. Few of us ever forget the connection between "travel" and "travail," and I know that I travel in large part in search of hardship—both my own, which I want to feel, and others', which I need to see. Travel in that sense guides us toward a better balance of wisdom and compassion—of seeing the world clearly, and yet feeling it truly. For seeing without feeling can obviously be uncaring; while feeling without seeing can be blind.

Yet for me the first great joy of traveling is simply the luxury of leaving all my beliefs and certainties at home, and seeing everything I thought I knew in a different light, and from a crooked angle. In that regard, even a Kentucky Fried Chicken outlet (in Beijing) or a scratchy revival showing of *Wild Orchid* (on the Champs-Elysées) can be both novelty and revelation: In China, after all, people will pay a whole week's wages to eat with Colonel Sanders, and in Paris, Mickey Rourke is regarded as the greatest actor since Jerry Lewis. If a Mongolian restaurant seems exotic to us in Evanston, Illinois, it only follows that a McDonald's would seem equally exotic in Ulan Bator—or, at least, equally far from everything expected.

Though it's fashionable nowadays to draw a distinction between the "tourist" and the "traveler," perhaps the real distinction lies between those who leave their assumptions at home, and those who don't. Among those who don't, a tourist is just someone who complains, "Nothing here is the way it is at home," while a traveler is one who grumbles, "Everything here is the same as it is in Cairo"—or Cuzco or Kathmandu. It's all very much the same.

But for the rest of us, the sovereign freedom of traveling comes from the fact that it whirls you around and turns you upside down, and stands everything you took for granted on its head. If a diploma can famously be a passport (to a journey through hard realism), a passport can be a diploma (for a crash course in cultural relativism). And the first lesson we learn on the road, whether we like it or not, is how provisional and provincial are the things we imagine to be universal. When you go to North Korea, for example, you really do feel as if you've landed on a different planet—and the North Koreans doubtless feel that they're being visited by an extraterrestrial, too (or else they simply assume that, like them, you receive orders every morning from the Central Committee on what clothes to wear and what route to use when walking to work, and that, like them, you have loudspeakers in your bedroom broadcasting propaganda every morning at dawn, and that, like them, you have your radios fixed so as to receive only a single channel).

We travel, then, in part just to shake up our complacencies by seeing all the moral and political urgencies, the life-and-death dilemmas, that we seldom have to face at home. And we travel to fill in the gaps left by tomorrow's headlines: When you drive down the streets of Port-au-Prince, for example, where there is almost no paving and women relieve themselves next to mountains of trash, your notions of the Internet and a "one world order" are usefully revised. Travel is the best way we have of rescuing the humanity of places, and saving them from abstraction and ideology.

In the process, we are saved from abstraction ourselves, and come to see how much we can bring to the places we visit, and how much we can become carrier pigeons—an anti–Federal Express, if you like—in transporting back and forth what every culture needs. I find that I always take Michael Jordan posters to Kyoto, and bring woven ikebana baskets back to California; I invariably travel to Cuba with a suitcase piled high with bottles of Tylenol and bars of soap, and come back with one piled high with salsa tapes, and hopes, and letters to long-lost brothers.

But, more significantly, we carry values and beliefs and news to the places we go, and in many parts of the world, we become walking video screens and living newspapers, the only channels that can take people out of the censored limits of their homelands. In a closed or impoverished place, like Pagan or Lhasa or Havana, we are the eyes and ears of the people we meet, their only contact with the world outside, and very often the closest—quite literally—they will ever come to Michael Jackson or Bill Clinton. Not the least of the challenges of travel, therefore, is learning how to import—and export—dreams with tenderness.

By now all of us have heard (too often) the old Proust line about how the real voyage of discovery consists not in seeing new places but in seeing with new eyes. Yet one of the subtler beauties of travel is that it enables you to bring new eyes to the people you encounter. Thus even as holidays help you appreciate your own home more—not least by enabling you to see it through a distant admirer's eyes—they help you bring newly appreciative—distant—eyes to the places you visit. You can teach them what they have to celebrate as much as you celebrate what they have to teach. This, I think, is how tourism, which so obviously destroys cultures, can also resuscitate or revive them, how it has created new "traditional" dances in Bali and caused craftsmen in India to pay new attention to their works. If the first thing we can bring the Cubans is a real and balanced sense of what contemporary America is like, the second—and perhaps more important—thing we can bring them is a fresh and renewed sense of how special are the warmth and beauty of their country, for those who can compare it with other places around the globe.

So travel spins us round in two ways at once: It shows us the sights and values and issues that we might ordinarily ignore; but it also, and more deeply, shows us all the parts of ourselves that might otherwise grow rusty. For in traveling to a truly foreign place, we inevitably travel to moods and states of mind and hidden inward passages that we'd otherwise seldom have cause to visit.

On the most basic level, though I'm a teetotaler who usually goes to bed at nine P.M., when I'm in Thailand I stay up till dawn in the local bars; and in Tibet, though I'm not a real Buddhist, I spend days on end in temples, listening to the chants of sutras. I go to Iceland to visit the lunar spaces within me, and, in the uncanny quietude and emptiness of that vast and treeless world, to tap parts of myself generally obscured by chatter and routine.

We travel, then, in search of both self and anonymity—and, of course, in finding the one we apprehend the other. Abroad, we are wonderfully free of caste and job and standing; we are, as William Hazlitt puts it, just the "gentleman in the parlour," and people cannot put a name or tag to us. And precisely because we are clarified in this way, and freed of inessential labels, we have the opportunity to come into contact with more essential parts of ourselves (which may begin to explain why we may feel most alive when far from home).

Abroad is the place where we stay up late, follow impulse, and find ourselves as wide open as when we are in love. We live without a past or future, for a moment at least, and are ourselves up for grabs and open to interpretation. We may even become mysterious—to others, at first, and sometimes to ourselves—and, as no less a dignitary than Oliver Cromwell once noted, "A man never goes so far as when he doesn't know where he is going."

There are, of course, great dangers in this, as in every kind of freedom, but the great promise of it is that, traveling, we are born again, able to return at moments to a younger and more open self. Traveling is a way to reverse time, to a small extent, and make a day last a year—or at least forty-five hours—and traveling is an easy way of surrounding ourselves, as in childhood, with what we cannot understand. Language facilitates this cracking open; when we go to France, we often migrate to French, and to the more childlike self, simple and polite, that speaking a foreign language educes. Even when I'm not speaking pidgin English in Hanoi, I'm simplified in a positive way, concerned not with expressing myself, but simply with making sense.

So travel, for many of us, is a quest for not just the unknown, but the unknowing; I, at least, travel in search of an innocent eye that can return me to a more innocent self. I tend to believe more abroad than I do at home (which, though treacherous again, can at least help me to extend my vision); I tend to be more easily excited abroad, and even kinder. And since no one I meet can place me— no one can fix me in my résumé—I can remake myself for better, as well as, of course, for worse. If travel is notoriously a cradle for false identities, it can also, at its best, be a crucible for truer ones. In this way, travel can be a kind of monasticism on the move: On the road, we often live more simply (even when staying in a luxury hotel), with no more possessions than we can carry, surrendering ourselves to chance.

This is what Camus meant when he said that "what gives value to travel is fear"—disruption (or emancipation) from circumstance, and from all the habits behind which we hide. That is why many of us travel not in search of answers, but in search of better questions. I, like many people, tend to ask questions of the places I visit; I relish most the ones that ask the most searching questions in return. In Paraguay, for example, where one car in every two is stolen, and two-thirds of the goods on sale are smuggled, I have to rethink my every Californian assumption. And in Thailand, where many young women give up their bodies in order to protect their families—to become better Buddhists—I have to question my own too-ready judgments. "The ideal travel book," Christopher Isherwood once said, "should be perhaps a little like a crime story in which you're in search of something." And it's the best kind of something, I would add, if it's one that you can never quite find.

I remember how, after my first trips to Southeast Asia, more than a decade ago, I would come back to my apartment in New York, and lie in my bed, kept up by something more than jet lag, playing back, in my memory, over and over, all that I had experienced, and paging wistfully through my photographs and reading and rereading my diaries, as if to extract some mystery from them.

Anyone witnessing this strange scene would have drawn the right conclusion: I was in love.

For if every true love affair can feel like a journey to a foreign country, where you can't quite speak the language, and you don't know where you're going, and you're pulled ever deeper into the inviting darkness, every trip to a foreign country can be a love affair, where you're left puzzling over who you are and whom you've fallen in love with. All the great travel books are love stories, by some reckoning—from the *Odyssey* and the *Aeneid* to the *Divine Comedy* and the New Testament—and all good trips are, like love, about being carried out of yourself and deposited in the midst of terror and wonder.

This metaphor also brings home to us that all travel is a two-way transaction, as we too easily forget; if warfare is one model of the meeting of nations, romance is another. For what we all too often ignore when we go abroad is that we are objects of scrutiny as much as the people we scrutinize, and we are being consumed by the cultures we consume, as much on the road as when we are at home. At the very least, we are objects of speculation (and even desire) who can seem as exotic to the people around us as they do to us. We are the comic props in Japanese home movies, the oddities in Malian anecdotes, and the fall guys in Chinese jokes; we are the moving postcards or bizarre *objets trouvés* that villagers in Peru will later tell their friends about. If travel is about the meeting of realities, it is no less about the mating of illusions: You give me my dreamed-of vision of Tibet, and I'll give you your wished-for California. In truth, many of us, even (or especially) the ones who are fleeing America abroad, will be taken, willy-nilly, as symbols of the American Dream.

That, in fact, is perhaps the most central and most wrenching of the questions travel proposes to us: how to respond to the dream that people tender to you. Do you encourage their notions of a Land of Milk and Honey across the horizon, even if it is the same land you've abandoned? Or do you try to dampen their enthusiasm for a place that exists only in the mind? To quicken their dreams may, after all, be to matchmake them with an illusion; yet to dash them may be to strip them of the one possession that sustains them in adversity.

That whole complex interaction—not unlike the dilemmas we face with those we love (how do we balance truthfulness and tact?)—is partly why so many of the great travel writers, by nature, are enthusiasts: not just Pierre Loti, who famously, infamously, fell in love wherever he alighted (an archetypal sailor leaving offspring in the form of Madame Butterfly tales), but also Henry Miller, D. H. Lawrence, and Graham Greene, all of whom bore out the hidden truth that we are optimists abroad as readily as pessimists at home. None of them was by any means blind to the deficiencies of the places around them, but all, having chosen to go there, chose to find something to admire. All believed in "being moved" as one of the points of taking trips, and in "being transported" by private as well as public means; all saw that "ecstasy" ("ex-stasis") tells us that our highest moments come when we're not stationary, and that epiphany can follow movement as much as it precipitates it. I remember once asking the great travel writer Norman Lewis if he'd ever be interested in writing on apartheid South Africa. He looked at me astonished. "To write well about a thing," he said, "I've got to like it!"

At the same time, as all this is intrinsic to travel, from Ovid to O'Rourke, travel itself is changing as the world does, and with it changes the mandate of the travel writer. It's not enough to go to the ends of the earth these days (not least because the ends of the earth are often coming to you); and where a writer like Jan Morris could, a few years ago, achieve something miraculous simply by voyaging to all the great cities of the globe, now anyone with a Visa card can do that. So where Morris, in effect, was chronicling the last days of the Empire, a younger travel writer is in a better position to chart the first days of a new Empire, postnational, global, mobile, and yet as diligent as the Raj in transporting its props and its values around the world.

In the mid-nineteenth century, the British famously sent the Bible and Shakespeare and cricket around the world; now a more international empire is sending Madonna and the Simpsons and Brad Pitt. And the way in which each culture takes in this pool of references tells you as much about it as its indigenous products might. Madonna in an Islamic country, after all, sounds radically different from Madonna in a Confucian one, and neither begins to mean the same as Madonna on East Fourteenth Street in New York City. When you go to a McDonald's outlet in Kyoto, you will find Teriyaki McBurgers and Bacon Potato Pies. The placemats offer maps of the great temples of the city, and the posters all around broadcast the wonders of San Francisco. And—most crucial of all—the young people eating their Big Macs, with baseball caps worn backwards and their tight 501 jeans, are still utterly and inalienably Japanese in the way they move, they nod, they sip their oolong teas; they are never to be mistaken for the patrons of a McDonald's outlet in Rio, Morocco, or Managua. These days a whole new realm of exotica arises out of the way one culture colors and appropriates the products of another.

The other factor complicating and exciting all of this is people, who are, more and more, themselves as many-tongued and mongrel as cities like Sydney and Toronto and Hong Kong. I am an increasingly typical specimen, if only because I was born, the son of Indian parents, in England, moved to America at seven, and cannot really call myself an Indian, an American, or an Englishman. I was, in short, a traveler at birth, for whom even a visit to the candy store was a trip through a foreign world where no one I saw quite matched my parents' inheritance, or my own. And though much of this is involuntary and tragic—the number of refugees in the world, which came to just 2.5 million in 1970, is now at least 27.4 million—it does involve, for some of us, the chance to be transnational in a happier sense: able to adapt anywhere, used to being outsiders everywhere, and forced to fashion our own rigorous sense of home. (And if nowhere is quite home, we can be optimists everywhere.)

Besides, even those who don't move around the world find the world moving more and more around them. Walk just six blocks, in Queens or Berkeley, and you're traveling through several cultures in as many minutes; get into a cab outside the White House, and you're often in a piece of Addis Ababa. Technology compounds this (sometimes deceptive) sense of availability, so that many people feel they can travel around the world without leaving the room, through cyberspace and CD-ROMs, videos and virtual travel. There are many challenges in this, of course, in what it says about essential notions of family and community and loyalty, and in the worry that air-conditioned, purely synthetic versions of places may replace the real thing—not to mention the fact that the world seems increasingly in flux, a moving target quicker than our notions of it. But there is, for the traveler at least, the sense that learning about home and learning about a foreign world can be one and the same thing.

All of us feel this from the cradle, and know, in some sense, that all the significant movement we ever make is internal. We travel when we see a movie, strike up a new friendship, get held up. Novels are often journeys as much as travel books are fictions; this has been true since at least as long ago as Sir John Mandeville's colorful fourteenth-century accounts of a Far East he'd probably never visited, and the distinction is even more shadowy now, as genre distinctions join other borders in collapsing.

In Mary Morris's *House Arrest*, a thinly disguised account of Castro's Cuba, the novelist reiterates, on the copyright page, "All dialogue is invented. Isabella, her family, the inhabitants and even la isla itself are creations of the author's imagination." On page 172, however, we read, "La isla, of course, does exist. Don't let anyone fool you about that. It just feels as if it doesn't. But it does." No wonder the travel-writer narrator—a fictional construct (or not)?—confesses to devoting her travel magazine column to places that never existed. "Erewhon," after all, the undiscovered land in Samuel Butler's great travel novel, is just "Nowhere" rearranged.

Travel, then, is a voyage into that famously subjective zone, the imagination, and what the traveler brings back is—has to be—an ineffable compound of himself and the place, what's really there and what's only in him. Thus Bruce Chatwin's books seem to dance around the distinction between fact and fancy. V. S. Naipaul's recent book *A Way in the World* was published as a nonfictional "series" in England and as a "novel" in the United States. And when some of the stories in Paul Theroux's half-invented memoir, *My Other Life,* were published in *The New Yorker,* they were slyly categorized as "Fact and Fiction."

Since travel is, in a sense, about the conspiracy of perception and imagination, the two great travel writers to whom I constantly return are Emerson and Thoreau (the one who famously advised that "traveling is a fool's paradise," and the other who "traveled a good deal in Concord"). Both of them insist on the fact that reality is our creation, and that we invent the places we see as much as we do the books we read. What we find outside ourselves has to be inside ourselves for us to find it. Or, as Sir Thomas Browne sagely put it, "We carry with us the wonders we seek without us. There is all Africa and her prodigies in us."

So, if more and more of us have to carry our sense of home inside us, we also—Emerson and Thoreau remind us—have to carry with us our sense of destination. The most valuable Pacifics we explore will always be the vast expanses within us, and the most important Northwest Crossings the thresholds we cross in the heart. The virtue of finding a gilded pavilion in Kyoto is that it allows you to take back a more lasting, private Golden Temple to your office in Rockefeller Center.

And even as the world seems to grow more exhausted, our travels do not; some of the finest travel books in recent years have been those that undertake a parallel journey, matching the physical steps of a pilgrimage with the metaphysical steps of a questioning (as in Peter Matthiessen's great *The Snow Leopard*), or chronicling a trip to the furthest reaches of human strangeness (as in Oliver Sacks's *The Island of the Color-Blind,* which features a journey not just to a remote atoll in the Pacific, but to a realm where people actually see light differently). The most distant shores, we are constantly reminded, lie within the person asleep at our side.

So travel, at heart, is just a quick way of keeping our minds mobile and awake. As Santayana, the heir to Emerson and Thoreau with whom I began, wrote, "There is wisdom in turning as often as possible from the familiar to the unfamiliar; it keeps the mind nimble; it kills prejudice, and it fosters humor." The Romantic poets inaugurated an era of travel because they were the great apostles of open eyes. Buddhist monks are often vagabonds, in part because they believe in wakefulness. And if travel is like love, that is, in the end, mostly because it's a heightened state of awareness, in which we are mindful, receptive, undimmed by familiarity, and ready to be transformed. That is why the best trips, like the best love affairs, never really end.

Acknowledgments

When David Talbot and I were editors at the *San Francisco Examiner* in the early 1990s—he as arts and features editor, I as travel editor—we would often share our frustrated dreams of starting magazines devoted to great writing.

In the fall of 1995, David broke away from the *Examiner* to pursue his dream in the just emerging world of online publishing, creating a journal of criticism and commentary called Salon. About a year later, when he felt Salon was ready to expand its editorial base, he called me and asked if I still wanted to create that literary travel magazine I had always talked about.

Of course, I said, but it was just too expensive to start a print magazine. There was a pause and then he said, "Why not join us and do it online?"

And so a great editorial adventure, which we called Wanderlust, was born.

This compilation of essays and tales would simply not exist without David's editorial vision and courage, and so, first of all, I want to thank him for allowing me to pursue my dream at Salon.

I also want to thank all of the wonderful staff people at Salon—my fellow editors, and the great people in the art, tech, and business departments—who helped nurture and build that dream.

I want to thank my excellent agent, Amy Rennert, for finding just the right publisher for this book and then for steering it safely through the contractual shoals.

I want to thank my equally excellent editorial counterpart at Villard, Oona Schmid, for understanding and appreciating the vision behind this book from the very beginning, for sharing her unwavering enthusiasm, critical acumen, and marketing savvy throughout the editing and production process, and for becoming a cherished cheerleader, ally, and mentor along the way.

I especially want to thank all the extraordinarily talented writers represented herein, who offered me the great gift of publishing their most intimate and moving travel tales.

I want to thank all the friends, fellow editors, readers, travelers, and writers who have enriched and inspired my life along the way.

And last and most important, I want to thank my family for supporting and guiding and delighting me, and for teaching me that sometimes the world's greatest wonders are literally right before our very eyes.

Contents

Introduction

WANDERLUST

Don George

You probably have your own definition of wanderlust. My trusty *Webster's* defines it as "strong or unconquerable longing for or impulse toward wandering," and that pretty well sums it up for me.

It also sums up the fundamental inspiration for *Salon.com's Wanderlust*: a collection dedicated to putting the romance and the passion—the "unconquerable longing"—back into travel writing.

Remember the first time you traveled to a foreign place? If you are like me, you were overwhelmed and exhilarated. Every moment seemed unbearably precious, every outing an extraordinary lesson in a new culture and a new people—full of thrilling sights and smells, tastes and textures, thoughts and values, encounters and connections: a whole new world!

The stories in this collection recapture and celebrate that feeling: Isabel Allende discovers inspiration in the green depths of the Amazon; Simon Winchester is surprised by romance in rural Romania; Jan Morris explores the hallucinatory power of Gdańsk; Carlos Fuentes conjures an unforgettable conjunction of the imagined and the real in Zurich.

Yet it is not only famous writers who enliven these pages. I think you will long remember Amanda Jones's erotically entangled encounter with a stranger on a crumbling island; David Kohn's mind-marinating, tastebud-tantalizing tour of the Memphis World Championship Barbecue Cooking Contest; Susan Hack's all-too-true tales of desperately seeking Tampax in far-flung pharmacies; Jeffrey Tayler's detour toward death on a spontaneous Sahara side-trip; and Edith Pearlman's richly rejuvenating "junior year abroad" at the tender age of sixty—to mention just some of the adventures herein.

What unites all the accounts in this collection is writing of the highest order combined with a sense of courage, passion, and wonder: courage to explore and confront the larger worlds outside and within; passion to pay deep attention to and care profoundly about what those worlds reveal; and wonder at their illuminating intersections and at the mundane marvels that make up our planet.

The epiphany at the heart of my own wanderlust goes back a quarter century to one sunny June morning in Paris, where I had gone to work for the summer as a brief interlude, I thought, between undergraduate and graduate schools. As I did every morning, I took the rickety old filigreed elevator from my apartment—right on the Rue de Rivoli, looking onto the Tuileries—and stepped into the street: into a sea of French. Everyone around me was speaking French, wearing French, looking French, acting French. Shrugging their shoulders and twirling their scarves and drinking their *cafés crèmes*, calling out *"Bonjour, monsieur-dame,"* and paying for Le Monde or Le Nouvel Observateur with francs and stepping importantly around me and staring straight into my eyes and subtly smiling in a way that only the French do.

Until that time I had spent most of my life in classrooms, and I was planning after that European detour to spend most of the rest of my life in classrooms. Suddenly it struck me: This was the classroom. Not the musty, shadowed, oak-paneled, ivy-draped buildings in which I had spent the previous four years. This world of wide boulevards and centuries-old buildings and six-table sawdust restaurants and glasses of *vin ordinaire* and fire-eaters on street corners and poetry readings in cramped second-floor bookshops and mysterious women smiling at you so that your heart leaped and you walked for hours restless under the plane trees by the Seine. This was the classroom.

This volume is for anyone who has been touched by the wand of that wanderlust: travelers who understand that the true grit and gift of travel is encountering alien landscapes, peoples, values, and rites, finding yourself in a situation where you have absolutely no idea what to do, navigating and embracing worlds of newness day after day after day, not knowing how the story is going to end.

Because the story never ends. There's always a new corner, a new chapter—and who knows what wonders await there?

I hope you are inspired and moved by the accounts herein, and I invite you to e-mail me your tales and reactions at dgeorge@ salon.com.

Enjoy the journey!

San Francisco
May 2000

WANDERLUST

ON THE AMAZON

Isabel Allende

A powerful dream led me to the Amazon. For three years I had been blocked, unable to write, with the feeling that the torrent of stories waiting to be told, which once had seemed inexhaustible, had dried up. Then one night I dreamed of four naked Indians emerging from the heart of South America carrying a large box, a gift for a conquistador. And as they crossed the jungles, rivers, mountains, and villages, the box absorbed every sound, leaving the world in silence. The songs of the birds, the murmuring of the wind, human stories, all were swallowed up. I awakened with the conviction that I must go there to look for that voracious box, where perhaps I could find voices to nourish my inspiration. It took a year to realize that wondrous journey.

THE LARGEST FOREST IN THE WORLD

How shall I describe the Amazon? It occupies 60 percent of the landmass of Brazil, an area larger than India, and extends into Venezuela, Colombia, and Peru. From the airplane it is a vast green world. Below, on the ground, it is the kingdom of water: vapor, rain, rivers broad as oceans, sweat.

I approached the Amazon through Manaus. The city is far from the Atlantic coast, and appears on the map as solid jungle. I imagined a village on stilts, ruled over by an anachronistic baroque theater. I had been told that during the height of the rubber boom, the city was so prosperous that its ladies sent their clothing to Paris to be laundered, but probably such tales were only legend.

It was a surprise to land in an effervescent city of a million inhabitants, a free port, a center of a broad spectrum of businesses and trafficking, both legal and suspect. A wall of heat struck me in the face. The taxi took me along a highway bordered with luxuriant vegetation, then turned into twisting little streets where the homes of the poor and the middle class were democratically interspersed, both far from the neighborhoods of the wealthy, who live in luxurious fortresses under heavy guard.

The famous opera theater, remodeled, is still the major tourist attraction. During the last century, Europe's most famous opera stars traveled to Manaus to delight the rubber barons. The surrounding streets are paved with a mixture of stone and rubber to mute the wheels and horses' hooves during performances.

After seeing the theater, I had *piracucú,* the best freshwater fish in the world—delicious, but horrifying in appearance—served on a terrace facing the incredible river, which in times of flood stretches out like an ocean.

INTO THE JUNGLE

I stayed in Manaus only a couple of days, then set out on a boat with a powerful outboard motor. For an hour we traveled upstream at a suicidal pace, following the Rio Negro to Ariaú, an eco-hotel constructed in the treetops. The hotel consists of several towers connected by passageways open to monkeys, parrots, coatis, and every insect known to man. Chicken wire everywhere prevents animals from coming in the rooms, especially the monkeys, which can wreak as much destruction as an elephant.

I took a walk through the thick undergrowth, led by a young

caboclo—a jungle dweller—as guide. It seemed to me that we walked for an eternity, but afterward I realized that the walk had been ridiculously short. Finally I understood the meaning of the last line in a famous Latin American novel: "He was swallowed up by the jungle." Compasses are useless here, and one can wander in circles forever.

The jungle is never silent; you hear birds, the screeching of animals, stealthy footfalls. It smells of moss, of moistness, and sometimes you catch the waft of a sweet odor like rotted fruit. The heat is exhausting, but beneath the dark canopy of the trees you can at least breathe. Out on the river the sun beats down unmercifully, although as long as the boat is moving, there is a breeze.

To inexpert eyes, everything is uniformly green, but for the native, the jungle is a diverse and endlessly rich world. The guide pointed out vines that collect pure water to drink, bark that relieves fevers, leaves used to treat diabetes, resins that close wounds, the sap of a tree that cures a cough, rubber for affixing points on arrows. Hospitals and doctors are beyond the reach of the *caboclos*, but they have a pharmacy in the forest's plants—barely 10 percent of which have been identified. Some with poetic names are sold in the hotel: *mulateiro*, for beautiful skin; *breuzinho*, to improve memory and facilitate concentration during meditation; *guaraná*, to combat fatigue and hardness of the heart; *macaranduba*, for coughs, weakness, and lugubrious chest.

LIFE ON THE WATER

Another day we went to a native village that was in fact the habitat of a single extended family. These were Sateré Maué Indians who had been evicted from their lands and forced to immigrate to the city, where they ended up in a *favela*, or slum, dying of hunger. The owner of the Ariaú Hotel had given them some land where they could return to living in harmony with their traditions. We arrived at their village late one afternoon by boat, at the hour of the mosquitoes. We climbed a muddy hill to the clearing in the forest where, beneath a single palm roof, a bonfire blazed, and a few hammocks were strung. One of the Indians spoke a little Portuguese, and he explained that they had planted manioc and soon they would have the necessary tools to process it. From the root they make flour, tapioca, and bread—even a liquor.

I walked over to the fire to see what was cooking, and found an alligator about a meter in length, quartered like a chicken, with claws, teeth, eyes, and hide intact, sadly roasting. Two piranhas were on a hook, along with something that resembled a muskrat. Later, after I got a good look at the skin, I saw it was a porcupine. I tried everything. The alligator tasted like dried and reconstituted codfish, the piranhas like smoke, and the porcupine like petrified pig. The Indians were selling the modest crafts they make from seeds, sticks, and feathers—and a long, badly cured boa skin, brittle and pathetic.

The *caboclos* are Indians with European or African blood, a mixing of races that began during the sixteenth century. Some are so poor they don't use money; they live from fishing and a few crops, trading for fuel, coffee, sugar, flour, matches, and other indispensable supplies. There are a few villages on land, but as the water rises more than forty-five feet during the annual floods, submerging thousands of acres, people prefer to build houses on stilts or live in floating huts. The dwellings are not divided into rooms, as the *caboclos* do not share the white man's urge for privacy. They have few possessions, barely what is needed for survival. The incentive of acquisition is unknown; people fish or hunt for the day's needs, because anything more than that spoils. Sometimes, if they catch more than their daily need, they keep the live fish in bamboo baskets in the water. They cannot understand the white man's greed or his drive to get everywhere quickly.

All communication and transportation is by river. News can take weeks to travel by word of mouth to the nearest radio, where it awaits its turn to be transmitted in the form of a telegram. As a result, word of a family member's death may come a year after the fact, and news of a birth when the child is already walking. For the *caboclos*, time is measured in days by boat, life in rainy seasons. What sense is there in rushing? Life, like the river, goes nowhere. The whole point is to keep afloat, paddling through an unchanging landscape.

CONNECTIONS

A few months ago on the Alto Yavarí River, on the border between Peru and Brazil, explorers discovered a tribe that had never had any contact with white civilization. To record that first encounter, airplanes and helicopters laden with television cameras filled the air, while on the ground the Indians, surprised in the midst of the Stone Age, readied their arrows.

I admit with a touch of embarrassment that I bought a blowgun, arrows, and a pouch of powerful poison, curare, that came directly from that tribe. The blowgun is nearly ten feet long and I was not allowed to take it on the plane, but I hope that someday it will arrive in the mail. The arrows and curare are on my desk as I write, but I need to find a safer place for them. It would be difficult to explain if someone pricked a finger on a curare-poisoned arrow.

In comic contrast, Avon Ladies have invaded the Amazon, women who go from door to door selling beauty products. I learned that one had recently been eaten by piranhas—a direct contradiction to the soothing words of the guide when he invited us to swim in the Rio Negro.

The Negro is as smooth as a dark mirror when it is calm, frightening when storms erupt. In a glass, the water is a kind of amber color, like strong tea. It has a delicate, almost sweet flavor. One day we left before dawn to see the sun rising on a red horizon and to watch the frolicking of rosy dolphins. Dolphins are among the few fish that are not eaten; the flesh tastes terrible and the skin is unusable. The Indians, nonetheless, still harpoon them to rip out their eyes and genitals to make amulets for virility and fertility. In that same river, where the water is as warm as soup and the dolphins frolic, where the previous afternoon we had watched some

German tourists catch dozens of piranhas with a pole, a string and a bare hook, I had swum naked.

That night we went out in a canoe with a huge, battery-powered spotlight to look at the alligators. The light blinded the fish, and in their terror some leaped into the boat. We saw bats and huge butterflies flying in the darkness. The boatman, an adolescent *caboclo* who spoke a little English and laughed openly at our discomfort, would beam his light into the tree roots and when he spotted a pair of red eyes would jump into the water. We would hear a great thrashing and soon he would reemerge holding an alligator by the neck in his bare hand if it was small, with a cord around its muzzle if it was larger. We saw photographs of one they had caught the week before; it was longer than the boat. There are also more than thirty species of manta rays in those same waters, all very dangerous. And to think I had swum there!

After ten days, we had—reluctantly—to leave. I did not find the four naked Indians with their magic box, but when I returned home, I carried some bit of that vast greenness within me, like a treasure. For the sake of discipline, and because of superstition, I begin all my books on January 8. On January 8, 1997, I finally ended the three-year block I had suffered and was able to write again. My dream of the jungle was not without its reward.

ONCE UPON A TIME IN ITALY

Bill Barich

I am on a cruise ship bound for Italy. I am twenty years old, a wayward student escaping from a small snowbound all-male college in upstate New York. I have never seen so much snow before, in fact. It starts falling in October and continues through the winter and into the spring. Our classrooms border a frozen quadrangle students must reach by hiking up a steep, icy hill. Only young men desperate for a formal education make the climb on a regular basis.

I am in rebellion myself, desperate to be educated, but in a different, less punishing way. Maybe I can find out what I need to know by exploring, through trial and error. The world is big, and I want to see it. I imagine my future as a great romance. I have read too much Hemingway and not enough Dostoyevsky.

The sea has been very calm so far. I stand for hours at the rail and watch the wheeling birds and the spume-dappled water. There is nothing else to watch. We haven't seen any land for days, not since leaving Manhattan. This creates a curious sensation of being outside time, without a particular destiny.

When the Azores appear on the horizon at last, every passenger comes out for a look. The islands are hunks of rock in the ocean, nothing more, but everybody looks and comments. One man even sighs. He will write a postcard home that begins, "Today we saw the Azores . . ."

Lisbon is our first port of call. A beautiful beach at Estoril, actual Portuguese people on the boulevards. That excites me. "Yes, I've been to Portugal," I say to myself, practicing. We stop in Morocco the next afternoon, in Tangier. Huckster merchants in fezzes ring the shore, shouting and waving. Oranges, parrots, a tempting strangeness. I wish I could follow them down a dank alley to taste forbidden pleasures, but I am too wary, still too American, unwilling to commit experience.

Not so Gregor, my roommate. I share a cabin with him and two other guys, all of us headed for Florence and a semester abroad. Gregor grew up in Chicago. He is hip to the streets and the first truly cool person I've ever met. He has a wonderful voice and sings wherever he is, performing gorgeous front-stoop doo-wop tunes. In Florence, he will sing to the swans in a park one evening, and the swans will rise up and flap their wings in tribute.

Gregor smokes marijuana. It is 1963, so he keeps this a deep secret. He will later turn me on in Arezzo, after our failed attempt to see some famous frescoes by Piero della Francesca. I will ask him, accepting the joint at a crummy pensione, "Am I going to become an addict?" I am still too wary, too American, etc.

I don't know about the marijuana yet, not in Tangier. I do know that Gregor is unaccountably happy and singing his brains out as we sail away. He has made some friends among the crew, fellow druggies, and he invites me to join them at a party that night. The prospect thrills me. I, too, am dying to be cool, and I need all the help I can get.

The crew deck is down below. Gregor leads the way. As we descend, I hear dance music echoing from a portable record player, some kind of rumba or cha-cha. It's a merry scene, all right. The crewmen have hung colorful paper lanterns from overhead cables and put out a cut-glass bowl of punch. They have swapped their uniforms for casual clothes—Hawaiian shirts and neatly pressed khakis. They dance with women in slinky dresses, who have elaborately styled hair and painted, doll-like faces.

I move closer and see that I'm mistaken. Those aren't women. Those are crewmen in wigs. In drag! I've been at sea for less than a week and already the scales are falling from my eyes. Life in its amazing fullness is reaching out to me, so I grit my teeth and try not to run.

Beer bottles clink; the engine rumbles. The indigo sky is alive with stars. When a tall sailor in a Rita Hayworth–style wig asks me to dance, I decline politely. I expect to be tossed out for being a spoilsport, but instead the sailor pats my cheek, calls me honey, and urges me to enjoy myself. And I do.

This worries me a little. It goes against my upbringing. My mother, through her psychic powers, can probably see me now. I sense her disappointment. A man in a dress is supposed to be depraved, a monster. So why am I having a good time at a party where half the men are wearing dresses? Because it goes against my upbringing? Yes, it's possible. Fun may be had in new and unexpected places. That is the traveler's first lesson.

The ship rolls on. We pass through the Strait of Gibraltar and along the Algerian coast to Naples, where we tour the harbor. Cobbled streets; the Tyrrhenian Sea blue and implacable. Sunshine, cottony clouds riding the breeze, a pervasive smell of salt. The city looks ancient to me, historic and filled with mystery. I am aware of barnacles and rotting wood.

The glassy-eyed fish at an open-air market are arranged precisely, as in a Dutch still life. The fat market women wear wedding rings, the shapely ones do not. Men huddle in doorways nearby and smoke cigarettes with a furious energy. They argue, they gesticulate, they stomp their feet and comb their hair. Their only job is to observe.

They are the fabled *ragazzi*, boys forever, even at the age of forty-five or fifty. They visit their mothers every Sunday unless they live at home, as many do. Priests—black crows—spook them. They're behind in going to confession. Their fathers work as barbers and listen to opera on the radio. The music drifts from shop windows, sublime arias floating above the racket of the crowd.

I eat at a pizzeria. I eat a real Italian pizza—no cheese, a sauce of fresh tomatoes, herbs sprinkled on top. The red wine is raw but good. Gregor is still happy. He imitates Frankie Lymon and sings "Why Do Fools Fall in Love" to a tattered bunch of urchins, who ask him for coins and pretend to steal his wallet. In England, the Beatles are busy being born.

We get off the ship for good in Genoa, dragging our bags behind us. In the morning, we will go by bus to Florence and settle in for the long haul. The thought of impending study fills me with dread. Professors, classrooms, dead air, responsibility—but there won't be any snow, at least. That's a plus, I tell myself. Meanwhile, we have a last night free to wander. I plan to make the most of it. I am a youth with a mission.

I walk from our hotel at twilight, into another ancient city that seems in a state of perennial decay. The colors are muted and faded, touched with an ashy pallor. Everything human has already happened here, I realize, and it will keep happening, infinitely repeated. The idea is new to me, and comforting somehow. Genoa has already witnessed every mistake a young man can make. I count this as a blessing.

It's nasty out. The clouds open and rain batters the old stones, but I ignore it. My mission is to find a woman—a prostitute, to be more accurate. This, too, goes against my upbringing, but in Europe, women are part of the deal. It says so in every novel. The hero is always ducking into a bordello with some sleazy tart. I almost expect to see signs that read, "This way to the whorehouse."

Cafés, narrow alleys, the reek of gutters. I feel anxious and high on adrenaline, like a thief about to pull off a crime. I check the railroad station and the waterfront without success. Maybe it's too early for the girls to be on duty. What do I know about the rules of whoring? Soon I am hopelessly lost. The rain drenches me to the bone. A driver hurrying home toots his horn and shouts at me, *"Cretino!"*

I am about to give up the search when I bump into a friend. It's Gregor, of course. He is also on a mission, same as mine. We laugh about this and order espressos at a bar, where old men in fedoras are playing cards for money. Gregor takes off the beret he bought in Lisbon and wrings it out. Water splashes on the counter; it forms a tiny lake on the worn linoleum floor. You wouldn't think a swatch of wool could hold so much liquid.

Then we spot them, two hookers on their rounds. *Miracolo!* They are dressed alike, in tight red sweaters and short black skirts, and they carry shiny little purses of patent leather. Their stiletto heels click on the paving stones. Our mouths must be agape, because they pause by the bar and stare at us. The petite one is attractive in a hard-bitten way, but her partner is huge, built like a professional wrestler.

We have a problem, obviously. Gregor, being a man of the world, will solve it, I assume. He'll do me a favor and choose the wrestler. But no, he wants the petite one, too! We stand in the rain and debate the issue until he has a bright idea. How about a coin toss? Okay, I agree. I flip a lira coin. I lose.

I'm sick at heart, reeling with envy. I watch Gregor disappear with my beloved, wishing I had a knife to stick in his back. The hooker has become immensely desirable in the moment, a prize, a trophy. Yes, I would gladly kill on her behalf. The wrestler chews gum and stands waiting with her arms crossed, but I send her away. "I'm sorry, *signorina*," I tell her, adopting a forlorn expression and gripping my stomach to show that I'm indisposed. I keep an eye on her purse. For once, I'm lucky. She doesn't hit me with it.

I sit on a dry ledge and mope. I can return to the hotel, or I can go second. There isn't any other option. I remember my father, who's paying for this trip. I remember how my mother, a devout Lutheran, stuffed me with religion. My sense of sin is deep and Gothic, stoked by fire-breathing preachers from the Middle West. Clearly, I am a fallen being, a wretch. I belong in one of their sermons.

There is no justice in life. That is the traveler's second lesson.

Our bus the next morning is a drab Mercedes. It rattles and belches as we proceed along the coast. Suitcases are strapped to a luggage rack on top, and the driver seems to be hung over. FIRENZE, it says on a little destination card above his head. Florence, the city of flowers, kingdom of the Medici, where we will live with local families for the next few months and my new freedom will surely be compromised.

We follow a road that overlooks the Ligurian Sea. Fishing boats can be seen in the distance. The view is dramatic and inspiring, but I have the blues. Gregor is sitting up front, his beret at a jaunty angle, as dry now as an autumn leaf. He even has the nerve to whistle, unconsciously celebrating his victory.

The Riviera di Levante is below us. There are resort hotels and pleasant beaches, along with some spas where you can indulge in a hot sea bath. I imagine skinny rich women in bikinis lounging under the September sun and tanning to a buttery bronze. They are lovely but hairy. Their husbands are titans, industrialists, technocrats. They all resemble Carlo Ponti, who won the hand of Sophia Loren. Stubby men radiant with power, endowed with an acute sexual energy.

I'm daydreaming. Portofino, a fishing village, is as lovely as a postcard. Houses in subtle tones of gold and rose-red, their window shutters closed against the heat. Balconies hung with laundry, a good clean scent of soap on the wind. America is all primary colors, a giant kindergarten. I like the softness of the Italian palette, the flaking paint, the disrepair, the palpable presence of the past.

How does the song go, that one about Portofino? Just a little moonlight, a little serenade. Mandolins, violins. I picture Dean Martin crooning it, or maybe Perry Como in his avuncular cardigan sweater. His brother Al was my high-school basketball coach. When he got angry with our play, he'd shout, "Boys, I don't have to put up with this. I can make more money carrying Perry's bags!"

The bus chugs up a hill, and a suitcase slips from its binding and lands in the road. The latch springs. Clothes go blowing about. Underwear, socks. *Che peccato!* What a pity! It's among the only phrases I know, because I skipped the shipboard language lessons to stare at the ocean. *Mi chiamo* Bill. Hello. I am a kindergartner from America.

We stop for lunch in Portovenere, on the Gulf of La Spezia. It's called Golfo dei Poeti, because so many poets have sung its praises, including Dante and Petrarch. Lord Byron once swam from Portovenere to San Terenzo, across the bay of Lerici, to visit Percy Shelley at his rented digs. An incredible swim, really, for a wastrel.

Shelley's house, Casa Magni, still stands. It has an open ground floor and seven arches in a sort of loggia. The sea washes up almost to the front door. Shelley was as mad as a hatter at the end, pursued by horrible visions. He died in a sailing accident when he was twenty-nine. His boat, a schooner, had lounge chairs and bookshelves built into it.

Casa Magni has a plaque to commemorate Shelley's stay, I learn from my guidebook. The plaque says, "Sailing on a fragile bark, he was landed by an unforeseen chance to the silence of the Elysian Fields." Shelley did not write the words himself.

I am touched by these facts, anyhow. I have never been to a village where poetry matters, where it has worked its way into the fabric of everyday life. Those British Romantics, they lived like hippies, strumming their guitars and fathering children out of wedlock. I'm all for them. Am I not slightly Byronic myself? I believe there might be a poem or two in me, if I can just get them out.

Portovenere marches up a mountain slope, toward a fortress wall. There are olive trees, dark-green pines, and a bell tower with a clock. Tables are reserved for us at a trattoria by the harbor, on a vine-covered patio. We dine on pasta and roast chicken. The white wine comes in liter carafes and helps me to forgive Gregor. After a glass, he's not such a bad fellow. After two glasses, he is my bosom pal again. We are a couple of poets on the loose in Italy and decide to chat up two women in our group, Jessica and Cynthia.

Jessica has the severe but compelling manner of a campus intellectual. She uses words like "deliquesce" and "ramification" and bites her nails. Her clothes are often black. Jessica scares me a little, but Cynthia has the opposite effect. Blond and guileless, she will be barefoot on Haight Street in a few years, her hair threaded with wildflowers and a curly-haired cherub on her back.

We talk about poetry, of course. Gregor quotes a line he swears is from *The Divine Comedy*. I think he's about to sing, but he doesn't. The wine goes around. Is it Jessica who mentions the famous grotto? The place where Byron launched his epic swim? It becomes apparent to us all that we must visit this grotto, and right away.

Into the hills we go, without any idea where the grotto might be. Jessica speaks the best Italian, so we elect her to ask for directions. Byron? The swimmer? Heads shake, people give us strange looks. A big silence hangs over Portovenere. Most shops are closed. Lunch has ended, the peasants are bedded down for their siestas.

The grotto remains elusive, but we don't care after a while. Our search loses its importance as the wine wears off. The afternoon is bright and warm, and the bay is sparkling. Such beauty! We are young and optimistic and wildly poetical, so we tumble to earth on a grassy hillside, where Gregor promptly falls asleep.

Time passes. A lot of time passes, in fact. We roust ourselves at last and stroll back to the harbor, but everything seems different. There are shadows where the sun once shone. The village is awake again, citizens are bustling about. The waiters at the trattoria have moved the tables from the patio, and it's as if we've never been there. We've been erased.

"The bus is gone," Jessica says.

This is true. We've been erased and left behind! We will not be in Florence when our families come to claim us. We are orphans. We will have to pay some hideous price. Cynthia is crying. She's afraid she'll be sent back to Delaware. What could be worse?

Gregor swings into action. We'll pool our money, he says, and hire a taxi. I throw in the ten-spot I hide in my wallet's secret compartment. There go dozens of *espressi*, bottles of Chianti, books of poetry, and fateful assignations. We find a taxi stand and negotiate a fare. Thirty bucks, plus tip. The cabbie is a scoundrel, but he has us where he wants us.

In a cramped little Fiat, we turn inland from the bountiful sea and race toward Florence on the autostrada. Cynthia has stopped crying and sits on my lap. That would be a positive turn of events, if we didn't have so far to go. I feel her weight on my thighs. My feet are getting numb, plus I'm tired and mourning the loss of my ten dollars. The literary life can be costly. That is the traveler's third lesson.

Our taxi speeds toward the center of Florence and the piazza where our college is located. We are late arrivals, bad students who have missed the school bus in Portovenere on account of wine, sunshine, Byron, and Shelley. The director rolls his eyes at the sight of us. A fleshy, operatic man, he wears an ascot, leans on a walking stick, and affects a British accent. Probably he has read too much Henry James.

Cynthia is still nervous, thinking she might be expelled, but there's no way. The college has already banked our tuition. Instead, the director reprimands us—irresponsible behavior, detrimental to the group, blah blah blah. It's silly. In fact, my free-form education on the Continent is progressing nicely. In the last week, I've almost danced with a sailor in drag and almost made it with a hooker in Genoa. Who knows what I'll learn next?

In another room, Italian families are waiting. They will be our hosts for the next few months, taking us in as boarders. They're dressed in their church clothes and look uneasy about the deal they've struck. To invite an uncultured young American into your home is no laughing matter. It's best to lock up the jewelry and the majolica.

Cynthia is claimed, and so are Gregor and Jessica. Finally, the director summons me and introduces me to an elderly woman with bright blue eyes—eyes that men must have fallen into, swooning, when she was younger. This is the Marchesa. She has on a black dress shiny from wear, and her white hair is in a tight bun held fast with an elegant tortoiseshell comb. Her cheeks are round and rosy. She smiles at me in a serenely accepting way.

I am drawn to her immediately. Some people age with a special grace, without any bitterness, and the Marchesa is among them. It's her smile that gets me. She can see right into my soul. Absurd, yes, but I'm certain of it. It can happen like that at a first meeting—no barriers, no sense of opposition, a kind of purity. She knows I'm up to no good in Italy, but that doesn't faze her. What's youth for, if not for adventure?

I will bring her a dozen roses one day, and she will weep.

At twilight, we set out on foot for her flat. The Marchesa limps a bit, favoring her left side. Still, she's cheerful. The walking is tough on me, though, what with a heavy suitcase on my shoulder. My feet are sore from the long taxi ride. I had Cynthia on my lap for hours, and she cut off the blood flow to my legs. How unfair! I've often wished for a woman on my lap, and when I get one it hurts.

It turns out the Marchesa has fallen on hard times. Her flat occupies the ground floor of an old palazzo, where she has six cold, dark rooms hung with sun-bleached tapestries. Touch an armchair and you raise a cloud of dust. Ancestors in antique gilt frames loom large. They are brooding presences, distant and unfathomable. I can hear them whispering.

The Marchesa calls for her family. They assemble in the parlor. Here's her son, Aldo, a fortyish bureaucrat, who lives in the flat, too, along with his shy wife, Lucrezia, and their son, Giorgio, who's thirteen and—incredibly—a baseball fan. He says to me, in perfect English, "Hello, sir. You are from New York. Tell me, please, how are the New York Yankees?"

I am thrown off-stride. The few responses I've mastered in Italian will not suffice. "Well, they need a starting pitcher if they hope to win the pennant next year," I say, also in English.

"And Mickey Mantle?"

"He's been injured. It's been a rough year for him."

Giorgio dashes to his bedroom and returns with his baseball glove, scuffed and ragged. He keeps the pocket soft by rubbing it with olive oil. It could be a sacred icon, by his tender caress.

We sit down to supper. The Marchesa serves thin vegetable soup, chewy bread, and a stringy piece of boiled beef, but not a drop of wine. Hardly anyone speaks, mostly because of Aldo.

Frankly, he's a pain. He imposes order. He reminds me of the hawk-nosed Florentine merchants you see in paintings, bent over a pile of coins. My soul is a blank to him and always will be.

For dessert, there is a special chestnut pudding. It tastes awful to me, but I don't let on. Instead, I kiss my fingertips and sing its praises, a gesture for which I pay dearly. Soon chestnut pudding shows up on the table almost nightly, until the stuff is coming out my ears! Only Gregor suffers a worse fate. He lands in a house with a family that worships fennel, and they feed him endless plates of it over pasta, sautéed, deep-fried, or raw in salads. By the end of the semester, he stinks of anise.

Classes start. It is a torture. Every morning around seven, the Marchesa raps on my door and asks, *"Permeso?"* Sometimes I am awake and dressed, but more often my head is buried under a pillow. She sets a plastic tray on my bureau, always the same—a hard roll, butter, marmalade, and a pot of strong coffee. Always, too, she is smiling. I envy her, really. I crave such equanimity myself, such a perfect balance on earth, but I fear I'll never gain it.

The streets teem with children in school uniforms. They tote books, they run in packs, they are adored by passing adults, who chuck them under the chin and pat them on the head. Kids are the true royalty in Florence, little princes and princesses whose every whim must be indulged. Childhood flies, after all. The Madonna's glow? It comes from the glowing infant she clasps to her breast.

The traffic is intense. Diesel fumes, belching old buses, motor scooters that buzz like mosquitoes. I am forever dodging hell-bent drivers and also soccer balls. The kids kick them back and forth, bouncing them off walls, cathedrals, monuments, and cars. No surface is spared from serving as a temporary goal, not even the statues in the piazza across from my college.

Our school building has many windows, and that's too bad. I spend my classroom time staring at the piazza and wishing I were out there, where real life is going on. I watch the ancients seated on benches, their bodies bundled in overcoats despite the autumn warmth. Leathery faces, a white stubble of whiskers, intricate debates over who remembers what, and why. The sun shines on *bambini* playing in the dirt. All the young mothers are beautiful, even when they're ugly.

The professors drone on. They have an amazing capacity to block out our snoring. It's tedious to listen to a packaged lecture on the Renaissance, when the Renaissance is alive outside. I touch it almost daily, in fact. San Marco is near my flat, and I go there and sit in awe before Fra Angelico's extraordinary frescoes. *The Mocking of Christ, The Annunciation.* He painted them from 1438 to 1445, but they could have been done yesterday. The frescoes are rich in emotion, in spirit, in longing—a longing I am beginning to share.

What do I long for? I want to be part of a civilized world, not the kindergarten of America. A world where art, literature, and music matter, where history is present and palpable. The old palaces in Florence, they alert me to how every human endeavor ends— chipped, battered, in debris. It's not so bad. I can accept it. That's what I think at the moment, but I am still young and not yet on familiar terms with grief.

Daydreaming again. There's a song running through my head, one by Rita Pavone, a pint-sized belter from Torino, who's a teen sensation. She rules every jukebox in town and will be mentioned in a Pink Floyd lyric someday and even perform on *The Ed Sullivan Show.* We hear Rita when we escape into a café after class—*un bicchiere di vino rosso,* maybe a game of eight-ball if we can find a pool table.

In the cafés, we talk with astonishing energy. We cook up new theories about the nature of existence and advance arguments to celebrate our own brilliance. It's no use, though: The Italian guys put us to shame.

How sophisticated they are as they linger for an eternity over a single aperitif, their jackets draped over their shoulders and their manicured hands free to punctuate their words! The only thing that interrupts their weary languor is a pretty woman passing by. Then they pant like dogs.

I've decided cigarettes are essential to the pose. Sartre, he's always pictured smoking, isn't he? Hanging out with that Simone de Beauvoir? It must be imperative for an intellectual to smoke, so I spring for a ten-pack of Nazionale *con filtro* and fire up a couple every day. My eyes water at first, and my throat gets raw. I have coughing fits, but I stick to the program, cancer be damned. Gradually, I do start to feel smarter, although I can produce no objective evidence to support those feelings.

A month goes by. The grapes are harvested, the Tuscan landscape flames with color. I buy a cheap bicycle and ride into the countryside. I ride along the turbid brown Arno and watch the men fishing with long poles. The rains come in November, but the days are often still sunny, if bitingly cold. I go to the Mercato Nuovo for a new wool sweater and rub the snout of Il Porcellino, the famous bronze boar, for good luck.

But things are changing, winding down. Cynthia has an Italian boyfriend, for instance. It's inevitable, really, since those guys will pursue an American blond to the ends of the earth. Guido isn't a bad sort, though, despite his enameled hair and open-necked shirts. He is a pacifist guitar player who lives in a ruined villa in the hills of Fiesole along with his mother and two brothers, one a Marxist and the other subtly and sweetly loony.

We all take the bus up for a visit one Saturday morning. Gregor sings to the other passengers. He's ripped, as usual, on the last of the dope he bought in Tangier. Guido's mother is in her garden, plucking bugs from plants and polishing off a big glass of Chianti. Blowsy yet seductive, the Signora shows us around the villa. I have never seen such wreckage, but she doesn't mind it. At an old cistern, she pushes a few rocks into the water. Minutes later, they splash. She knocks stones from a retaining wall with a backhand swipe. Let it collapse, she appears to be saying. Collapsing is our fate.

She serves us lunch on a patio. Some prosciutto and cheese, more wine, fruit in a wicker basket. Guido strums Joan Baez folk songs while his Marxist brother offers criticism and correction. Politics in Italy are hopeless, a form of entertainment at best.

Florentines care about the basics, good bread and olive oil, the closeness of family, the soul's ardor. Even the peasants can recite some Dante.

After our meal, the loony boy excuses himself to chase small birds through the ruins. He loves the game. Here's happiness on the wing! His laughter echoes as he runs down a hill, vanishing into a grove of olive trees.

I go for a walk with Jessica. I'm still awkward around her. She is intelligent, academic, and forceful in her opinions. Also clever and witty. I am attracted to her mind, and that's a first for me. All my previous girlfriends have been cheerleaders. Thinking was not required of them (or of me), but now I've entered an epoch of discovery and am eager to share my epiphanies. Jessica is the designated muse, whether or not she wants to be.

I light a Nazionale, cough, and tell her how lately in the afternoon I've been sitting on the loggia in the Piazza Signoria and writing in a notebook. It's pleasant now with the tourists gone. She doesn't blink, so I confess I'm writing poems. Terrible poems, to be sure, but the act makes me happy. Maybe that's my way of chasing birds, I say. Jessica could slash me to bits at any instant, but she doesn't. Instead, she listens. Soon we will be lovers.

By December, time has become my enemy. The days whip by, and I must face the distressing prospect of returning to my snowbound university in upstate New York. The idea makes me sweat at night, even in winter. I'm irritable around the flat, sick of Aldo and his clerkish routines. *"Va via!"* I want to shout. Get out of here, Aldo! The Marchesa sees how upset I am and puts a chocolate bar on my breakfast tray.

Giorgio and I are still the best of pals, at least. He treats me like a weird older brother from a faraway planet, somebody who can handle a baseball bat and hit fly balls for fielding practice! That's a valuable talent in Florence, bankable even. A crowd gathers whenever we play catch outside, and I make peppy chatter and embarrass Giorgio by saying he'll be the next Joe DiMaggio.

I bring the Marchesa a dozen roses, and she weeps.

The longing just gets worse! I skip classes to visit galleries and museums. I am devouring the paintings, swallowing the sculptures, storing up impressions to nourish me in the dark times ahead. The guards at the Uffizi know my face by now and nod to me on their silent rounds. Can they be laughing inside? Poor young American in love with art, he must return to the land of Norman Rockwell!

Gregor and I plan a farewell weekend. We lie to our families and say we're going to Rome by train. We go nowhere. We wallow in Florence instead, soaking up the city. We roam from café to café, we get drunk and sappy and find ourselves near Santa Croce, at a medieval open-air bar jammed with grotesques. They're pounding shots of grappa and eating roasted pig ears. We sleep both nights on park benches and wake covered with dew. Sunday, we climb up to the Piazzale Michelangelo and watch the sun rise over red tile roofs.

Our city! we cry. Gregor sings to Florence, a lullaby. Then there are the inevitable stupidities of term papers and exams. The hiss of radiators, those professors with hair sprouting from their noses. How can they issue us grades, when we've been studying the ineffable?

We throw a big party at the end of the semester, but it is a hollow affair. Gregor, in his wine-soaked beret, will head to Paris and try (but fail) to be a painter. Guido proposes to Cynthia; then he unproposes. She accuses him of being unreliable, a Romeo. In reply, Guido shrugs. Cynthia will wind up in San Francisco, hiding her hash pipe in the fine leather purse Guido bought for her on the Ponte Vecchio.

Jessica and I will travel together to Switzerland, Germany, France, and England. We'll stop at many clubs and pubs and hammer many pinball machines, pretending we don't have to go home. Rita Pavone is still on every jukebox, no matter what country we visit.

But first I am in the piazza across from our college by myself—
one more time, taking stock. Church bells toll, pigeons flap, doves
are cooing. The sky turns pink. At that moment, I should be writing in my notebook, "Youth fades, the loving memories endure,"
but I don't have the words yet. They are the traveler's final lesson,
one that approaches with the speed of light, years after the fact.

NAXOS NIGHTS

Laurie Gough

No single incident in my life has been so strange, so hard to grasp, so totally lacking in feasible explanation. It's the weirdest thing that has ever happened to me, and it happened on a Greek island.

I came to Naxos by mistake, but maybe there are no mistakes. Maybe sometimes we're meant to be led here and there, to certain places at certain times for reasons beyond our understanding, beyond our will or the spell of the moon or the arrangement of the stars in the sky. Maybe all the dark and eternal nameless things lurking around us have their own purpose and vision for us. Who knows?

When I was twenty-three, I was traveling alone through Europe. Traveling alone seemed to come naturally to me, and that solitary trip was just the beginning of what would become a habit in the years to come. I'd been in the rain for two months in Britain and discovered I didn't like being wet. I wanted to dry out. And perhaps I wanted more than that—an inner light, a deeper understanding of life's complexities, a friend. With all those rainy days traveling alone, a fire had been extinguished within me and I needed rekindling. One morning I woke up soggy. I was on a beach in Scotland at the time, so sogginess was to be expected, but I was also shivering and miserable. I decided to escape to Greece as fast as possible.

Three days later I was on a midnight flight to Athens. At six in the morning, dragging my sleepless, jet-lagged body around the port of Piraeus, I came to a clapboard sign with a ferry schedule for various Greek islands. I was still dripping wet—although that was probably psychological—and dead tired, but I wanted things: a beach, the sun, a warm, dry place to sleep, a Greek salad. I bought a ticket for the island of Paros because the ferry was leaving in ten minutes. Arbitrary, yes, but I was twenty-three and still arranged my life that way.

Six hours later we pulled into the Paros harbor. From the wooden bench on the boat where I'd been napping, I looked up to see a large crowd of passengers jamming the exit doors. Since I was groggy and exhausted, I decided to stay on the bench a few more minutes and let the crowd disappear. When I looked up again, in what seemed just a few minutes, I was appalled to see the boat pulling away from the harbor, the passengers all gone, and me left alone on the boat. For the next two hours I worried we were sailing back to Athens, but I was too embarrassed to ask the men who worked on the ferry about it.

Fortunately, in two hours we arrived at another island. I got off the boat on Naxos and walked with my backpack along the dock, where I was immediately swarmed by a sea of short, round, middle-aged women in black polyester dresses and black socks who wanted me to stay at their guesthouses or sleep on their roofs. Assuming the roles of eccentric aunts, they took my arms and patted my hands, trying to pull me into their lives, their doughy bodies.

I didn't go to the houses of any of those women. In the recesses of my drowsy mind I remembered I needed a simple combination of a beach and sleep. Leaving the busy little port town, also called Naxos, behind me, I headed south along the beach, walking for a long time through scatterings of bodies lying on the white sand, topless French women playing Frisbee, nut-brown boys throwing balls, incoming waves at my feet, and tavernas off to the side. A pure Aegean light fell on my head like a bleached curtain draping from the sky. It was a lean and haunting landscape, savagely dry, yet the light was uncannily clear, with a blue sky big enough to crack open the world, had the world been a giant egg. The crowds thinned as I walked farther along the beach, and the music from the tavernas faded in the distance. Finally, I spotted something under the shade of an olive grove—a small bamboo wind shelter that someone must have constructed and recently abandoned. Perfect. I'd found the place to drop down and sleep. And although I didn't know it at the time, I'd found the place that would become my home for over a month.

I slept the rest of that day in the shelter under the olive grove, and when I woke up it was dark and all the people were gone. A night wind danced across my face and shooting stars crashed across the sky. I ran along the beach, delirious, exalted, and finally dry.

My days on the beach took on their own rhythm. In the morning, rose-colored rays of sunrise from behind a dark mountain would wake me, and if they didn't, the island's omnipresent roosters would. The sea would be calm at dawn and I'd go for a swim before the day's beach crowd arrived. Walking back to my bamboo shelter, I'd say hello and chat with the smiling waiter, Nikos, at the nearby taverna as he set out chairs for the day's customers. Nikos was handsome in the way many Greek men are handsome, which has more to do with the way they look at you than with how they themselves look. Nikos was good at looking rather than good-looking, which was almost the same thing in the end. When the sun got too high, I'd escape its burning rays and read books in the shade of my olive grove. I'm a redhead—an absolute curse in a desert climate like Greece's.

The waves would gather momentum as the day passed and at some point every afternoon they would be at their fullest. That's when the old men would appear. From seemingly out of nowhere, a gathering of weathered, mahogany Greek men with sunken chests and black bathing shorts would converge to stand on the shore and survey the sea. The Aegean in dark-blue spasms would reach its zenith there in the afternoon light and, from my olive grove, I'd watch it also. The old men would enter the sea together, simultaneously turn to face the shore, and hunch over with their knees slightly bent, skinny arms outstretched, waiting. They'd look over their shoulders at the ocean beyond, ready to jump up and join it at precisely the right moment. They always knew when that was. I would join them and always laughed when riding the waves, but I never saw those men crack a smile. I decided that when I was eighty, I would take waves that seriously also. After that many years of life on earth, what could be more important than playing in the waves?

Sometimes I'd walk into town to explore, buy fruit and bottled water, and watch old men argue politics over their Turkish coffee served in tiny cups. The coffee was sweet and strong and the cup was one-third full of gooey sediment. At sunset the men would turn their chairs to face the sun as it melted the day into the sea. They'd sigh and drink their ouzo or citron or *kitro*—a lemon liqueur that is a Naxos specialty—and stop talking until the sky was drained of color. Parish priests with stovepipe hats, long robes, and beards would stroll the narrow alleys with their hands behind their backs, looking exactly like movie extras. Old women in black would watch me as I passed and occasionally stop me to ask about snow. I'd wander through the maze of whitewashed houses, the stark lines of white and blue, and stumble back home over the rocky land of dry absolutes in a heady daze.

Nothing is murky on a Greek island like Naxos, nor hazy, nor humid, nor dewy. Lush doesn't live there. This part of Greece is a rock garden of shrubs and laurel, juniper and cypress, thyme and oregano. Wildflowers spin colors that surge out of a pure clarity, and in this clarity the forms of things are finer. In the hard heat of this arid place, donkeys sound off at all hours, as if agitated. They'd wake me even in the dead of night.

One evening at sunset a man on a moped zipped by as I was walking along the beach. He came to a stop in the sand ahead and turned to ask my name. I'd seen him before at the taverna, throwing his head back to laugh when Nikos the waiter told jokes. The man on the moped offered me a ride down the beach and I took it. Naxos has one entire uninterrupted beach and in twenty minutes or so we came to his village, a cluster of houses and an outdoor restaurant overlooking the sea. The man let me off, smiled without speaking, and disappeared. I went to the restaurant for dinner and chatted with some tourists. We didn't say anything significant. Mostly we watched the sky, which by then was bloodred, cracked apart with amber shots of whiskey. Shortly after, I found a bus that took me back to the town of Naxos.

By the time I finally arrived at the olive grove, it was dark except for the light of the moon heaving itself full over the mountain. I came to my bamboo shelter and found it creaking in the wind, desolate, as it was the day I arrived, abandoned by its inhabitant. My backpack and the little home I'd made with my sleeping bag and pillows were gone, taken.

For approximately three seconds I felt panic spread through me. This didn't seem healthy, so I looked at the moon. Seeing that dependable milky rock hovering up there like the planet's eccentric uncle made me smile, and I remembered that in the great scheme of the universe, this kind of thing didn't matter. I had my money, traveler's checks, and passport with me and could buy the few things I needed. My backpack had been too heavy anyway and traveling light would be a relief, a new challenge, something to write home about in postcards. Sitting on the sand I thought of the stolen things I would miss: my journal, my camera, some foreign change, a pair of Levi's, my toothbrush, my shoes. My shoes!

I fell asleep surprisingly quickly under the full moon that night. Luckily the thieves hadn't stolen the floor of the wind shelter—the bamboo mats—and I was comfortable and warm, but an hour or so later a group of hysterical German women came and woke me. They'd been staying at a campground down the beach and they, too, had been victims of an annoying petty crime. Standing with them was a quiet, tall Dutchman with a blond beard and thick glasses. His belongings had been stolen also, even an expensive camera, but I noticed that, unlike the women, he wasn't the least perturbed by it. In fact he was calm, even amused, and I felt an instant affinity for this unusual man. In the midst of the German panic, three Scottish backpackers came along and asked if this was a safe place to camp. I laughed, which seemed to irritate the German women, while Martin, the Dutchman, said it was safe except for the occasional theft, but really quite peaceful during the day. The German women went off to search for clues down the beach. Martin and I lay back on the sand and watched the stars swirl over the wine-dark sea as we discussed the lapses and betrayals of the modern world.

We should have been helping in the search, but what was the point? Our possessions gone, we felt free in a funny way. We didn't care. We were two whimsical souls colliding in the land of Homer. Half an hour later, the German women came running back, exhilarated and out of breath. "We found everything! Our things! Come!" It was true. Over a sand dune not far away, most of our belongings, including my backpack, were piled together like a happy heap of children hiding in the dark. My backpack had been slashed with a knife and anything of value, like my camera, was gone, but my journal was there and so were most of my clothes, even my toothbrush. It felt like Christmas. I found my sleeping bag and tent in another sand dune, and since I hadn't used the tent since Britain anyway, I gave it to Martin because his had been taken. Somehow losing everything and so unexpectedly finding it again had given us a new perspective on what we valued. One of the German women gave me a book. A festive night! The best part of the thievery was that in the semicrisis of getting our stuff ripped off, I'd met the strange, fair-haired Dutchman and he made me laugh.

Martin and I spent the next two days together talking continuously. Just being with him filled me with an excitement and a calm, deep knowledge. There are people with whom you feel mute and around them you forget you have a head and a heart full of ideas and wonder, poetry and longing, and there are those who can reach straight into your chest and pull songs and stars out of your heart. Martin wasn't quite like that—I didn't sing around him—but he was close, and he was the best friend I'd made in months of traveling. Traveling is so temporary. Sometimes you forget you need friends. Then when you find one, you remember the miracle of another person and you remember yourself. Talking to Martin made me feel I was availing myself of whatever was extraordinary in the world. He had a special interest in the spirit world, and in plants and modern history. He was a storyteller, too, with stories of his long journey through India and Tibet, stories of love, betrayal, auto accidents. I told stories also, most of mine involving medical mishaps in Third World countries.

On the third day Martin left to catch a plane. I walked him to the ferry. He limped because he'd stepped on a sea urchin. He was sunburned. I waved good-bye from the dock to the man with gawky glasses and violet eyes and wondered if I'd ever see him again.

As the days passed, I found it increasingly difficult to leave my wind shelter. I had the moon, sun, stars, my books, the old men in the waves. Why would I leave? I'd seen enough of the world and I liked where I was. Perhaps the more you stay in a place, the more it grows on you, the way some people do. I'd wake up at dawn thinking today should be the day to go to another island, back to the mainland, or to another country. But then I'd go for a swim and read a little, take a walk, jump through the waves. The sun would sneak across the sky, making its way toward its great dip into the sea, and I'd still be there like a lotus eater—lazy, some would say, if they didn't know better. One day I decided to make an excursion away from my beach. I wasn't prepared to leave Naxos yet; I'd just see more of it. I took a bus to the other side of the island and was gone for four days. It felt like forever.

The bus driver could have gotten us killed several times as he rampaged around hairpin curves into the mountains. From the window, I watched the dramatic patchwork of Naxos, its gardens, vineyards, citrus orchards, villages, and Venetian watchtowers. Farmers plowed with donkeys in the fields. Children played barefoot along the roads. The people of the island may have had only a scruffy flock of goats or a small grape orchard, a rowboat to search the night waters for fish, or a taverna with three tables, but they weren't poor. Life brought them regular random encounters with friends and relatives each day, not just occasional carefully selected lunches with them. Their lives were rich, plentiful, and cheerful.

I stayed at a fishing village called Apollon on the roof of a house of one of the women in black. In Greece, a woman puts on a black dress when her husband dies, and often she wears a black dress the rest of her life. That's devotion. It also cuts down on clothing expenses. Some women rent out rooms to tourists, too, and if the rooms are full, they rent the roof. That's a good head for business. By this time I was so accustomed to sleeping outside, I chose the roof over an inside room. The woman in black gave me a fine example of a "tsk-tsk" (something people the world over do with their teeth and tongue when they disapprove of you), said something in Greek, which was truly Greek to me, and gave me an extra blanket. For hours I watched the stars and thought of our dark ancestral past far away, the stars where we originated in some distant, long-forgotten explosion. Under the weight of the stars I could hardly bear the full force of the universe, the randomness, the chaos, the chance of it all. What is one to do with a life when eternity surrounds us?

One could return to a wind shelter under an olive grove. That was one option.

So I returned. And that's when the strange thing happened, the one for which there is no logical explanation.

On the first night back from my excursion, I had fallen into a deep sleep in my shelter when I had the distinct and uncomfortable feeling that something was moving toward me along the beach and that I should wake up to chase it away. I tried with all my might to wake up, but my eyes felt glued shut and I couldn't open them. The thing was approaching fast, faster every second it seemed, and it was determined, perhaps running, and I knew it was looking for me. Although I couldn't fathom what it was, it felt horribly dangerous and I knew it was imperative I wake up to protect myself.

Yet waking was impossible. My body and eyes were paralyzed. Like a great black shadow, the thing was coming across the sand, and still my body was catatonic. Then I could feel it close by, and I knew suddenly this dark and unknown thing was with me in the olive grove. My heart seemed to bang out of my chest, loud enough to hear. I forced myself to climb up through layers and layers of a deep sleep, the sleep of centuries it felt like, and at last I broke out of it and woke up, or so I thought. Pulling myself up on my elbows, I saw what the thing was: a tiny woman in black, no more than four feet tall, and very old. She lay down beside me, curled her body against mine, and shivered.

Whatever she was, she was very cold and wanted inside. I knew she didn't mean inside my sleeping bag—she wanted inside me.

No, I said, you can't come in. I live here.

She pulled herself closer, and her long, damp silver hair fell like sorrow, like misery, like an ancient sad longing. She needed a home, a warm body to live in, a place with a fire. Her face was that of a crone and I could feel her wrinkled icy skin on my cheek. Even her breath felt like the frigid night air of winter. Her eyes seemed bottomless at first, empty, like black holes, but buried deep inside were two brilliant stars for eyes, blazing stars light-years away. Again and again I told her no, which seemed to make her unbearably sad. Please let me in, she pleaded. No, you can't. This is my body, this is me! For a moment an uncanny intimacy hung there between us as we stared at each other across the distance of two worlds. Her eyes shone so brightly, they burned my own, burned straight through to my inner core. No, I told her again firmly. No. With that, she raised herself up and drifted off down the beach, still shivering and still wanting a home. She left as she had come, with the night breeze.

The incident itself I could easily have dismissed as a bizarre dream, and did in fact do so the next morning, when I awoke to the call of the roosters, shaking my head at the previous night's dark madness. Although the dream had been unusually vivid, tangible, and oddly lucid, it had to be a dream nonetheless. A four-foot-tall woman in black trying to pry her way into my body? How rude. Crazy. What happened later that day, however, made me wonder how far dreams travel into the waking world.

That afternoon, the taverna near my wind shelter, where I always ate lunch, was closed, the tables, chairs, and Nikos nowhere in sight. Strange, I thought, since I had never seen it closed in all the weeks I'd been there. Perhaps Nikos was taking a holiday. I decided to walk down the beach to the campground restaurant instead. By chance, my table happened to be next to some backpackers who were discussing where they would travel after Greece. As I ate my fruit salad, I listened to their conversation, which fortunately was in English, since they were of several nationalities. The conversation took a twist when a German woman began to tell the others about a strange dream she'd had the night before:

"It was horrible, a nightmare. I dreamed a little woman came floating along the beach. She was kind of like the women here in Greece, the ones who wear the black, but she was tiny. She was cold. It was terrible, terrible. Such a clear dream."

My spoon fell from my hand and I felt a sudden constriction around my heart. Had I heard her right? Was this too a dream? "Excuse me," I said to the German woman, "I couldn't help overhearing you. What did the woman want?"

The German woman looked over at me, startled, almost familiar. Her face was pale.

"To get inside me."

In a land where myth and reality swirl around each other in a luminous haze, lessons clear and absolute can be found after all. I said nothing is murky in Greece, but I was wrong. A woman came to me on the mist. She crossed over from the other side and sent me a gift. In all my life I have never known such a moment as when those haunting eyes from eternity stared into mine. Although she may not have intended to, she gave me a message: A human life is an extraordinary treasure. She wanted to feel life, maybe feel it again as she once had, and she wanted it desperately. I was alive, breathing, warm, strong, with a fire and light inside me she ached for. When I pushed her away, proclaiming my life my own, never had I felt the life inside me so intensely.

I left on the ferry the next day. I didn't need to stay in Naxos anymore. I needed to see the rest of the world. To stay in my wind shelter and live amid the lure and myth of Greece would be to believe in magic and fate, superstition and dark mysteries. I had this world to explore first, the one with cities and rivers, foreign faces and Woody Allen movies. From the boat, I watched the island shrink on the horizon, getting smaller and smaller like a puddle evaporating in the sun. Yet I knew then, as I still know now, that from the shore where the sand dunes begin, the olive grove grows old, and from the bed where we sleep, the shadows of secret things lurk, forbidden, timeless, and forever calling our name.

PASSIONATE AND PENNILESS IN PARIS

Maxine Rose Schur

> We kept very still of course, and were satisfied
> with the idea of Paris.
>
> —*Elizabeth Barrett Browning*

I sure know what Elizabeth meant. We've been to Paris five times, but the very idea of Paris still seduces. I hunger for Paris and lust over memories. Yet at night, when I lie in my husband's arms, it isn't the recent, sybaritic images I conjure to lure him into that intimate realm of memory. No. At night, fancy restaurants, scenic boat rides, châteaux, and boutiques evaporate. In their place memories float up, strange and strong. Up floats an idea of Paris from my first visit, a quarter-century ago, when I was twenty-two and newly wed.

Of course, even then I had an idea of Paris. That's why, for our drive into the city in our VW van, I dressed in what I fancied were "Parisian clothes." Never mind they were Parisian clothes of some other century. In my long black skirt, black boots, hoop earrings, flea-market scarf of pink silk, I felt like Paris personified.

The moment I arrived in the City of Light, I was lit. "We must stay at least a month," I told Stephen, my husband. "Let's enjoy Paris!"

Paris was expensive and we had little money, but I made a fuss so at last he said, "All right, we'll stay—but we'll have to camp."

"Camp!" I cried. "In Paris? Nobody camps in Paris!"

We did.

That night we rolled our van, outfitted with no more than a mattress, down the ramp to the Quai de la Tournelle, where vehicles are forbidden. We parked at the edge of the river, just past the Pont de la Tournelle. When we looked left, we could see the stone bridge with its little statue of St. Geneviève, and beyond, the floodlit cathedral of Notre Dame. Looking right, we saw our quay merge with the next, then vanish in murky shadows. In front of us, across the narrow arm of the river, rose the elegant apartments of the Ile St. Louis.

We climbed in the back of our van, lay face up on the mattress, and looked out the windows.

Magic.

The effect was as if we were both inside the van and out of it. At once cozy in an enclosed, secret place, and right out in the city. In its very heart. Above us, apartments loomed into the stars, their lacy iron balconies bathed in light, and at our feet, the Seine flowed discreetly southward.

"Let's enjoy Paris," Stephen murmured.

Now, a lot of practical things can get in the way of romance—such as the need for a bathroom. But we had the courage of youth and didn't let it. The next afternoon we sat on the riverbank planning just which cafés we would discreetly visit at what times of day when a van, big and white as an ambulance, pulled up next to ours. A young man stepped out. He wore no shirt and balanced a hammer vertically on his nose.

"Gidday," he said.

This was Basil Didier, a Mormon New Zealander who'd come to Paris to research his genealogy.

His trick turned the wheel of camaraderie. We had a few laughs together, then seeing our interest in his Citroën delivery van, he asked, "Would you like a perv?" which is New Zealandese for "Would you like to take a look?"

We were awed by the ingenious cabinetry: the seat that evolved into a bed, the stove built into the counter, the table hung on the wall like a picture, and the sink with its clever foot pump, small as a piano pedal.

"I'm a carpenter," Basil said with Down Under modesty. But when I opened a narrow door and discovered a flush toilet, I knew he was more than a carpenter. He was our friend.

There must have been something in the air that August 1971. The next day two more vans arrived. One was inhabited by a young New York couple who'd just returned from North Africa. The other, a rusted black Fiat, contained a bearded artist from Hawaii named Hayden and his black dog, Mahler.

Of an evening, the couple would regale us with their adventures in Morocco and Hayden would recount the curious theatrics performed by a tribe of Gypsies he'd lived with in Toulouse. For the next month, the six of us shared food, opinions, toilets, and, at sunset, *vin rouge*. Surely there was alchemy at work, for though it was totally *défendu* to camp there—directly across, as we learned, from the island home of Prime Minister Pompidou—the gendarmes never told us to leave.

Au contraire! Each night a gendarme would stop by our van to check passports and to see that we were all right.

"*Ça va, jeunes Americains?*"

"*Ça va.*"

One warm evening, as Hayden was inside his van painting on its walls by candlelight what he called his private vision of Paris, and the New Yorkers were playing gin rummy, and Mahler was barking at every kerosene barge that chugged up the river, Basil, Stephen, and I sat on the quay, dangling our feet over the water. Stephen and I were drinking wine and trying in vain to get Basil to taste the marked-down cheese we'd bought from the Monoprix. But Basil was too busy preaching how French cheeses were decadent.

"Food should be just matter to fill up space," he said.

Then he went on about sex.

Mormonism forbids sex before marriage, and in his opinion that was "too right," for any fool could see sex is merely a fad. A style! A kind of fashion!

"Sex," Basil explained, "is just Gucci hootchie-kootchie."

Bored with his ideas, we told him one of ours: to drive from France to India. "And what we need," Stephen said, "is a camper, fixed up like yours."

Basil was happy to take the bait. He said he was "right tired of dead Didiers," and would be pleased to help us make our van into a camper. Our joy turned to dejection, however, when we realized the impossibility of a project that required power tools, for we had no electricity nor any access to it.

"Too bad, too," I said, "when there's electricity all around us . . ."

The maintenance crew at the Collège de France looked up from their lunches, astonished, when we drove into the courtyard.

"Why are you driving your vehicle in here?" demanded a gray-haired man in overalls.

"Where else would we outfit it for the expedition?" Stephen retorted.

"What expedition?" the man asked as the rest of the crew stared.

"What expedition?" I asked silently.

Then in the same ringing tone used to call out Métro station names, Stephen announced, *"L'expedition à l'Afrique du Nord!"*

The questioner looked skeptical and the other men laughed. But Stephen began relating the details of our *"expedition scientifique,"* how we needed to collect flowers in Morocco and how outfitting the van for this botanical study was part of the project. Stephen blended gobbledygook with what the New Yorkers had told us about Morocco.

The man threw his cigarette butt on the ground. "I'm sorry, but my men cannot help. Union rules absolutely prevent involvement."

"Monsieur!" Stephen cried. "We wouldn't dream of troubling you. We only need to use the electricity here—and some power tools."

The man paused, looking hard at Stephen and me. And in that pause I dared hope he'd play accomplice to honeymooners.

Finally, in a voice low and sly, like beer trickling out of a jug, the man said, "Well then, it's not impossible . . . is it?"

For the next three weeks we spent our mornings in construction. Basil drew a blueprint copying the classic VW camper interior. The crew chatted with us every day and cheered us on. They not only supplied power tools but gave us steel rods and rollers from the lab to make the couch scoot into a bed. They also told us where to find scraps and army surplus items. While Stephen and Basil built the cabinetry, I bought the supplies and sewed curtains.

Then, each afternoon, when Basil went off to his French class at the Alliance Française, Stephen and I fell in love all over again. With each other and with Paris.

We strolled the Left Bank bookstores, plunging headfirst into musty books, anticipating delight in finding just the right one—for each other. We read Baudelaire at twilight in the spooky ruins of the Arènes de Lutèce, a Roman amphitheater off the Rue Monge. We sipped tea in tulip-shaped glasses in the garden of the Paris mosque, and every other day crossed the bridge to the Ile St. Louis to bathe at the municipal baths. In our private washroom, as we splashed each other with warm water from the copper pail, we were serenaded by the soulful tunes of the Muslim men who sang in their showers. "Mustafaaaa, Mustafaaaaaaaa!" they wailed. Their mellifluous voices washed us in music. Then, damp-haired, we'd stroll at dusk along the riverbank, our sandals clapping on the cobblestones while above us, softly and silently, chestnut leaves fluttered like the wings of giant butterflies.

The day our van was finished was also the day Basil ran off to Toulouse with his French teacher, Jacqueline. It was also the day before Pompidou was to return and the day the gendarmes told us to go. "We have to leave all this beauty!" I cried. To cheer me, Stephen said we'd have a farewell feast in a restaurant. That evening we climbed up the steep market street, the Rue Mouffetard, but found all the restaurants full. Ambling down an alley we came upon a Chinese restaurant jammed with boisterous diners at tables no bigger than record albums.

"*Entrez! Entrez!*" the diners shouted at us. We were lured inside and before we understood what was happening, tables were squeezed together and we were seated with two men plowing through some inscrutable Chinese dish.

The two were as different as Gruyère from gruel. One was tall and elegant with dark, wavy hair. An architect, dressed in a chic suit. The other was short, fat, and had a ruddy face. He appeared to be some sort of factory worker, for he wore the blue working-class jacket. In minutes we were drinking wine, enjoying mushy chow mein, and listening to the men bemoan how Paris was no fun anymore as nowadays people were obsessed with making a living.

"What a pity we have forgotten the zany little ways of life!" the architect wailed, and we all drank a toast to this loss, feeling giddy with joy.

As the evening wore on, I no longer cared that our intimate tête-à-tête had turned into a tête-à-tête-à-tête-à-tête. We drank a lot of wine and laughed like crazy. In fact, the whole restaurant was a boat of merrymakers on the brink of capsizing.

When the lugubrious waiter asked if we'd like dessert, and I declined, the architect appeared offended.

"Do you mean to say, Madame, that you won't even try *la banane du chef*? It is the specialty of the house!"

"I don't have room for it," I answered.

"No room! Nonsense! You will have the room when you taste it!"

"Very true," the ruddy-faced man said. "It tastes like nothing else in the world! Am I not right?" he asked the waiter. The waiter nodded as one might on identifying a body in a morgue.

"Why don't you try it, if it's that good?" Stephen urged, knowing my fondness for sweets.

"I'll have *la banane du chef!*" I said to the waiter.

As conversation and wine flowed, it occurred to me (through a little haze) that this dessert was taking quite a long time. I was about to question the waiter when the lights in the restaurant went out, plunging us into darkness and eliciting a collective scream from the patrons. Then the kitchen door was flung open and our waiter walked through the black restaurant holding high a tray with a flaming dessert. Somberly, he made his way to our table, guided by the blue-yellow light of the flames. He set the plate in front of me and announced gravely, *"Madame, la banane du chef!"* To my amazement, these words brought a hand-clapping and foot-stomping from the other diners. I looked down.

Banana fritters formed in the shape of a male's private parts.

Every eye in the place was on me, waiting for me to take a bite, but I was giggling so much, I couldn't. At last, when I did take that first bite, loud cries of *"Ooh-la-la!"* went up and the lights came on. All four of us shared the dessert, which was delicious.

After dinner, Stephen took my hand and led me up the Rue Mouffetard. Up and up we wound our way along the medieval street. The night was bright with moonlight, which gave the ancient gray houses the look of tarnished silver. We stopped and kissed, our bodies like clasped hands.

"Where are we going?" I whispered.

"You'll see."

For some time, we threaded up and around some side streets until suddenly Paris was spread before us. How beautiful it looked! Exactly like my idea of Paris. Like everyone's idea of Paris. Vibrant and askew. The gold-lit Eiffel Tower tilted jauntily, and for a beret, wore the moon. The *bâteaux-mouches* were now spaceships floating on a black iridescent ribbon, while, at the Place de la Concorde, the obelisk was a rocket taking off. And far at the city's cusp sailed Sacré-Coeur, a white ship guided by stars. Yes, that night, it seemed Paris, in sympathy with us, twinkled and trembled, and leaned too in fervent anticipation. An excited city listing toward love . . .

So if in the day, I recount some delightful French meal, shopping discovery, historical site, or museum exhibit, you'll understand if I say that at night, a more passionate nostalgia beckons. At night, when I lie in my husband's arms, I need only whisper "Gucci hootchie-kootchie" or *"l'expedition scientifique,"* or, if feeling particularly naughty, *"la banane du chef,"* to lure us into the realm of memory. Lure us back to that long-ago couple, fearless and fanciful. Back to the quivering nights of a time-distant Paris when the air was dusty with miracles and the stars were hung lower. Closer to our hearts.

SLEEPING WITH ELEPHANTS

Don Meredith

"If you had pitched your tent over there"—Godi, our Tanzanian cook, waves a hand toward a solitary thorn tree—"the earth would now be trembling."

It's a few minutes before sunrise. Coffee's on and bacon sizzles over an acacia-wood fire. A few yards beyond the tree where Godi points, two dozen elephants splash and rumble at the rim of a borehole—mothers and young, some old matriarchs the size of firehouse pumpers.

When we arrived yesterday afternoon, the *nyika*, the arid plain surrounding our camp, was empty of game. Not a bird or lizard tracking the dust. A flat place in the shade of the thorn tree, a few yards from the borehole, seemed a perfect campsite. I spread the canvas and pounded the stakes. Godi stood nearby, watching from under his hat. A tall man with the sweetness and patience of a Fra Angelico saint, he waited a long time before he spoke.

"Not a good place, bwana."

"Really? Why not?"

"*Tembo*," he said. Elephant.

"What elephant?"

Now, at first light, I observe the bearing-out of Godi's caution. If I'd pitched my tent where I wanted, I'd have been flattened.

Tsavo East National Park lies two hours west of Mombasa, East Africa's principal port, and Tsavos East and West make up Kenya's biggest national park, which is among the world's largest wildlife sanctuaries. Established in 1948 and now combined with Chyulu Hills, it covers over eight thousand square miles and marks Kenya's commitment to its natural heritage.

We left Mombasa early and by noon turned off the Nairobi Highway to enter Tsavo East at Buchuma Gate. Instantly, herds of gazelle and zebra appeared, grazing along the road, and within a mile a solitary bull elephant shambled out of a gray ocean of thorn-tree scrub. This was not just any bull, but a creature of enormous size and age, carrying a massive pair of gleaming tusks—hundred-pounders, in the parlance of white hunters.

When he spotted the old bull, Limo Ndungu, driving our Land Rover, jerked to a halt and stalled the engine. Limo is an experienced safari hand, and he thought he'd seen everything wildlife could offer—but here was an elephant he could not believe had survived. In the 1960s, the Tsavo elephant population was so large—between fifty thousand and sixty thousand—that a battle had raged over the need to cull them; by the close of the 1970s, as a result of slaughter by ivory poachers, only four thousand remained. Yet despite the odds, here loomed a beast that had seen generations of native Akamba trackers, then the age of the great white hunters—Bror Blixen, J. A. Hunter, Denys Finch Hatton, and so on—and finally decades of decimation by poachers. Somehow he'd hung on, a symbol of the will to endure.

We followed him through featureless bush for a quarter-hour before he veered from the road and was lost in the expanses of the heat's shimmer.

Scarves of dust spread above herds of zebra and impala gathered at the lake near Aruba lodge. We turned south toward camp. The high African sky was crystalline, shot here and there with white puffs of cloud. Elegant Masai giraffe paused in their cropping to watch us pass. By four we'd made camp, my fragile tent pitched to Godi's satisfaction, and were off again, Limo at the wheel.

North of camp the laterite soil of Africa turned a vibrant terra-cotta, and dust boiled behind us as we sped toward Manyani. The bush was thicker here, the thorn trees taller, leafier, though branches had been snapped off by feeding elephants and in places whole trees had been uprooted. Rounding a curve beyond a deep cut, Limo hit the brakes and the Land Rover slid sideways. As he slammed into reverse, I saw her—an aged tusker bearing down on us, ears flared, trunk hoisted threateningly. An expert will tell you this is only a bluff charge, but who cares? We shot backward. Beyond the elephant were others, mothers and young, but the old matriarch blotted out the sky with her menace. Swaying from side to side, she barricaded the road as the others hurried across and lost themselves in the bush. The matriarch trumpeted once, loud and long, then swung behind the stragglers and was gone.

The sun was setting when we got back to camp. Our three tents and the palm-thatch *banda* looked terribly vulnerable as darkness approached. It seemed more vulnerable yet when I saw large gray shapes moving about the borehole and discovered five elephant cows with three generations of young—one pair only weeks old—at their evening ablutions. They snorted and blew, sucking up water to shower themselves and drink. The ceremony continued until the last was washed and replenished. Then, one by one, they melted into the bush.

It was dark when Godi dished up dinner—pan-fried tilapia fish and boiled potatoes. A full moon the color of country butter rose over the *nyika* as we ate. By now a new family of elephants was at the borehole, just forty yards from our campfire. When I'd forked in the last of the fish and cleaned my dishes, I decided to take a stroll near the animals.

I'd walked only a few steps before the old cow at the edge of the group turned to face me. She fanned her ears and tested the wind. I backed rapidly away, then moved through the campfire's glow to

the far side of the *banda*. Here, though I was nearer the elephants—barely twenty yards separated us—I was downwind and
in deep shadow. The shaky palm thatch gave me confidence—
though had it occurred to her, the old cow could have flattened it,
and me, in an instant.

Soon the group broke up. Their path led past a corner of the
banda. First a cow, her half-grown youngster, and her month-old
calf swayed toward me, passing between the *banda* and the thorn
tree. Had I been foolish enough I could have tossed a stone and
struck them, or touched them with the end of a stick. As it was, I
wasn't making perfect sense. No one in his right mind would get
this close to six tons of wild African elephant. I was moonstruck in
the moonwashed *nyika*, transfixed by the nearness, the size, the
beauty of these creatures.

They passed one by one, the old cow last, pausing at the corner
and looking my way as if to say she'd known I was there all along.
I counted as they vanished into the moonlit bush: twenty-two.

A half-hour passed before the next group came, this one accom-
panied by a pair of young bulls. At a pace of five miles per hour,
elephants cover twenty to thirty miles a day in their journeys to
and from water. The Tsavo animals were on a tight schedule: a
half-hour to assemble, bathe, and drink; a half-hour to disperse
while another group moved cautiously into the nimbus of moonlit water.

I stood in the shadows until the tropical moon was directly
overhead. It was not flat like some moons but visibly globular, a
pale sphere rolling in space, its light falling like yellow dust over
the *nyika*. Once, far across the bush, I saw lights, a string of them
moving swiftly, and heard a distant whistle: the night train to
Nairobi.

Meanwhile, the elephants came and went beneath the pallid
stars. It was late when I crawled into my tent. I slept little. As one
group of elephants left, another arrived. All night the sounds of
their drinking and bathing reached me. Occasionally there was
trumpeting with their steps.

I woke up before first light. Godi had the fire going, a pot of coffee brewing. We drank it scalding from tin mugs and, while Godi started bacon, I went back to my post at the *banda*. Elephants were moving into the bush, a young female leading, a matriarch, one tusk broken, bringing up the rear. The moon had set; the sun's crimson rim shone at the farthest edge of the world. The borehole was silky as a lagoon. The last elephant had watered and bathed. It was morning on the *nyika*. Sunup at Tsavo.

ROMANCE IN ROMANIA

Simon Winchester

It was as I was starting to climb the stairs to the bedroom that I first heard her voice. Later she told me she had been calling for quite a while, but I, what with having to go over the details of the next day's drive to Budapest, must have been distracted. It took some time before I realized that Elena, as her name turned out to be, had been trying to attract my attention.

"Please stop!" she cried. "Just for a moment!"

She was standing behind the reception counter. When she saw that she had made contact, she put up a hand, palm out and fingers spread, and waved at me like a child, evidently relieved. Her face lit up with a thankful smile.

I have to admit I was taken with her from the start. She was very pretty, with short and glossy brown hair cut neatly to frame her face, a pert little retroussé nose, and a sprinkling of faint freckles on her cheeks. She couldn't have been much over five feet tall, and so the massive old wooden reception desk that stood between us—and which had been built in the town's more prosperous days, no doubt—rather blocked the rest of my view. But she seemed to be slender and trim. She wore a neat white blouse, aged but well washed, and she had twisted a bright pink cotton scarf around her neck, as if she might have been a Parisian.

Or might have wanted to be, more like. The whole effect was of a wholesome and dignified young girl from a rather poor family— but then, who wasn't poor, in those dying days of Communist Romania?—who would have liked to go to college or live in another, more contented country, but had had to take this hotel job instead. She was probably twenty, though the dark Gypsy faces of these young Carpathian girls could be deceptive, and she might have been fifteen, or perhaps even younger.

But I am getting ahead of myself. She hadn't even spoken; I had no idea who she was, or what she wanted. Quite probably it was something administrative—hotel receptionists having only a limited menu of official interests—and probably to do with my bill.

Only it wasn't that at all. "I am Elena," she said. "The boys are telling you have a wonderful car outside. A Rolls-Royce? Is this true?" She smiled, hopefully.

It had been in London three months before that I had first hatched the plan. I was organizing the last of a series of six journeys around Europe for an editor who thought that we Britons knew far too little about our continental neighbors. My remit was as broad as it could be: I could go wherever in Europe I wanted, and I was to take along a photographer. The only condition was that each of the six journeys should make use of a different form of transport, something that was perhaps appropriate to the country through which I traveled.

So, during the first two months or so of the assignment, I had contrived to sail a yacht across the Baltic, I had motorcycled from Munich to Turin, had walked for half a week from Cádiz to Gibraltar, had ridden a horse through the Black Forest, and had taken a train from Victoria Station in London to the Hotel Victoria in Brig, Switzerland. All that remained, come September, was to drive a car the whole way across—to drive from the westernmost point of northern Europe to the continent's most easterly extension.

I rather roughly defined this as being a trip from the cliffs that overlooked Ushant in France to the point where the continent-dividing line of the River Volga has its estuary, at Astrakhan, in what was then still Soviet Russia. It would be a passage of four thousand miles or so, slicing neatly across the Iron Curtain from the Loire to the Caspian: in all ways, an admirable expedition.

At first I had supposed that my own car, a perfectly pleasant Volvo, would prove more than up to the task. But one afternoon, perhaps emboldened by a long lunch with a couple of scheming Fleet Street types, I had another idea altogether: I thought I might ask Rolls-Royce if they could lend a hand. Taking such transport would change a merely admirable expedition into something with dash and style. I dialed the number of the firm's headquarters, and asked if it might be possible.

A man in public relations said he would have to think about it. He rang back ten minutes later—suspiciously double-quick time, I thought. I assumed it was an immediate rejection. But it was quite the opposite. The marketing people had apparently thought it was a nifty idea.

He had, he said, a brand-new Silver Spirit. It was in ocean blue, and it had white upholstery. It was due off the assembly line in two days' time. It was a canceled order. The production manager had said I could borrow it for three months. I had merely to promise to try to look after it. Would a Spirit—that's how one apparently refers to Rolls-Royces, by the second name of the mark—be acceptable?

I put my hand over the mouthpiece. "White upholstery?" I mouthed to the photographer. "*White?*" He slapped me with a folded newspaper. "Of course," he said. "*Of course* we'll take it," I said to the man up in Crewe. Great, he replied. Come up by train and pick the car up tomorrow. After we give you lunch.

By the time I met little Elena, the ocean-blue marvel was well on her way home. The photographer and I had swept across six thousand flawlessly comfortable miles together in it. We had duly reached the banks of the Volga, had taken photographs showing that we had done so, had collected a ragbag of impressions about Europe that we thought might be useful for the piece, and had turned around, toward France.

We had driven through the grim plains of Georgia and the Ukraine, and the night before our brief encounter we had crossed the frontier between the Soviet Union and Romania, leaving the gray land of Brezhnev for what seemed (for what did we know then?) the genial invigilation of Ceauşescu.

At the frontier it didn't appear as though we were passing from one totalitarian state to another; it was more like escaping from prison to freedom. The Soviet border guards had taken a remarkable six hours to clear us. For a while the dignity of the Spirit had seemed in danger of serious compromise, as she was taken off to a lead-lined hut and X-rayed, to make sure we had hidden neither icons nor gold—nor escapees—in any of her secret compartments. When we passed out of the sight of barbed wire and searchlights and watchtowers, we breathed a deep sigh of relief. Romania by contrast was a Latin paradise, it seemed: Everyone appeared so happy, and looked so handsome.

The little town where we spent our first night was called Cîmpulung Moldovenesc, a grubby and not very attractive home to twenty thousand or so souls, a place tucked untidily in a fold of the hills beside a fast-flowing river. There was only one decent hotel—the Castle, I think it was called—and it had two clean rooms and a reasonable restaurant, and that night Patrick the photographer and I ate rabbit pie and drank apricot brandy.

The great car was parked outside, at the back; as had become usual on the journey, a small crowd gathered outside it during the evening, and—as also seemed customary—a couple of young boys volunteered to wash it for us. It was as though people just wanted to be able to touch the car, to stroke her gleaming flanks, and to have their pictures taken alongside her.

This was early September. The Carpathians must be tucked into the western edge of a time zone, because it stayed light long into the evening, and the dusk was a long and lazy thing. Patrick was tired, and at ten or so, even though there was still a purple gloaming outside, he went up to bed. I was left alone, so I hung around in the bar. I spent a while talking to an elderly doctor who had once been to England; and then, at about eleven, I decided to go up to bed as well. It was as I was about to go that Elena called to me.

Yes, I said, it is entirely true that we have a fine motorcar outside. You haven't seen her yet? Why not have a look now? I'll show you around. Perhaps I wouldn't have said this had Elena been a homely sort. But she seemed so pleased, and she skipped with delight as she cleaned up her desk, and I knew that what lay ahead was going to be fun.

She raced out into the lobby, called out her good nights to her colleagues, and half-ran down the stairs, beckoning to me as she did so. She was wearing a very short skirt; it fluttered in the evening breeze as she tripped her way down the stairs, and more so as she ran to the car and stood, breathing hard, beside it.

"My heavens!" she said, running her fingers over the cold blue metal. "This is just—so beautiful. I have never seen a car so lovely."

She looked up at me, right into my eyes, and smiled.

"What is the story? Why you have it?"

There was a magnificently fatal charm about her, and her directness. I was quite lost to her.

"Get in," I said. "Why not come for a ride?"

It goes without saying that there is something inescapably special about riding in a Rolls-Royce. The solid thunk of the closing doors. The cathedral silence before the engine fires. The cold softness of the leather beneath your thighs. The gleam of the polished walnut. I felt all this once again, and I am quite sure Elena did. I watched her from the corner of my eye as she settled herself onto the passenger seat, tossed her hair back, straightened her skirt, made herself as respectable as the car demanded.

I started the engine, and we purred away from the hotel. Elena gave directions—I wanted to head up into the hills, away from the down-at-heel nastiness of the town. I swung the car this way and that through the narrow streets. Passersby looked at us open-mouthed.

Steadily the houses thinned, the town fell away. Soon there were fields, and then foothills, and after five minutes or so we found ourselves climbing, on a narrow road that ran up the ridge. There was a river to the right, and once we were above the valley haze, the moon shone down from a clear evening sky, and the stream flashed silver among the trees. In the distance I could see round mountaintops, capped by a dusting of early frost. Some evening stars were twinkling in the east.

The car sped quite effortlessly up the road, more than two tons of luxury and comfort being hauled up the hillside by the hushed engine. Elena was quiet, too—gazing at the panorama, taking pleasure, I felt sure, in being here. She nestled down into the seat. Once I caught her stealing a glance at me. She grinned, impishly.

The gradient slackened, and then we were at the top of the pass. This was as far as we were going. I stopped the car, then turned her around so we were facing the way we had come.

It was perfectly quiet. The moon was full, and down below the lights of the town pierced the valley gloom. We sat there together for a few moments. I looked at her: She seemed to be breathing hard, her small breasts rising and falling under her blouse. She looked wonderful.

But then I put my foot on the accelerator, and we swept off downhill again. I turned on the sound system, and punched the stereo button. A sudden flood of music poured through the car. It was what Patrick had been playing a few hours before, the theme from *Chariots of Fire*. It was powerful, seductive, perfect for the moment, and it seemed to bear us along as we sped down toward the town. Elena reached out and clutched my hand, squeezing it hard, her fingernails digging into my palm.

And then it was all over. The road became flat and better paved; there were streetlights, and houses on either side. Soon there were buildings I recognized, and streets I knew from thirty minutes before, and soon I was in the square in front of the hotel, and then in the car park.

I slid the car into its place, switched off the music, doused the headlamps, turned the ignition key to off. The low roar of the engine stopped, and the car became cathedral-silent once again. I turned to Elena.

"What did you think?" I asked.

For a moment she didn't say anything. She had her hand up to her face.

I asked again. This time, after a while, she slowly turned her head toward me. I could see why she had hesitated. She had been crying.

"What's the matter?" I asked. It seemed mysterious, odd. Surely she should have been happy.

She shook her head. I pulled a clean handkerchief from my pocket and gave it to her. She blew her nose noisily.

"I'm so sorry, so sorry," she said. Her voice was husky with tears, but she was recovering. She paused, then spoke again.

"I'll tell you why.

"This has been an unbelievable experience for me. You must forgive my bad English. I never know anything like this.

"Romania is very poor country, you must know. The people have nothing. There is no possibility for anyone. I work here at hotel—not a good job. Little money.

"I live three miles away, in a village. I have a bicycle. But it is not working. Bad tire, something like that. So I walk, and then take trolley. It is so crowded. I never get to sit. It is very dirty, rusty, broken down.

"Very few people have cars. Sometimes I get ride. But usually it is the same—walk, and then trolley-bus. Is not happy.

"Now, of course I know of the Rolls-Royce car. Everyone knows of the car, I think. I have seen pictures. Film stars getting out of car, that kind of thing. But I never seen one. Never. Not possible to imagine.

"And yet—see what happens. Two men come from foreign country, and they drive such a car into my town. It is the most exciting thing to happen here for years. All the boys in the hotel tell me about it. 'Elena, Elena, you must see it,' they say. They know I would like it. And then I do get to see it. You are so kind. You show the car to me, and then you let me ride with you.

"Ride in the car! Can you imagine what it feels like for me? A Romanian girl like me, riding in a Rolls-Royce? It is absolutely, absolutely, the last thing I can imagine. Is so wonderful. The silence. The soft leather. The music.

"And then where we went—the moonlight, and the river like silver, and the stars. I get to see all this, and in such a car. And with such a nice man. I see only few foreigners. It is not easy to meet them.

"I think—how can I say?—I think this for me was like flying. Yes, like flying. So impossible to imagine, something just to dream about. And so yes—that is what I feel. I have been flying, up in the air, soaring into the sky like a bird."

She stopped, breathless. She looked up at me with large, sad eyes. There were tears, half dried, on her cheeks. I gazed down at her.

"But why—why are you sad?" I said. "If it was so wonderful— and I'm happy it was—why this?" I dabbed her cheek with the back of my finger, wiping a tear away. I waited.

"Oh yes—why I am so sad? Easy to answer. I think you know already. You must do this many times.

"I am sad because I think: Tomorrow, you and your friend will go away from here, and tomorrow night you will be in another town, and there will be some other nice moment for you. A nice dinner, or a pretty girl, or a great mountain or some good thing. You will forget me, just like that. If you ever think of me, you will say, 'Oh, that silly girl in that town in the mountains.' That will be all. I will just be a silly girl. A small memory. And perhaps not even a memory.

"But for me—for me I shall never, never forget. For all of my life I will think of this. Me and you, alone in a Rolls-Royce car, under the stars and the moon. Taking me away from this town, away from my normal life.

"That is why I am sad. You will forget. I will never."

And she reached over to me, and she kissed me very gently on the lips. And then in one swift moment she was out of the car, running to the stairs, back to the hotel, and somehow back to her home.

I wondered if I might take her there. But I couldn't find her. All that was left of her was a damp handkerchief, a salty taste on my lips, and a faint warmth on the leather seat. And that was cooling fast, and soon it was as though she had never been there, and so I went to the stairs, and climbed alone, to bed.

LOOKING FOR ABDELATI

Tanya Shaffer

Here's what I love about travel: Strangers get a chance to amaze you. Sometimes a single day can bring a blooming surprise, a simple kindness that opens a chink in the brittle shell of your heart and makes you a different person when you go to sleep—more tender, less jaded—than you were when you woke up.

This particular day began when Miguel and I descended from a cramped, cold bus at seven A.M. and walked the stinking gray streets of Casablanca with our backpacks, looking for food. Six days earlier I had finished a stint on a volunteer project, creating a public park in Kenitra, an ugly industrial city on the Moroccan coast. This was my final day of travel before hopping a plane to sub-Saharan Africa and more volunteer work.

Miguel was one of five non-Moroccans on the work project, a twenty-one-year-old vision of flowing brown curls and buffed golden physique. Although having him as a traveling companion took care of any problems I might have encountered with Moroccan men, he was inordinately devoted to his girlfriend, Eva, a wonderfully brassy, wiry, chain-smoking Older Woman of twenty-five with a husky scotch-drinker's voice, whom he couldn't go more than half an hour without mentioning. Unfortunately, Eva had had to head back to Barcelona immediately after the three-week work camp ended, and Miguel wanted to explore Morocco. Since I was the only other person on the project who spoke Spanish, and Miguel spoke no French or Arabic, his tight orbit shifted onto me, and we became traveling companions. This involved posing as a married couple at hotels, which made Miguel so uncomfortable that the frequency of his references to Eva went from half-hour to fifteen-minute intervals, and then to five as we got closer to bed-time. Finally one night, as we set up in our room in Fès, I took him by the shoulders and said, "Miguel, it's okay. You're a handsome man, but I'm over twenty-one. I can handle myself, I swear."

This morning we were going to visit Abdelati, a sweet, gentle young man we'd worked with on the project in Kenitra. He'd been expecting us to arrive in Casablanca for a few days, and since he had no telephone, he'd written down his address and told us to just show up—his mother and sisters were always at home. Since my plane was leaving from Casablanca the following morning, we wanted to get an early start, so we could spend the whole day with him.

Eventually we scored some croissants and overly sugared *panache* (a mix of banana, apple, and orange juice) at a roadside café, where the friendly proprietor advised us to take a taxi rather than a bus out to Abdelati's neighborhood. He said the taxi should cost twenty or twenty-five dirham—under three dollars—and the buses would take all day.

We hopped into a taxi, which took off with a screech of rubber before we'd agreed on a price.

"Forty or forty-five dirham!" the driver shouted over the roar of his engine. He was already careening around corners at top speed.

"Why isn't the counter on?" I asked.

"Broken!" he said.

Miguel rolled his eyes. "Eva would hate this," he whispered.

"If I had the counter, it would cost you fifty," the driver said.

Since the man in the café had told us twenty or twenty-five, I asked the driver to pull over and let us out. At first I put it politely:

"We'd like to look at other options," but he simply said okay and kept driving. After four such attempts, I said sharply, *"Nous voulons descendre."* We want to get out.

Reluctantly he pulled over, saying we owed him ten dirham. "Fine," I said. "Let me just get our bags down first—the money's in there." We yanked our backpacks off the overhead rack and took off, while the taxi driver shouted after us.

Miguel shook his head. "Eva would've killed that guy," he said.

It was an hour before we caught another taxi. Finally one pulled over, and a poker-faced man quoted us an estimate of eighteen or twenty dirham.

"Très bien," I said with relief, and we jumped in.

Apparently the address Abdelati had written down for us was somehow suspect, and when we got into the neighborhood, our driver started asking directions.

First he asked a cop, who scratched his head and asked our nationalities, looking at our grimy faces and scraggly attire with a kind of bemused fondness. After more small talk, he pointed vaguely to a park a few blocks away. There a group of barefoot seven- or eight-year-old boys were kicking a soccer ball. Our driver asked where Abdelati's house was, and one of the boys said Abdelati had moved, but he could take us to the new house. This seemed a bit odd to me, since Abdelati had just given me the address a week ago, but since a similar thing had happened in Fès, I chalked it up as another Moroccan mystery and didn't worry about it too much.

The little boy came with us in the cab, full of his own importance, squirming and twisting to wave at other children as we inched down the narrow winding roads. Finally the little boy pointed to a house, and our driver went to the door and inquired. He came back to the cab saying Abdelati's sister was in this house visiting friends and would come along to show us where they lived.

Soon a beautiful girl of about sixteen emerged from the house. She was dressed in a Western skirt and blouse, which surprised me, since Abdelati's strong religious beliefs and upright demeanor had made me think he came from a more traditional family. Another thing that surprised me was her skin color. Whereas Abdelati looked very African, this young woman was an olive-skinned Arab. Still, I'd seen other unusual familial combinations in Morocco's complex racial mosaic, so I didn't give it too much thought.

We waited in the yard while the sister went in and returned accompanied by her mother, sisters, and brother-in-law, all of whom greeted us with cautious warmth. Unlike the younger girl, the older sisters were wearing traditional robes, though their faces were not veiled. You see a range of orthodoxy in Moroccan cities, caught as they are between Europe and the Arab world. From the younger sister's skirt and blouse to the head-to-toe veiling of the women gliding through the streets with only their eyes in view, the women's outfits seem to cover the entire spectrum.

We paid our taxi driver, tipping and thanking him profusely, until he grew embarrassed and drove away.

We were ushered into a pristine middle-class Moroccan home, with an intricately carved doorway and swirling multicolored tiles lining the walls. The mother told us in broken French that Abdelati was out, but would be home soon. We sat on low cushioned seats in the living room, drinking sweet, pungent mint tea poured at a suitable height from a tiny silver teapot and eating sugar cookies, while the family members took turns sitting with us and making shy, polite conversation that frequently lapsed into uncomfortable silence. Every time anything was said, Miguel would say "What?" with extreme eagerness, and I would translate the mundane fragment into Spanish for him: "Nice weather today. Tomorrow perhaps rain." At this he'd sink back into fidgety frustration, undoubtedly wishing Eva were there.

An hour passed, and as the guard kept changing, more family members emerged from inner rooms. I was again struck by the fact that they were all light-skinned Arabs. How did Abdelati fit into this picture? Was he adopted? I was eager to find out.

After two hours had passed with no sign of Abdelati, the family insisted on serving us a meal of couscous and chicken.

"Soon" was the only response I got when I inquired as to what time he might arrive.

"You come to the hamam, the bath," the young sister said after we'd finished lunch. "When we finish, he is back."

"The bath?" I asked, looking around the apartment.

The sister laughed. "The women's bath!" she said. "Haven't you been yet?" She pointed at Miguel. "He can go to the men's; it's right next door."

"What?" said Miguel anxiously, sitting up.

"She wants to take us to the baths," I said.

A look of abject horror crossed his face. "The—the bath?" he stammered. "You and me?"

"Yes," I said, smiling widely. "Is there some problem?"

"Well . . . well . . ." I watched his agitation build for a moment, then sighed and put my hand over his.

"Separate baths, Miguel. You with the men, me with the women."

"Oh." He almost giggled with relief. "Of course."

The women's bath consisted of three large connecting rooms, each one hotter and steamier than the last, until you could barely see two feet in front of you. The floors were filled with naked women of all ages and body types, sitting directly on the slippery tiles, washing each other with mitts made of rough washcloths. Tiny girls and babies sat in plastic buckets filled with soapy water—their own pint-sized tubs. The women carried empty buckets, swinging like elephants' trunks, to and from the inner-most room, where they filled them at a stone basin from a spigot of scalding-hot water, mixing in a little cold from a neighboring spigot to temper it.

In a culture where the body is usually covered, the women's ab-solute lack of inhibition surprised me. They sat, mostly in pairs, pouring the water over their heads with small plastic pitchers, then scrubbing each other's backs—and I mean scrubbing. Over and over they attacked the same spot, as though they were trying to get out a particularly stubborn stain, leaving reddened flesh in their wake. They sprawled across each other's laps. They washed each other's fronts, backs, arms, legs. Some women washed themselves as though they were masturbating, hypnotically circling the same spot. Two tiny girls, about four years old, scrubbed their grandmother, who lay sprawled across the floor face down. A prepubescent girl lay in her mother's lap, belly up, eyes closed, as relaxed as a cat, while her mother applied a forceful up and down stroke across the entire length of her daughter's torso.

I was struck by one young woman in particular, who reclined alone like a beauty queen in a tanning salon, back arched, head thrown back, right at the steamy heart of the baths, where the air was almost suffocating. When she began to wash, she soaped her breasts in sensual circles, proudly, her stomach held in, long chestnut hair rippling down her back, a goddess in her domain.

Abdelati's sister, whose name was Samara, went at my back with her mitt, which felt like steel wool.

"Ow!" I cried out. "Careful!"

This sent her into gales of laughter that drew the attention of the surrounding women, who saw what was happening and joined her in appreciative giggles as she continued to sandblast my skin.

"You must wash more often," she said, pointing to the refuse of her work—little gray scrolls of dead skin that clung to my arms like lint on a sweater.

When it came time to switch roles, I tried to return the favor, but after a few moments Samara became impatient with my wimpiness and grabbed the washcloth herself, still laughing. After washing the front of her body she called over a friend to wash her back, while she giggled and sang.

"What was it like in there?" asked Miguel when we met outside. He looked pink and damp as a newborn after his visit to the men's baths, and I wondered whether his experience was anything like mine.

"I'd like to tell you all about it," I said eagerly, "but . . ." I paused for emphasis, then leaned in and whispered, "I don't think Eva would approve."

When we got back to the house, the mother, older sister, and uncle greeted us at the door.

"Please," said the mother, "Abdelati is here."

"Oh, good," I said, and for a moment, before I walked into the living room, his face danced in my mind—the warm brown eyes, the smile so shy and gentle and filled with radiant life.

We entered the lovely tiled room we'd sat in before, and a handsome young Arab man in nicely pressed Western pants and shirt came forward to shake our hands with an uncertain expression on his face.

"*Bonjour, mes amis,*" he said cautiously.

"*Bonjour.*" I smiled, slightly confused. "*Abdelati—est-ce qu'il est ici?*" Is Abdelati here?

"*Je suis Abdelati.*"

"But . . . but . . ." I looked from him to the family and then began to giggle tremulously. "I—I'm sorry. I'm afraid we've made a bit of a mistake. I—I'm so embarrassed."

"What? What?" Miguel asked urgently. "I don't understand. Where is he?"

"We got the wrong Abdelati," I told him, then looked around at the assembled family who'd spent the better part of a day entertaining us. "I'm afraid we don't actually know your son."

For a split second no one said anything, and I wondered whether I might implode right then and there and blow away like a pile of ash.

Then the uncle exclaimed heartily, "*Ce n'est pas grave!*"

"Yes," the mother joined in. "It doesn't matter at all. Won't you stay for dinner, please?"

I was so overwhelmed by their kindness that tears rushed to my eyes. For all they knew we were con artists, thieves, anything.

Still, with my plane leaving the next morning, I felt the moments I could share with the first Abdelati and his family slipping farther and farther away.

"Thank you so much," I said fervently. "It's been a beautiful, beautiful day, but please . . . Could you help me find this address?"

I took out the piece of paper Abdelati had given me back in Kenitra, and the new Abdelati, his uncle, and his brother-in-law came forward to decipher it.

"This is Baalal Abdelati!" said the second Abdelati with surprise. "We went to school together! He lives less than a kilometer from here. I will bring you to his house."

And that was how it happened, that after taking photos and exchanging addresses and hugs and promises to write, Miguel and I left our newfound family and arrived at the home of our friend Abdelati as the last orange streak of the sunset was fading into the indigo night. There I threw myself into the arms of that dear and lovely young man, exclaiming, "I thought we'd never find you!"

After greetings had been offered all around, and the two Abdelatis had shared stories and laughter, we waved good-bye to our new friend Abdelati and entered a low, narrow hallway, lit by kerosene lamps.

"This is my mother," said Abdelati.

And suddenly I found myself caught up in a crush of fabric and spice, gripped in the tight embrace of a completely veiled woman, who held me and cried over me and wouldn't let me go, just as though I were her own daughter, and not a stranger she'd never before laid eyes on in her life.

SPECIAL DELIVERY

Lindsy van Gelder

I certainly didn't volunteer to deliver the postcard because I wanted to make new friends in exotic foreign lands. *Au contraire*, I'm a person whose travels are motivated by nature, architecture, and food—in other words, all the attractions Barbra Streisand isn't referring to when she natters on about "peeeeeeople who need people." But there I was on Floreana Island, at the ass end of the Galápagos, six hundred miles off the coast of Ecuador, and I wanted to send a postcard home to my partner, Pamela, in Miami. If I expected hand delivery of my own mail, *mano a mano*, it seemed only sporting to pick up somebody else's.

The Floreana post office is really just a raffish wooden barrel plunked down in the middle of the sand, a descendant of one installed in the eighteenth century by whaling crews. In those days it was an optimally efficient system: Sailors who were passing through checked the mailbox for letters addressed to their ships' ports of call. Today the barrel is stuffed with postcards from tourists of all nations. You could schlep them home and stamp them, obviously, but the true spirit of the olde mail barrel, according to our guidebook, demands the personal touch.

The day my daughter Miranda and I were in Floreana, most of the mail was addressed to Norwegians and Argentines. But there was one postcard with frolicking sea lions on one side and *"Saluti"* scrawled on the other, intended for someone named Gina at an *erboristeria,* or herbal pharmacy, in Bassano del Grappa, Italy. I knew this was the home of grappa, the firewater liqueur. I had even been through it once on a train, so I also knew it was located at the foot of the Alps, in the Veneto region, about fifty miles from Venice. Pamela and I had frequent-flier tickets to go to Venice in a few months. I pocketed the card.

Still, I wasn't prepared just to show up cold. When I got back home, I decided to write Gina a letter. I speak a little Italian—that is, I know a lot of hotel and menu words, which I sometimes say in Spanish by mistake. But with the help of a dictionary, I managed to explain all about the mailbox traditions. I assured Gina that there was no social obligation that went along with her receipt of the postcard—although I'd be glad to buy her a beer.

"Mom, you can't send this to strangers," warned Miranda, who majored in Italian. "They'll understand you, but they'll think you're a serial killer."

She rehabilitated my felonious grammar. Off went a letter to Bassano del Grappa. A month later I got an e-mail from someone named Luca. There was a note in Italian, plus a serial-killer-English translation:

> Dear Sirs VAN GELDER, let off ourself for the postpone what we replay at your letter, but we were outside for a travel. We are very happy to meet yuo in Veneto for make a friendship. If yuo send to as the date of yuor travel we can organize ourself for meeting. Reverence, Gina

It was around this time that Pamela, who speaks no Italian at all, began asking me pointed questions about exactly how much of our time in Venice was going to be devoted to this project. But I had made a commitment to the spirit of the mailbox, damn it. I sent the dates. Gina/Luca e-mailed back phone numbers and said we should call when we got to Venice.

A woman answered the phone.

"Buon giorno," I burbled, *"é Gina chi parla?"*

No, it wasn't Gina. It was Edda. Whoever Edda was, she knew exactly who I was—"You're coming on Monday, yes?"—and we managed, despite my rotten Italian, to communicate some particulars about the railway schedules. "Just go to the counter in the station," she instructed.

When I got off the phone, I realized that I had no clue which counter she meant. The ticket booth? The postcard had been addressed to a pharmacy. Could it be in the train station? Did it have a counter? A few hours later I called again, and this time a male voice answered. No, Gina wasn't there. Neither was Edda. The male voice belonged to Luca, my e-mail buddy, who explained to me in halting English that the train station was not very big and I shouldn't worry. Then he added: "You perhaps don't know that Gina really doesn't speak any English? As you will see when you meet her on Monday."

I was beginning to doubt her existence altogether. Was Gina actually a dog, the mascot of the pharmacy? Was I the butt of a joke that had already traveled seven thousand miles?

"You really don't have to come if you don't want to," I told Pamela. No, no, she'd come. But we just wouldn't stay any longer than we had to.

Our doubts began to melt the second we got off the train. There, carrying a single red rose and a big sign that said, "Welcome Lindsy to Bassano del Grappa," were a college-aged guy and two grinning sixtyish ladies. One of them—an Italian leprechaun—immediately grabbed me in a bear hug. The more bashful of the two, dressed in brown and wearing eyeglasses, turned out to be Gina. My new best friend was her sister Edda, dolled up in bright red and wearing major eye makeup. The guy was Luca, their younger sister's son, an engineering student who, alone among the group, had once studied English. He had his dictionary out. So did I.

Before I could proffer the small piece of cardboard that had gathered us together in this spot, Pamela and I were whisked off to a restaurant for lunch. It was like being plopped down in the middle of *Amarcord:* We were joined by Luca's mother, who tooled in on a bicycle, and briefly by his father, as well as a parade of cooks and waiters to whom we were introduced as the Girls from America Who Brought the Postcard. Mounds of antipasto arrived at the table, followed by enormous platters of pasta with lobster and heaps of delicate baby greens. Prosecco, the champagne of the Veneto, flowed like the Adriatic. And a good thing, too, since most of the conversation that we could all muster had to do with the cuisine of the region. Someone would proclaim *sarde en saor,* and the rest of the group would mmmm and ahhhh, and then someone else would chime in with *spaghetti vongole* or *radicchio al griglia,* followed by more orgasmic choruses. From time to time one of us would raise a glass and toast, "From the Galápagos to Bassano del Grappa!" and we would all whoop. I noticed that Pamela was not looking at her watch.

The family's *erboristeria* was currently closed for renovations, we learned, and perhaps they all had some time on their hands. But that alone didn't really explain the brass-band welcome. Nor did the famous postcard, which I finally presented to Gina over sorbet laced with a lethal dollop of grappa. She glanced at it, remarked that it was from a customer, and packed it away in her purse, not to be referred to again. The postcard was merely the message. Making friendship was the medium.

And what was a little translation technicality among friends? By the time the check was paid—the family refused to take our crumpled lire notes—we were all feeling punchily pleased with our ability to leapfrog over the language barrier. A tour of the town was proposed. Bassano is actually a gem of a place, with a spectacular Palladian wooden bridge spanning the Brenta River and a sinister castle on its banks—the home, Luca explained, of Ezzelino III da Roma, a bloodthirsty tyrant so infamous that he was cited in Dante's *Inferno.* Then we strolled on a bluff above the river past a row of lollipop-like trees. Bassano was notoriously active in the Resistance, Gina told us, and in 1944 the German army hanged thirty-one of the town's young men in retaliation—one for each tree. "I wrote a poem about it once," Gina added shyly. How nice, I thought with the genteel condescension of the professional journalist, a pharmacist who expresses herself in poetry. We tramped around to churches, Roman ruins, even a Museum of Grappa, where Gina insisted on buying us not one but three bottles of the stuff—regular, honey, and blueberry—as souvenirs.

Certainly we would also like to see a little of the region? *Sì, sì, certo.* Into the family station wagon we piled, Luca trying to drive and riffle through the dictionary at the same time. By then, we more or less had our schtick down. The Italians spoke slowly, with infinite patience and maximum hand-jive. Dictionary pages flipped like decks of cards. Somehow we managed to progress beyond cuisine to pets, gambling, art, birth order, the weather in Miami, the allure of Venice, Edda's arthritis, my bad knee, our feelings about spirituality versus organized religion, even politics and politicians (for that one we all used the international sign of stuffing one's finger down one's throat). We took pictures of each other in the main square of Marostica, where the residents dress up as bishops and queens every other fall and enact a days-long chess game. We climbed to the fort above the town. By then it was getting dark, and, alas, we had a train to catch.

But it was decided that we would meet the family cats and dogs. At Gina and Edda's house we got another surprise. Gina had written poetry, all right—she brought us out copies of all her books, as well as a CD on which several of her verses had been set to modern classical music and sung by the soprano Isabella Frati. These, she insisted, were gifts: one set for us, and one for Miranda . . .

By now we were sagging under the weight of three bottles of grappa and a small library, plus the CDs and a multilingual guidebook to Marostica that Gina had impulsively bought after Luca and I had exhausted our dueling dictionaries in the search for words to describe chess pieces and military architecture—all in exchange for one lousy postcard. Nor would the sisters dream of letting us take the train back to Venice. They drove us all the way to Piazzale Roma, the last niblet of mainland before one has to switch to a waterbus or gondola. We kissed, cried, offered our respective spare rooms any time, promised to be fluent in each other's language the next time we met. And indeed, with the help of my dogeared dictionary, I am slowly reading Gina's poetry. The one about the thirty-one martyrs is a favorite, but there are also sexy, smoldering love poems. Pamela has been stockpiling South Florida culinary goodies to send the ladies. Luca and I have become e-mail pen pals. I correct his English; he corrects my Italian and tells me what the family is up to. Edda was recently in Australia. Somehow I feel certain she made herself understood.

Meanwhile, the postcard I mailed home to Pamela from Floreana hasn't turned up yet. I find myself getting oddly excited at the idea of meeting whichever stranger, speaking whatever language, eventually shows up with it. I may have been the one who went to the Galápagos. But it was Gina and her family who taught me about real adventure travel.

ENGLAND'S DECADENT DELIGHTS

Douglas Cruickshank

One of the most satisfying things about the English countryside is how much it looks like the English countryside. Consider the view here at Stapleford Park, a spectacular old estate near the village of Melton Mowbray in Leicestershire. An hour north of London by train, Leicestershire is the heart of England's impossibly pastoral hunt country, Stilton cheese country, and "hand raised" pork pie country. Out the bedroom window, just visible through my hangover, a morning mist cloaks the sheep meadows, liberally sprinkled with the pea-witted beasts, and oozes down to the lake, where a single swan, white as sugar, glides along with such measured grace that it must be one of those animatronic track-mounted kind they have at Disneyland. As if that weren't enough, a rainbow arcs over the nearby woodland.

Indeed, the scene is so excruciatingly exquisite that I've got a good mind to call Mr. Merchant and Mr. Ivory and tell them to get their softly lit Panavision asses up here and bring along Helena Bonham Carter and Jeremy Irons, or some other members of the Supremely Sensitive Pallid Performers Academy, and knock off another of those precious extravaganzas that they've been pumping into cineplexes for the last decade or so. Instead, I walk to the mir-ror—starkers—to see if I look as ravaged as I feel.

I look worse. One glance and it's frighteningly apparent: some kind of untamed, passion-crazed, hydrophobic *Cat People*–type creature has indulged in most unwholesome sport at my expense. I have been clawed, gnawed, or pawed by a love-hungry humanoid of unnatural inclinations and insatiable appetite. My right shoul-der is a mass of lacy crimson stripes. They'd be beautiful, if it weren't for the pain. That's the good news.

The bad news is that I can't remember any of last night's gym-nastics. Stapleford has been described to me as the "one-time home of the Naughty Earl," but that doesn't explain my wounds, because the randy old scamp vacated long ago. My room, my lovely, splendid room—which was personally decorated by Lady Jane Churchill (a specialist in rose hues that exacerbate hang-overs)—is wobbling lazily, first in one direction, then another. My clothes are neatly folded on the chesterfield; nothing seems to be out of place. It's all quite mysterious.

Suddenly, I hear the cry of a great blue heron in the distance, or maybe it's Mariah Carey warming up down the hall. Did I mention that Mariah Carey is also staying in this mansion, that she arrived late last night in a black Saab stretch limousine (yes, Saab) accom-panied by two cell-phone-addicted bodyguards and two personal assistants? No, of course not, I've barely got started telling about the house. Lordy, where is my brain? Let's back up a bit.

This entire junket—I'm here with a small group of assorted media types—has been conceived as a luxurious blitzkrieg tour. These excursions are particularly seductive to freelance freeloaders such as me who are never likely to travel in such exalted style un-less we somehow secure a middle management position with the Medellín cartel (but then when would there be time to write, what with all the money-laundering and gun-running?).

The odyssey began with a British Airways first-class "sleeper service" flight from San Francisco to London. At more than $10,500 round trip it is one of the best reasons I've come across for getting rich. The flight is more than ten hours long, but who cares? At the touch of a button, the motor-operated recliner seat will bend you any which way you desire—including stretched out flat (and I'm six foot one). What's more, you get your own "sleeping suit," plus what I call a sleeping bag and the airline calls a duvet ("No camping references please, we're British").

Flying in such rarefied fashion is nearly as good as not flying at all. Luxuriating in one's own private wood-grain lounging pod in the first-class cabin all but obliterates the fact that you may be rocketing toward eternity in a giant tube of machinery. Instead, and especially after a glass of claret or three and a bit of liquid-velvet watercress soup, you find yourself serenely suspended above the clouds and sea over the Lost Planet of the Barbarians, snug in a Jules Verne airship while being coddled by the last representatives of civilization. Remember the times when you were a child, a late-night drive home, dozing in your mama's lap? It's like that, but with free movies and cognac.

Which brings us back to Stapleford Park. The main residence at Stapleford is what the English call "somewhat old." That is, it's mentioned in the Domesday Book, the record of the Norman survey carried out by order of William the Conqueror in 1085–86—though the present structure has been around only since the fourteenth century. Of course, it's had some improvements since then. (A high-relief inscription on one exterior wall reads, "William Lord Sherard Baron of Letrym Repayred This Building Anno Domini 1633.") Stapleford comprises five hundred parklike acres (down from the original 4,500), the Gothic eighteenth-century church of St. Mary Magdalene, a graveyard, thatched cottages, gatehouses, a lavish stable, a school of falconry, and a folly in the woods built, the story goes, as headquarters for the naughtiness of the Naughty Earl and his mistress. Some say there is a tunnel from the main house to the folly. Others say they're not so sure. I say, If you're an earl, why bother with a tunnel—don't you get to do whatever the flock you want?

Stapleford now caters to those who are different from you and me in that they think little of dropping as much as $900 (double oc-

cupancy, canines welcome for $8 extra) on a night's lodging, break-
fast included (kibble extra). The house and grounds fulfill even the
most idealized imagining of English country splendor and privilege. The cuisine is good to excellent: the venison was the richest
and most tender I've ever eaten—so aromatic, so succulent, I
wanted to get up on the table and roll in it the way my dog rolls in
dead cormorants at the beach. The wines, brandies, and single-
malt scotches are superb and free-flowing. And the service is im-
peccable, which is why people like Margaret Thatcher, Henry
Kissinger, Tom Jones, Tom Cruise, Nicole Kidman, and others of
their ilk come here to chill.

Stapleford is also imbued with that unmistakable air of cool dis-
cretion that naturally seeps from the pores of the celebrated and
wealthy. Mariah Carey and her two assistants hung out in the small
library/bar during the evenings and nobody even glanced in their
direction (except for me, who stared shamelessly and leaned my
chair back so far I almost fell over trying to hear what they were saying). Still, the atmosphere is friendly and in at least one case it bubbles over with a certain, outsize rural mirth—namely Malcolm.

Malcolm is the big, toothy, tweedy, constantly laughing man
who oversees outdoor activities at Stapleford. No sooner had I arrived than he piled me, a couple of fellow pilgrims, and several
shotguns into his Land Rover and drove us off across the wide-
wale corduroy meadow in search of the elusive clay pigeon. We
stopped a few hundred yards from the house and climbed out of
the Rover. Two boys were huddled behind a nearby mound, ready
to operate the catapult. They looked anxious—as well they should
have. Perhaps they could tell that I'd never fired a shotgun before
and was eager to get my hands on the thing as a means of releas-
ing the day's tensions. Malcolm gave us a brief lecture on gun
safety as a pregnant gray thunderhead approached from the south.
Then he handed me the shotgun. I raised it to my shoulder.
Malcolm watched nervously. The boys ducked out of sight. The
sheep stopped chewing and cocked their heads. All was silent. My
fellow travelers adjusted their ear protection. The thunderhead
moved in and dumped its water on us. I gave a sideways nod to

Malcolm. He yelled "Pull!" And a black flying saucer no bigger than a crumpet went sailing toward the horizon. I jerked the gun, squeezed the trigger, and the intact saucer fell to earth with a dull wet splat. The sheep moved quickly toward the lake and the swan on the bank fell over dead.

It went like that for the next half-hour or so as I briskly made my way through several hundred dollars' worth of ammunition and the dour, *Hindenburg*-sized cloud gave us a proper English soaking. "It's true," I conceded to Malcolm as we walked back to the Rover, "that I used a great deal of ammunition while refining my aim. I'm not proud of it. But the weather conditions were not the best, and think of how much money was saved by sparing all those clay pigeons." Malcolm glanced mournfully at the boys, who were running hither and thither gathering the pucks I'd failed to blast back to the Stone Age. "I always say," he remarked, "that you can't educate pork." I snorted and took it as a compliment.

Along with rapeseed and cheese, grand houses, castles, and abbeys are the prime cash crops in Leicestershire. Within an hour of Stapleford there are more than a dozen, most of which are open to the public. In addition to Althorp, the Spencer family's estate and the final resting place of Princess Diana, there's nine-hundred-year-old Rockingham Castle; Burghley House, a hysterically ornate Elizabethan hallucination of a place with a deer park capably landscaped by the famous Capability Brown; Belton House, with its orangery and Italian-style sunken gardens; the medieval Grimsthorpe Castle; Hardwick Hall; Calke Abbey ("crammed with all manner of curious collections," I'm told); Kedleston Hall; Fawlty Towers; Sudbury Hall; Newstead Abbey (once home to Lord Byron); Harlaxton Manor, the first Duke of Devonshire's Chatsworth estate; and Deene Park, ancestral home of those sweater-wearing maniacs, the Earls of Cardigan.

Granted, many people are bored delirious by being marched through such places, forced to look at moldy tapestries, dusky portraits of long-departed dukes, suits of armor, moth-eaten boar heads, kitchen walls hung with turtle skulls, a glove that Queen

Victoria left behind, a chair in which Disraeli once sat, rusty muskets, ancient billiard tables, and hideously painted ceilings. But some are never happier than when they're creaking around spooky eight-hundred-year-old hallways. For those of us who spent much of our childhood staring hypnotized out the windows of cars and classrooms while imagining ourselves anywhere but in the drear present, going to these places is like coming home. They are high-test fuel for the imagination—magnificent stages, as they were for centuries of human drama both political and personal. For the career daydreamer, there are few things more pleasant than wondering who did what to whom six hundred years ago in the very room where you're standing.

The place the locals call Beaver Castle (though it's spelled B-e-l-v-o-i-r), situated atop a hill about twenty-five minutes from Stapleford, fired my hope of lurid revelations. Unfortunately, all they could come up with was a snippet of sixteenth-century Chinese silk said to have been taken from the nightgown worn by Mary Queen of Scots the evening before she was beheaded. "But those embroidered, uh, paddles," I said, breathing heavily, "on the stands next to the fireplace. What were those used for?"

"Why, those are just pull screens," the elderly guide answered irritably. "They were used to protect ladies' faces from the direct heat of the fire. Back in those days they covered their faces with wax as a base for their makeup, to give a smooth surface. But if they didn't place the screen between themselves and the fire, why, their faces would melt right off. Terrible mess on the carpets, I should think."

"Yes, terrible," I agreed.

Later, in the picture gallery, standing next to a magnificent life-sized portrait of Henry VIII by Hans Holbein, I finally had to ask our guide about the castle's name. "How do you get the pronunciation 'Beaver' from Belvoir?" The old gentleman paused and looked at me as if I'd just asked the most absurd of questions. "We're British," he said abruptly, and took us into the King's Rooms for a close look at the hand-painted nineteenth-century wallpaper.

Back at Stapleford there was just time for a short horseback ride
before descending into the evening's menu of indulgences. I was
given a large, dark gelding and loaned a pair of black boots, and off
we went through the woodland and past the Naughty Earl's folly,
which now resembles a tumbledown chimney wrapped in vines. I
had horses when I was a kid, so riding usually returns me to those
days of contentment and abandon—ambling aimlessly through
the wilds of child dreamland atop a cordial beast. When we
emerged from the woods, we looked across the verdant sheep
meadow to the great house, lit up yellow by late-afternoon sunshine spilling through the clouds. The light, the air, the eager energy of the horses demanded that we gallop over the expanse of
grass and mud that lay before us. And backward in time I went—
almost.

The rain had left the ground soggy and the horses' hooves sank
in a good six inches or more with each impact. I watched my animal's pounding feet, felt the bracing English air against me, the
great body beneath me, his mane whipping my face, his tree-trunk
neck rocking back and forth in front of me, but I was not transported to childhood. Instead I was returned to my anxiety-ridden,
adult, media-besotted memory. And as I listened to the slog and
clump of the racing horses and watched the horizon bounce up
and down, two words came to mind: Christopher Reeve. And I immediately slowed my warm beast to a walk.

Such is the curse of adulthood, isn't it—graphically imagining
everything that might go wrong, so fast come undone; never able to
be-here-now the way the gurus say we're supposed to? I walked back
to the house from the stable through the gardens, past Mariah Carey,
who was nibbling a fruit salad at a table on the patio, and into the
back hallway, where I got stuck reading the old certificates displayed
on the walls. One of Stapleford's previous owners was a collector of
turn-of-the-century memorabilia from men's societies, and several
of the best examples still hang in the house. The "Registration
Certificate of the Worshipful Company of Farriers" was fine indeed;
another, for the "Ancient Order of Foresters Friendly Society," was

also a hit, as was the certificate for the "Otters United Ancient Order of Druids." But really the best, I thought—the winner hands down—was the superb specimen from "The Royal Antediluvian Order of Buffaloes" ("Antediluvian," mind you!), which read, "This is to certify that Brother William Jacques has been duly initiated into the mysteries of Buffaloism with all the ancient rites and ceremonies." We should all be so lucky, no?

As I turned to go to my room, Mariah Carey walked into the hall, assiduously avoiding eye contact with me (a skill the famous must perfect if they're to have any hope of making it through the corridors of a crowded, fawning world). She was followed by one of my shooting companions. He looked at my injured shoulder. I guess I was absentmindedly rubbing it. "Shoulder bothering you?" he asked.

"A little sore," I said, wondering if he'd heard any antediluvian buffalo howls emanating from my room the night before.

"Yeah," he said. "Mine, too. Those shotguns have a bit of a kick. They'll bruise you up good and red if you don't hold 'em firm." At which point Mariah Carey looked back at us with a very peculiar glance, then headed into the bar.

"Shall we kick off the evening with a glass of Cardhu?" my companion asked, nodding toward the door through which Ms. Carey had just disappeared. And we did. In fact, we had several, and the mass of lacy crimson stripes on my shoulder was all gone by morning.

I LOST IT AT CLUB MED

Po Bronson

I recently lost my Club Med virginity, spending a week at the Turkoise club in the Turks and Caicos Islands, just south of the Bahamas. What's a Club Med vacation like? It's sort of like watching *Melrose Place*. You don't want to think of yourself as the kind of person who likes it, because it preys upon your most base impulses, both sexual and slothful. You're embarrassed that it appeals to you, so you participate for a while with a mind-set that is somewhere between heckler and lowbrow camp. But eventually the calming endorphins kick in. Acceptance occurs. Then you are hooked, and you will go back.

I'd never been to an all-inclusive resort. The closest I'd come to a Club Med was four years ago, when I was staying in a $12-a-night bring-your-own-bath-towel motel near the municipal pier in Zihuatanejo, Mexico. For a quarter I bought a bag of rolls to keep from starving and snuck down to La Ropa beach, over the course of the day getting kicked off the lawn chairs belonging to one hotel after another. One day I took the city bus over the hill to the planned resort strip of Ixtapa, where every afternoon at four the shopping district is choked with an insect-killing fog. At the north end of that perfect beach, around another bluff, lay the tennis courts and bungalows of Club Med. Its Playa Quieta cove was dotted with wind surfers and Sunfish sailboats. I couldn't hear the bubbling laughter of a good time being had, but my mind could supply it—I looked upon Club Med the way a pimple-faced high school freshman looks upon the cool cliques in the senior class. I resented it simply because I did not belong, resented it because it sparked in me an envy I didn't want to feel.

To me, Club Med promised luxury. Not just nice accommodations, but a seamless luxury; the term "all-inclusive" didn't just mean "no tipping," it meant "Your every wish is anticipated." I soon found that this luxury expectation couldn't possibly be satisfied, because my concept of luxury is one formed entirely by television. Unless the terrain beat out *Gilligan's Island* and the hotel rooms improved on *Dynasty* and the staff put Pamela Anderson to shame, there was no way I wasn't going to be disappointed.

I should have seen it coming. On the charter from Kennedy I had the Row 1 first-class seat, where you can't stow your carry-on at your feet. The stewardess who enforced this rule refused to put my bag in the overhead compartment and made me do it myself. I was miffed and completely unable to take pleasure in the joys of having a seat wide enough for two. After we arrived at the Providenciales airstrip, a Club Med van immediately took a load of passengers to the club, but I was perturbed that I actually had to check in at Club Med. I figured checking in at Kennedy once would have been enough. They already had an impression of my credit card; why did they need it again? Then I had to go check out a beach towel, and leave a separate deposit. Most seven-day/six-night vacations, you arrive at the resort that first night after dark. Here I was on the beach before eleven A.M., but my luxury expectation was so rampant that smoke almost came out of my head when I was told by the lunch hostess I had to wear a shirt and at least sandals into the dining buffet.

Why was I so on edge? I think it came from guilt. Last summer, I hiked in the Andes at fifteen thousand feet, learning Quechua myths and exploring temples. This summer, I was going to lie beside a pool conducting experiments like seeing how much rum an orange slice can absorb and still float. No matter how wealthy I become, I will always believe I should spend my precious vacation making contact with some barely reachable indigenous tribe, improving myself by broadening my horizons. So I think I rationalized that Club Med was okay as long as it presented a sociological expedition into the realm of *Luxurius extremis*—the opposite end of the spectrum from popping in to a South-of-Market leather club just to see what it's all about, but the same principle at work.

Club Med is luxurious only in the sense that luxury implies waste—everything's prepaid, so you can grab conch fritters from the buffet but don't have to eat them, or you can take a bucket of tennis balls out to the court and quit after only ten practice serves. You're not constantly trying to get your money's worth. The best way I can describe the accommodations is that they're like Ivy League college dorms. They're sufficient. A maid will clean the room and the air-conditioning works and the beds aren't lumpy. But there's no room service. There's no carpeting. There's no televisions or telephones. Most of Club Med could be cleaned with a fire hose. The pool doesn't have a little waterfall at one end or a Jacuzzi at the other. There's no cocktail waitress walking around the pool taking drink orders, no little native man at the beach offering you a towel when you come out of the ocean.

Club Med wasn't *Luxurius extremis,* it was merely pleasant. The sky wasn't even blisteringly blue; it alternated between hazy and cloudy. The staff didn't annoyingly attempt to make sure at every minute that I was having a good time, even when they found out I was writing about them. This was horrifying. It meant I was going to have to spend my week without my cloak of cynicism. It was going to be one of those weeks (and I would have to write one of those stories) where I would confront my own urbanized prejudices. Tomorrow morning was a mixed doubles Ping-Pong tournament, and after that water aerobics, and then tryouts for the Copacabana musical. I felt more naked than if I'd dropped my shorts.

I don't feel a need to intricately paint a picture of the Club Med compound, because it's so easily imagined. Think fairly uninhabited tropical beach, facing west for dramatic sunsets. Some palm trees, etc. The beach is about three miles long. Ten years ago Club Med was the only thing on the waterfront, but now there's a small hotel and a few houses in sight. Some people judge beaches by their scenic beauty, but I judge them by the quality of the sand and the pliability of the waves. At Turkoise there is a coral reef a half-mile out from shore that reduces the waves to about two feet—too small to bodysurf, but just big enough to constantly tease me into thinking how great it would be to bodysurf. The water temperature is not quite bathwater, a little too cool to fall asleep in. The sand is satiny. I found it interesting that it wasn't too hot to walk upon. Several times I made a mental note to ponder the physics of why this might be so, but I never actually got around to it.

Just off the beach there's a quarter-mile strip of zigzagged three-story dormitories, accommodating up to six hundred guests, which is perhaps not as many as it may seem; within three days you can feel like the big man on campus. The activity centers are scattered around like croutons in a tossed salad. Over here are the tennis courts, surfaced with a porous Astroturf that lets real blades of grass mingle with the plastic carpet. Over there is the circus center, with full trapeze, a trampoline, and a tightrope. There's a soccer field, a scuba shack, a water-ski dock, a gazebo where classical music plays in the afternoon. The pool is just special enough that a postman from Brooklyn, on the last day of the week, took a roll of pictures of it, which he intended to show to all of the customers on his mail route. "We don't have pools this big in Brooklyn," he enthused. "At home they won't believe me unless I have evidence."

Near the bar there's a couple of pool tables and four slot machines. I'm not sure if the slots pay out. A retired and widowed legal secretary, who felt somewhat out of place among all the young 'uns, spent a lot of her time making friends with the quarter-ante slots. She stood four foot eight on her cork heels and her only exercise was the upper-body lunge for each inhale of her cigarette, which she never let get more than a few inches from the ashtray. It took her about four days to lose all her money.

Most of the activities at Club Med are very low-commitment efforts. They require no investment. The catamarans are prerigged. The snorkeling equipment is provided. In the crafts center, where you can paint patterns on silk banners, the paints and waxes are all premixed. Participating is much like watching television: activity-surfing. Though the daily schedule is organized in hour-long chunks, I often would windsurf for about twelve minutes, and then as soon as I felt a boredom coming on, swim ashore and join the stretch class by the weight room. Twenty minutes later, boredom again nipping at the edges of my mind, I would zap stretch class in favor of water volleyball. Every night after dinner there was some form of stage entertainment in the open-air theater, and every night I sat down in one of the back rows, but except for the circus night, the longest I remained sitting was for twenty minutes.

I watched the circus intently because I spent an hour each morning on the trampoline and tightrope and spent several afternoons on the trapeze. I would like to offer some Marin County guru explanation for why the circus training was a compelling experience—for example, "Flipping and bouncing reinvigorated my childlike desire to play"—but I don't think that's it. I think it's fun in the way that people who enjoyed school relate to: it's fun because it's hard.

Because the circus is the only activity at Club Med at which it's possible to break your neck, the circus instructors take themselves very seriously and expected me to do the same. It was the only time during the week that I was trying to impress an instructor, the only time I feared I would let someone down, the only time I wanted to avoid the embarrassment of making a mistake. The circus instructors expected me to pay attention. They expected me to watch while other guests were going through the routines I would soon repeat. To make sure they could be heard, they spoke in a sharp bark that seemed to promise, by its very inflection, a swift caning for disobedience. On the backswing of the trapeze, I was supposed to bring my feet up to my hands in an upside-down crouch and then hang by my knees. This requires a flexibility that is not anatomically possible for me, but unless I learned the maneuver I could not get into the next stage of the routine, where I fly from my bar into the hands of another. All of this created a commitment and a goal. As I fell asleep at night, I found my mind rehearsing the motions, breaking it into steps. It had never been so important to me to be able to get into a tight crouch.

This was in stark contrast to the windsurfing lesson, in which our instructor, who barely spoke English, sort of pointed to the water and the wind and said, "Go to it." Windsurfing is probably just as difficult as trapeze, but the sport was regarded so casually that I didn't get into the challenges that make it interesting.

You can skip the tennis tourney and you can stay clear of the disco scene and you can ignore the nightly lip-synced Broadway musicals, but at Club Med it's pretty hard to completely avoid people if you want to eat. For meals, we would grab from the buffet and be seated on a first-come, first-served basis at round tables for eight. At first it was intimidating—every meal, new strangers to befriend. I would poke at my food and sip my wine, hoping someone would strike up a conversation so I wouldn't have to make the first move. It was a sort of just-add-water instant company. There was a lot of tentative recounting of that day's activities, a lot of repeating that I'm from San Francisco and have lived there ten years but grew up in Seattle, and that yes, it really does rain there all the time, but no, that's not why I left.

But good nuggets got through. Club Med is expensive enough (about $999 a week, plus airfare) that most who can afford it have relatively interesting jobs. Since I've come back I've described Club Med to many friends, and this is the one point that raises their eyebrows and makes them scoff. Club Med has never shaken its swinging seventies image; it still conjures topless orange-passing games. What kind of lame person would go? The only accurate generalization is: Guests first come to Club Med because they didn't have time to plan a vacation. They're likely to be workplace overachievers. If you were ever going to suffer a broken bone in some foreign country, you'd want to do it at Club Med, because at any moment there are a half-dozen young doctors within shouting range.

The guests turned out to be no less stimulating than college classmates at a ten-year reunion. Among the conversations I had: how violence among British soccer fans isn't an expression of working-class frustration; how to layer watercolor pigment when working on canvas; ways an author can manipulate bookstores to reorder; failed expeditions on the north face of Mount Everest; why professional hockey is popular in Italy; why Microsoft bought WebTV; how Haitians arriving at Miami International Airport for the first time think the automatically flushing urinals are possessed with voodoo; whether Queens has been taken over by Korean immigrants; that the French for "window shopping" translates literally as "licking the windows"; the unfairness of labor laws in Spain; and tips for maintaining a long-distance love relationship.

One more way that Club Med resembles television is the way you can follow other people's dramas like *Love Boat* plots. A mother and her twentysomething daughter arrived from Jersey, hoping to break out of their mother-daughter roles and bond as friends. They were both good-looking enough to play themselves in the Movie of the Week version of their own lives—the older a sandy blonde, the younger a glossy brunette. Their first night, the mother couldn't find her daughter for an hour, panicked, and made the Club Med security comb the perimeter and the coastline, looking for a raped or washed-up body. Then the daughter appeared, walking hand in hand with a guy who is a professional hockey player in Europe. (Probably, in the movie version, this wouldn't be the first night. A night where they seem to be getting along splendidly would be inserted.) For the rest of the week, mother and daughter sat at different dining tables. (In the movie version, you would be getting out your hanky about now.)

Club Med is a French-owned company, and at Turkoise about half of the staff and a quarter of the guests are non-Americans. Most of the entertainment is repeated in both English and French. This put me in a culturally receptive mood that defused my hair-trigger skepticism. I didn't want to make a faux pas and come across as an insensitive American. So I openly accepted a lot of campy Club Med customs under the small possibility that they were French decorum. The simplest example was the custom of saying hello when I passed by a staff person on the walkways. All the staff people say hello, and of course I said hi in return. But there's a lot of staff; Club Med Turkoise can house six hundred guests, who are served by three hundred staff. My week there were only four hundred guests. So every other person was staff, and many of them were in bathing suits without their badges. I didn't want to accidentally offend a staff person by not saying hello, so I made it an easy rule to say hello to absolutely everybody. Within thirty-six hours of our arrival, everyone was saying hello to everyone, and this forced friendliness became self-fulfilling. Tony Robbins, the guru of positive thinking, is on to something. I felt an honest friendliness toward everyone. I was experiencing a chumminess that we in heterogeneous America have lost. Maybe they've lost it in other cultures too, but it's been regained at Club Med. Scuba diving with the sea turtles and the afternoon thundershower during the volleyball game and the beef Wellington for dinner became our shared experience. It was like summer camp, with the difference that we weren't plagued by teenage shyness.

The flip side of this multiculturalism-within-the-compound is the way Club Med often cloisters its guests from the poverty-stricken natives living just beyond the bougainvillea-covered fences. But that wasn't really an issue in Turks and Caicos. The island is entirely limestone and sand, covered in scrub. The highest elevation is about twenty-eight feet above sea level. It's a tax-free haven, so the island has offices from all the Big Six accounting firms, one KFC, an IGA grocery store, and some liquor stores. There are no indigenous craft trinkets to take home and hang in your living room to remind you that you're a worldly person. There just isn't much native culture to ignore. The music blasting from local cars is a reggae rhythm under a pop-synthesizer melody. Being a soccer fiend, I can usually use my soccer skills in foreign countries to befriend locals, and did so here. I had the occasion to referee a grudge match between the Club Med staff (with so many foreigners, they fielded a respectable eleven) and the native all-stars, who spoke combinations of French, tony British English, and pidgin squawk. Despite every advantage I could give the Club Med squad, they were walloped by the much faster locals, 6–nil. After the game, I got several invitations from the locals to stay an extra week and live with them, in their two-bedroom apartments, scuba-diving every morning. Locals showed up for the daily five-thirty basketball game as well, would-be Michael Jordans of every height, all wearing some newfangled Nike high-top that must have cost at least $150.

This isn't to suggest that there aren't plenty of jobless locals living in cement-block huts. It's just that as a guest at Club Med Turkoise, you don't have to shield your eyes and hum loudly to block out sights that remind you that you're a fat-rich-lazy American. As seems a recurring theme at Club Med, it's a relatively guilt-free trip.

At twelve-thirty every day the staff leads everyone near the pool in a sun dance, which is a dorky quasi-aerobics routine mangling the Charleston, the twist, the hustle, and a sort of *Saturday Night Fever* body origami. It goes on for several interminable minutes. The first day, I chose then to use the toilet. The second day, I was in the pool playing water polo when it started, and I couldn't escape. It's the sort of silliness that if you did it with your friends during the seventh-inning stretch at a baseball game it would be campy fun, but when you do it with complete strangers it makes you think, Thank God my friends aren't witnessing this. I was amazed so many people willingly participate, and at the lunch that followed afterward, I said so.

"Lay off, Mr. Cool Police," said a systems engineer from Manhattan. "I don't get to be silly back home."

There were a few more moments of this forced cheeriness—we were expected to applaud when the snorkeling boat driver introduced his lifeguards—but they were less frequent than I had anticipated. Mostly, the staff were kind, encouraging, and attentive. By Club Med custom, they are called G.O.'s, which is French for "gracious organizers," and the guests are called G.M.'s, "gracious members." For about an hour, this terminology seems hokey. But soon it's good they've coined catchy terms, because no word quite conjures the casual distinction between guests and staff. They are not quite formal employees; they're more like guests who have just been here a long time and know the ropes. They are paid about $450 a month, plus room and board and some drink tickets. At that low pay, it's not a career—they're here to spend a year or two slacking in the sun. Every six months, they are transferred to a different Club Med. On average, they are a bit younger than the guests. They dress like guests, in bikinis and cutoffs. They are seated at meals with guests, in the same first-come manner. Many of the workers from the kitchen played in the afternoon soccer game with guests. I didn't feel waited upon by the staff, which was great, because when I stay at a hotel I'm always uncomfortable with having a porter carry my bag or a bellhop open the door. Once again: no guilt. The G.O.'s drink in the bar with guests and they dance in the disco with guests and, when they're in the mood, they sleep with guests.

It would have been irresponsible for me as a journalist not to pay attention to the singles scene. Most nights I was in bed by ten, exhausted from the sports and sunshine, but one night I hung upside down with the nocturnals. We were at the bar until eleven-thirty, the disco until one, the beach bar until three, and skinny-dipping until four-thirty. Over the night I received completely contradictory reports. One woman said it was an obscene meat market, with men requesting, after only five minutes of small talk, to retire to her room. If she refused, they wrote her off and moved on. Another woman insisted the men here must be blind not to pick up her comely posture's implication. "Do I look like I have herpes or something?" she asked.

I met a couple of guys from Minnesota, professionals in their thirties. "At Martinique, it's ninety-five percent singles," one said, "but I'm too old for them." He pointed to his hairline. "I tried Cancún, but the male staff there are Adonises, and toward the female guests are, how should I say, predatory—I had no chance against them." He delivered his analysis in the same authoritative-yet-patient tone he might use to present a client with a marketing plan. "The men here don't make me feel like Pee-wee Herman. I met this woman last night, she was telling me that one of the staff dropped his shorts in the middle of their conversation. How childish, she thought, and walked away. She's looking for someone more mature. I think I've got a chance."

It was very easy to meet people, easy to start a conversation— "Hey, I saw you on the trapeze"—and pretty safe to assume that anyone hanging out past midnight was willing if the chemistry was right. Some people lowered their standards for the week. Others, fearing the loss of self-respect from lowering their standards, actually raised them, and then complained at the lack of six-figure-income cardiologists with herculean pecs.

Over the week, the following romantic activity occurred: One couple came for a parting fling and ended up engaged; one couple came to get married and did; two men met women and fell in love; and I would estimate that about one-third of the single people got laid, which is exactly the percentage that gave getting laid any effort at all, even just a coy wink during the karaoke or a faked stumble at the bar into the arms of the executive from Sweden.

After my night with the nocturnals I spent my last full day failing to nap in a lawn chair at the edge of the bay. My verbal clumsiness with polite conversation had incited a self-disgust and despair that the sunshine did not calm out of me. In the afternoon, someone shrieked—a fin in the water! It was not a shark, though. It was JoJo the dolphin. JoJo is wild but swims without companions, and every few days he will follow a fishing boat in through the reef. I jumped up and tried to run into the water, but my legs collapsed under me and I tumbled in the sand. I got up but fell down in another two steps. What the hell was going on?

I grabbed my legs but couldn't feel my grip, and I realized that they had fallen asleep. One of the G.O.'s jumped on a catamaran. I got up once more and this time I stumbled into the water, where my arms took over, freestyling at full strength. I caught up to the catamaran and grabbed hold of a support beam and let it drag me to JoJo. We slapped the water to call him near, the same way you call a dog by slapping your thighs. The G.O. pointed. "Here he comes." I ducked my head and opened my eyes underwater. All those years of watching *Jaws* had given me a fear of this moment: a big gray beast approaching, my legs dangling, human sushi. I slowed my breathing to relax. JoJo eased by, a few feet under me.

He was about eight feet long and barrel thick, with tiny black eyes and a white stub snout. All those years of watching *Flipper* kicked in, and I was completely trusting. I let go of the catamaran and stroked along above JoJo. The sunlight shimmered on his gray skin. The catamaran tacked back and forth, and we followed. The G.O.'s had officially warned us not to touch JoJo, suggesting it makes his skin vulnerable to infection, but I'd also heard it whispered that a lawyer once sued the club, claiming JoJo bit him. (I've also heard that JoJo can get excited, and that the dolphin equivalent of humping your leg is to bump into you.) I played by the rules. For three minutes, JoJo swam with me gently, circling underneath me, then rising to the surface for air with enough grace to take the cynic out of anybody. He made no noise, but I kept squealing his name. The salt water made my mouth feel like rubber. JoJo was fuzzier now, which meant my contact lenses had popped out. When a bigger sailboat motored by, JoJo zipped away. Every few minutes he needs something new with which to play. I understood.

The next morning I packed my bags. At breakfast I was hit by a twinge of sadness: this would be the last stack of pancakes I would ever share with these people. I had to evaluate the kinship I had felt for other guests and offer a degree of willingness for future contact: I swapped phone numbers with three, told about a dozen to look me up if they ever made it to San Francisco, and said in all earnestness to about thirty others, "If our paths ever cross again, I will remember you." Feeling generous, I gave my extra drink tickets to my favorite circus instructor. Then I made sure I got the recipe for white chocolate bread. I was suffering the inverse of that first day's trauma: though it had seemed forced to sit down with seven strangers for dinner, it now felt just as unnatural to rupture the small telepathies that had evolved. I had drifted through the week, unaware of how attached I was becoming to the ritual.

Then we climbed onto an old school bus for the short ride to the airport. The entire Club Med staff stood on the terrace to wave good-bye. I sat beside my friends, asking about their life history with the vigorous curiosity they had deserved from me days earlier. The bus doors closed and we pulled forward, rounding the cul-de-sac. Then we paused to let a caravan of arriving minivans pull into the space we had just left. It was the next week's load of guests, checking in not ten seconds after we departed. What we saw as genuine waves of good-bye from the staff, the newcomers interpreted as waves of welcome.

"I feel like meat," said a friend.

But that's not how I felt. I felt fine about it. It's like this: When I watched *The Mary Tyler Moore Show* as a kid, my cognitive awareness that Mary was just an actress playing to millions of viewers didn't shatter my magical illusion that Mary Richards and I shared a mutual, private sympathy. And just as it was possible to feel "understood" by a fictional character in a mass medium, I could feel singular, even oddly genuine, about my week at Club Med.

ABSINTHE MAKES THE HEART GROW

Taras Grescoe

It drove Baudelaire to Belgium, then to an early grave; it left Paul Verlaine a hollow-eyed wreck, wandering from bar to bar in Paris's Latin Quarter accompanied by a misshapen shoeshine boy named Bibi-la-Purée. The deaths of Vincent van Gogh, Oscar Wilde, and the poet Alfred de Musset were hastened by their inordinate love for this poison, long since banned by the thinking men of all civilized nations.

Except, of course, death-defying, devil-may-care Spain, where 136-proof absinthe is about as common as orange Fanta.

I'd come to Europe determined to uncork the liquid muse of the avant-garde, the licorice-flavored, high-octane herbal alcohol popularized by a French doctor in 1792. I'd discovered that in the nation of his birth, absinthe's sale had been strictly prohibited since World War I, but that in Spain, absinthe is considered just another aperitif, as familiar as vermouth and Campari. I'd found what the Spanish call Absenta in liquor stores in Madrid and in just about every bar in Catalonia; hell, I'd even found liter bottles of the stuff in the window of Can Canesa, the great grilled-sandwich shop in Barcelona's Plaça Sant Jaume.

And now I was in Barcelona's Barrio Chino—the infamous warren of narrow streets where Jean Genet set *A Thief's Journal* and the Divine Dalí went slumming—finally face to face with my own glass of La Fée Verte, the nineteenth-century hallucinogen that, in its time, had ruined more lives than cocaine.

To tell the truth, I had been a little worried about my date with the Green Fairy. Before my trip, the only two people I'd met who'd actually tried absinthe—both mild-mannered Canadians—had gotten into fistfights after only a couple of glasses of the stuff. With this in mind, I'd chosen my drinking companions carefully: Mary, a Scottish painter who'd fallen in love with Barcelona in the eighties and stayed on through the booming nineties, and Henri, a gaunt Belgian pastrymaker with the sideburns of a rockabilly singer from Memphis. He'd left Ghent only two days before, using a Renault truck to transport fifty-five-pound blocks of chocolate across France at a top speed of about forty-five miles per hour, to fulfill his longtime dream of becoming the first trufflemaker for the sugar-loving citizens of Barcelona. As drinking partners, Mary and Henri may not have been Sarah Bernhardt and Arthur Rimbaud, but they had forged their friendship over countless glasses of absinthe, and knew its rituals. What's more, under their tutelage, I was pretty sure that I wouldn't finish the night in jail.

We had started the evening at midnight (this being Spain, after all) in the Bar Marsella, which, though recently purchased by two hefty Anglo-Saxons, has been preserved intact as a kind of monument to the fast-fading bohemia of the Barrio Chino. In the Marsella, yellowing posters for long-forgotten aperitifs curl on the walls, the paint peels suggestively, and half a dozen different tile patterns jockey for space on the undulating floor.

A young waiter had brought us small brandy glasses full of clear, oily-looking absinthe, along with all the attendant paraphernalia: a bottle of water, paper-wrapped lumps of sugar, and a three-tined trowel. In the classic procedure, one sets the trowel on the rim of the glass and slowly strains the water through the sugar cube into the absinthe until it dissolves. (Water wasn't the only mixer for absinthe, however; the singer Aristide Bruant drank it with red wine, and Edgar Allan Poe took his with brandy. And died, incidentally, at the age of forty of a heart attack after a prolonged drinking binge.)

Mary introduces me to a local variation: I allow a sugar cube, squeezed between forefinger and thumb, to soak up the absinthe, which is 68 percent alcohol. Then, placing the cube on the trowel, I set it on fire and burn the alcohol off. After stirring the dissolving cube into the absinthe, I fill the glass three-quarters full with water, provoking a remarkable transformation. The liquid turns milky green, a color Oscar Wilde described as opaline, though to my eyes it looks more like a happy marriage of crème de menthe and whipped cream. In the murky half-light of the Bar Marsella, my glass of absinthe appears to be glowing from within.

I pause before imbibing. Everything about absinthe, after all, is sinister. It proved the undoing of so many artists and writers that the best book on the subject—Barnaby Conrad III's excellent 1995 work, *Absinthe: History in a Bottle*—eventually starts to read like an obituary page. It's distilled from the grayish-green leaves of a shrub called wormwood—in Russia, the plant is ominously called *chernobyl*—and in large doses its active ingredient, thujone, is a convulsive poison. Even absinthe's Greek name, *apsinthion,* means "undrinkable." However, it was also one of the most popular aperitifs in fin-de-siècle France, the subject of a painting by Manet, a sculpture by Picasso, and innumerable anecdotes by Hemingway. A favorite among the women at Parisian bars such as the Nouvelle-Athène and the Café du Rat Mort, absinthe even made it to the New World, where Mark Twain and Walt Whitman drank it in New Orleans's Old Absinthe House. But the dead-eyed regard of actress Ellen Andrée, the barfly in Degas's 1876 painting *L'Absinthe,* had always haunted me, and the more I look, the more the small groups huddled conspiratorially around the other tables at the Marsella resemble the doomed characters out of Emile Zola's *L'Assomoir.* I imagine myself embarking on a long slide into debauchery, followed by months of hydrotherapy—a Belle Epoque cure for alcoholics, which consisted of purges and a half-hourly soaking with cold water—in some Gothic asylum.

Suppressing a sensation of vertigo, I drink. And then I smile. Not at all bad—reminiscent of pastis, the licorice-flavored French aperitif, but with a slightly bitter undertone. Loosening up, I start trading anecdotes with my drinking companions about our worst debauches. The Belgian wins hands down, naturally, with a sad saga of three bottles of red wine, abrupt eviction from the restaurant where he'd consumed them, and subsequent awakening to a curious sound: the slick hiss of car tires whipping past his ear in the gutter he'd chosen for his bed. Mary looks at the rapidly dwindling level of my glass and says with some concern: "You might want to slow down. This is brain-damage stuff." I, however, am eager to test Wilde's description of absinthe's effects: "After the first glass, you see things as you wish they were. After the second glass, you see things as they are not. Finally you see things as they really are, and that is the most horrible thing in the world."

In fact, as I finish my glass, the Bar Marsella is suddenly looking like the most wonderful place on God's earth. When I walked in, I had been pretty sure that I was surrounded by nothing more than particularly hip backpackers, but suddenly the people at the next table begin to look strangely fascinating. They must be artists, I think to myself. And, as I work on another glass, the second phase of Wilde's dictum begins to kick in: I start to see things as they aren't. Isn't that woman—the one with her arm around the redheaded guy with the goatee—staring at me through her half-lidded eyes?

My eyes, too, are playing tricks on me: When I focus on an ashtray or a beer spigot, the center of my field of vision becomes unusually clear, but the periphery looks watery, indistinct. Objects seem to be surrounded by yellowish haloes, as in a van Gogh painting (the Dutch artist was on an absinthe bender for much of his career, including the binge in which he ran at Paul Gauguin with a razor and then cut off the tip of his own ear). The overall effect is of wearing a pair of ill-fitting goggles in the bottom of a filthy but surprisingly comfortable aquarium.

Just as I'm beginning to think this bar would be a great place to live—like, for the next few decades—the owner starts to lower the metal curtains. In spite of this clear intimation of closing time, a couple of local roustabouts slip in and start insistently ordering wine. The bartender's repeated yelling of *"Tancat!"* seems to have no effect, and I consider getting up and helping to explain to these uncouth gentlemen that our host is employing the Catalan word for "closed." However, remembering my Canadian friends' warning about absinthe's tendency to lead to fistfights—and noticing that the woman at the next table has somehow vaporized—I instead suggest to Mary and Henri that we take our custom elsewhere.

Henri begs off, the combined effects of hard liquor and two days of driving with the French having taken their toll, but Mary and I continue our crawl through the Barrio Chino. Most of the rest of the *madrugada* (not surprisingly, the Spanish have a single word for the early hours of the morning) is a blur. We wander past the Franco-era prostitutes of Carrer d'en Robador, anarchist cafés, and the inevitable piles of street corner refuse giving off fascinating, unidentifiable odors. We stop at a nightclub called El Cangrejo, where a transvestite of the stature of the late Divine is performing beneath a wig the size of a sheep dog. We poke our heads into the Bar Pastís, a temple of francophilia where the jukebox has been playing Edith Piaf since the 1940s; the London Bar, where people come to worship swinging England; and finally the Bar Kentucky, which is what an American tavern might look like if Antonio Gaudí had been hired as a decorator. A barman who calls himself Pinocchio—he explains his sobriquet with a gesture to his bent nose—serves us our last absinthes of the night, and Mary and I ferry our drinks to the end of the mobile home–length bar.

As taxi drivers and prostitutes squeeze past us, we clink glasses, toasting what's left of Barcelona's rapidly gentrifying Barrio Chino. On this night, I won't make it to Wilde's ultimate phase of absinthism (it would take at least five more glasses), the one in which one's surroundings reveal themselves in all their horror. In the Kentucky, on the contrary, the seediness continues to look glamorous. I remember all those who succumbed to the allure of the Green Fairy, among them Toulouse-Lautrec, who carried absinthe around Montmartre cabarets in a hollow cane, and Alfred Jarry, the playwright, who dyed his face and hands green, toted pistols on his absinthe binges, and died at the age of thirty-four. With the opaline, nerve-damaging muse in hand, I drink to squandered talent and beautiful corpses. But I'm really drinking to danger— and to the grateful realization that, in this world in which people are increasingly protected from themselves, there are still places left where we are free to choose our own poison.

WHERE THE HULA GODDESS LIVES

James D. Houston

I first heard about the hula terrace from a Hawaiian dancer. We were talking about the spell cast by certain modern-day performers, whose voices and supple bodies seem empowered from an older time. She said that if I wanted to understand the true sources of hula, I should visit this place called Ke'e, on the island of Kauai. "It's mostly lava rocks," she said, "a kind of rocky platform out there by itself. It's dedicated to Laka, our deity of hula. You probably won't see any dancers. But you'll see where the dancing begins." This was an intriguing idea, a very Hawaiian idea: that a dance tradition could be linked to a gathering of rocks, might somehow originate there. I had to see the place, and last fall I finally had my chance.

Though it isn't marked on many maps, the old terrace was not hard to find. Kauai is a small island. There is only one road to the north shore. I followed it from the main town of Lihu'e, up the windward side, bore west toward Hanalei, with its glistening taro ponds, and on past Lumahai Beach, where they filmed scenes from *South Pacific*. Out that way razor-topped canyons notch the shoreline. About a mile past Ha'ena, the most northerly point in the main Hawaiian chain, the road ends at a sandy little cove called Ke'e Beach.

From there, as the dancer had instructed me to do, I hiked along the shore for a hundred yards or so. Beyond the last house on that side of the island, a wet path cuts inland through pandanus thicket. Nothing marks the route until you have climbed a while and come upon a simple sign saying "Ka-Ulu-O-Paoa-Heiau." "Heiau" means place of worship. "Paoa" had been a famous priest in this region. The corner of an old foundation loomed above me, the remains of the temple named for him, now a sloping stack of lava rocks.

Climbing out of the trees, I saw that a whole hillside had once been terraced with rock embankments rising from the temple toward a small plateau. On this uppermost level I found the platform, a rock-bordered and grassy rectangle, at the foot of a stone cliff splotched white with lichen.

It is called Ka-Ulu-O-Laka Halau Hula. "Halau" means a longhouse or meeting place. "Ulu" means to grow or increase, as well as to be artistically inspired by a god or spirit. Thus: "A Place of Dance Honoring the Inspiration of Laka." Whenever I come upon one of these revered Hawaiian sites, I have learned to stand still a while and listen and look around. Why here? I ask myself. Why not closer to the beach? Or at the top of this cliff? Or across that ravine? There is always some appropriate mix of features that gives the spot its own appeal and holding power.

In the case of Ke'e, it is important to bear in mind that hula in early Hawaii was much more than a form of entertainment. For dancers it was a sacred calling, to which you dedicated your life. Hawaiians had no written language. Chanters and dancers were the poets, historians, and keepers of the flame. Hands and arms and hips and feet were trained to tell the stories of the people— their gods, their origins, their voyages and exploits and affairs of the heart—and keep them alive from one generation to the next. Hula was the centerpiece of traditional culture, just as it has been the centerpiece of the current cultural renaissance. So any place dedicated to the deity of hula had probably been chosen with considerable care.

According to the famous myth of Pele and Hi'iaka, Ka-Ulu-O-Laka Halau Hula is where the high chief Lohi'au sat drumming for some dancers, when his compelling rhythms were heard by Pele, the volcano goddess, from her fiery home in Puna, on what is now called the Big Island. Drawn toward the sound, Pele's spirit-body traveled north from island to island until she reached the *halau hula*, where the handsome chief was instantly smitten by her great beauty. In his nearby house they spent three days together; then Pele's spirit-body left Kauai and returned home. Unable to get Lohi'au out of her mind, she sent a younger sister, Hi'iaka, on a mission to bring him to her.

Thus begins a complex epic of high adventure, love and rivalry, death and transformation. One of the Pacific's great legend cycles, the story of Pele and Hi'iaka links Ha'ena in the far north with the Big Island's active crater region in the far south, underscoring the significance of this old *halau hula* in both the geography and the mythology of the Hawaiian chain.

From the grassy terrace, looking north, it is all blue ocean, with nothing between this cliff and the Aleutians 2,400 miles away. Out of that infinity the swells roll toward you. Near shore, each rising edge becomes a pencil line across the blue, then breaks to gush over wet black rocks directly below, where the inshore swirl is marbled turquoise.

My dancer friend had told me that she and her troupe once flew here from the Big Island, 350 miles south and east, to pay their respects to the goddess who first brought hula to Hawaii. They began by dipping themselves in those waters, said to be healing and purifying for performers. They entered from Ke'e Beach, and then, with their leis and skirts and ankle-ferns dripping, they climbed barefoot up the trail and made an offering of their dance.

In the wall behind the platform there are niches and small ledges where the most recent offerings could be seen, nontraditional, left by visitors paying their respects—a bunch of wild daisies, a circular head lei of close-pressed flowers, a piece of starfruit, a polished kukui nut, a fresh mango wrapped in a ti leaf.

Root tendrils dangled from above. Higher up, ti plants and papaya trees had sprouted from the cliff. The plant-layered wall, with its natural altar, is framed by two narrow canyons that shape a bowl, a cathedral of eroded lava. The two canyon jungles, thick with palms and more papaya and ironwood and ferns, slope steadily toward the peaks and scoured ridges that cup around behind. One bold spire seems to rise like an obelisk, and above these peaks, the clouds spilled seaward, gauzy, urgent clouds floating down from Mount Wai'ale'ale, ten miles away, known to be the wettest spot on earth.

As these clouds poured over the ridges, they mirrored the panorama of rolling surf. Their gliding shadows could also change the colors of the sea, from turquoise to diamond blue to cobalt. I felt I knew then why dancers had been coming there for centuries to commune with hula's guiding spirit. I saw what my friend had meant by "sources."

The changing water, the spilling clouds, the creased and jagged peaks behind—all were bathed in an uncanny liquid light. A wind swept down to riffle the palms and the papaya trees, and the whole place had come alive, moving in its own kind of elemental dance.

IN A FRENCH CAVE

Beth Kephart

We have driven for many days now over the thin carapace of the earth, beneath a vast and vaporous sky. It is the end of the sunflower season. Like tired corn, the stalks take their beating from the sun, their faces the color of repentance, their fringes singed past glory. Where there are no flowers, there are loose-jowled cows, and where the cows have given ground, there are flocks of unimaginative sheep, and sometimes as we drive there is no ground at all. It's rocks on one side, piling up, and nothing but air on the other.

"Bill," I say to my husband, who's at the wheel. "For God's sake, Bill, we're going to fall." And then, because God has intervened, we are miraculously spared.

Earth, in this southwest knuckle of France, is a phantasma of layers. It is our planet left essentially alone or, more true, it is our planet respected. Ruined stone castles crumble down hills. Iron crosses sprout out of unlikely limestone pilings, like rusty bouquets to religion. I come from a place where land has been disregarded, pulped, and here, in this region of unblemished possibility, I suffer from a sadness that is also partly prayer.

On the day we leave for La Grotte Rose, the valleys are obscured by fog. It all burns off before noon, and by then we are already too far gone along the narrow necklace of road to turn back. Closing my eyes, I leave the navigation to Bill and the entertainment to our son, Jeremy, who is doing a fair impersonation of Ricky Martin in the back of the rented Renault.

At one hairpin curve some 860 meters up, Bill swerves and curses a camper barreling down wide on the opposite side of the single-lane road. I put one hand over my shut eyes and sip at the air through clenched lips. When the earth decides to level out again, I open my eyes to find a dull gunmetal-algae landscape, with evergreens that are stumpy and ill-shaped. We pass through a town big enough to have a name, small enough to be contained in a single photo. The roofs of its five houses scrape against the ground. A battalion of white geese honk their unilateral opinion.

The caves, when we reach them, are a relief. We are offered former visitors' discarded sweaters to wear, for it is cold—10 degrees centigrade—inside the earth. We are given the history, which sounds like folklore, about a shepherd named Sahuquet who, one crisp autumn day in 1880, saw a fox enter a fissure in the rocks. Being the good shepherd he must have been, Sahuquet set off in pursuit, fitting himself between the stones. It wasn't until his eyes adjusted to the light that he saw the ghosts knocking their heads against the smooth domed ceiling, the colored magic wands thrusting up from the nether world. At the very instant he let out a scream, others—invisible, haunted—let out screams back at him. This was hell of course, and Sahuquet ran from it, pawing his way back into the sun. Vowing never to return, he never did.

But he told his friends what he had seen and heard, and soon enough, Edouard-Alfred Martel, a fancy lawyer hungry for adventure, had brought the nascent craft of speleology to the caves. It is he we must thank for the lighted stairs we're about to descend.

In the sun, we fiddle with our adopted sweaters until the tour guide, his story over, finally steps aside to let us through. Inside the caves, the air seems more wet than cool, and we pull our arms in toward our chests, like birds settling their wings. There must be two dozen of us on this tour, and when I turn around there is already no sign of sun behind us, no evidence of the gray-green tundra, or of the nasty gap at the edge of the Jonte cliff, through which we are now walking.

Claustrophobia has no business here. Over the next damp hour, we will walk for two kilometers and go 120 meters down into the crepuscular belly of the earth.

It's a church we're looking at, and then a tortoise, a minaret, Father Christmas, a hall turned pink. It's the needles of stalactites hanging overhead and a burnished community of stout, determined stalagmites, some shaped like small-capped mushrooms, others like the free-form sand castles I used to pull through my fingers beside the tide pools of the Jersey shore.

The guide speaks in French. We pay acute attention, recalling what we already know. Look around, we imagine the guide saying to us, and remember the chemistry of caves. How rainwater is not neutral but acid; and yes, remember how curious rainwater is. How it creeps, trickles, and gropes between fissures and rock layers—breaking the earth's surface into clints and grikes and sinkholes, opening tunnels into which streams may disappear.

And how it keeps on running underground, dissolving rocks, chiseling out networks and passages, tunnels and caves, caverns and unreachable domes. How it sets the stage for the crenellated stalactites overhead, and for the stalagmites, which are both wrinkled and eerily smooth. And sometimes the stalactite and the stalagmite become one, as if columns were commissioned to serve the domes. Rainwater alone, dissolving the calcite of limestone, yields a single color: white. Where there is ferrous oxide, we are given red and yellow, pink. Where manganese oxide makes its presence known, there are shadows of charcoal and gray.

Down we go, farther down; I take Jeremy's hand into my own, wanting the comfort he always yields. *"Eeww-la-la,"* he whispers, *"eeww-la-la,"* in his very best French, with the innocent awe of childhood. I fumble around with my camera, certain all the while that I won't succeed. The colors will be wrong and how do you photograph a glisten anyway, how do you train your lens to measure the distance between yourself and a sky of stone?

We go down, and we go farther down, past a church pulpit, a flock of sheep, a forest of candles, something the guide calls the chaos of subsidence, into corridors, chambers, and halls. It takes a full century to produce five centimeters of petrification. And yet look at this petrified waterfall, one hundred meters long and twenty meters high. Look at the elephant ears hanging above us. Look where we have come to, far down now, and deep as we'll ever go.

"Jeremy," I whisper, still holding his hand, which has warmed slightly in mine. "Imagine cavemen living in this wild place. Imagine thinking that the dome overhead was the first important sky and the sky that we know, the cup of heaven. That the sound of the water ceaselessly dripping was the sound of the wind going by."

"*Eeww-la-la,*" he says. "They must have thought they lived in magic."

"I bet."

"They must have whispered."

"Sure."

"They must have been scared when they turned the lights out."

I take a deep breath. I fill my lungs with the fumes of the earth. I feel drops of mysterious mischievous rain burst on my head, wriggle toward my right earlobe. If I stood here long enough, I think, I'd be draped in a cloak of colored calcite. I'd be sealed inside the earth, in the dark, in a place 500,000 years old. A place that knows nothing of life on the other side, a place where nothing ever changes, not really, save the size and shape of all that glistens, and the echoes of astonished little boys.

HOW TO BUY A TURKISH RUG

Laura Billings

If there is something missing from the American Shopping Experience—and if you've been to the Mall of America, as I have, you know that not much has been overlooked—it is the act of bargaining. Not buying a bargain, a blandly experienced purchase of an item whose price has merely been called back to our atmosphere (e.g., "I saw these four-hundred-dollar shoes marked down to thirty-nine ninety-nine and I had to have 'em!"). No, I mean the act of bargaining, in which buyer and seller come together in the great mambo of marketing, which, in the best cases, makes each leave the exchange satisfied they've ripped off the other just a little bit. Bargaining may be disappearing from our commercial landscape (witness the rise of Saturn dealerships), but it lives on in the rest of the world. This is, in large part, why we travel.

Not long ago, a friend called to invite me on a cheap off-season tour of Turkey. She promised that I would see the ruins of Ephesus and the fairy chimneys of Cappadocia, that I would wake each morning to the sound of the Muslim call to prayer and go to bed each night with a belly full of aubergines. Yeah, whatever, I said, just as long as I get to buy a rug. The truth was that ever since I bought my first car and was introduced to the delirious back-and-forth of negotiating. I had dreamed of going toe-to-toe with the guys who invented the dealer showroom. Since flying carpets were our first automatic conveyance—and if you've read *The Arabian Nights* or seen *Aladdin* you know this is true—rug merchants were actually the world's first automobile salesmen.

And they're outstanding salesmen, living as they do in the busy confluence of Europe and Asia, a ripe spot for studying humanity and perfecting the salesman's credo: Tell the customers what they want to hear. On my first day in Istanbul, I nearly fell prey to a green-eyed charmer who accosted me in the Kapali Carsi, the famous covered bazaar that holds more than four thousand shops. (Take that, Mall of America!) "You are a great beauty," he said so wolfishly that it was clear the antiseptic threat of harassment charges hadn't drifted into this pungent corner of the world. "You must be Italian." Actually, I'm a poster girl for the corn-fed Midwestern look, and was so pleased to be deemed continental that I was opening my wallet when my Turkish tour guide dragged me away.

After another half-hour in Istanbul, I discovered that merchants' flattery flew almost as quickly as the prices they quoted, but it was the numbers I had to pay attention to. At the time I visited, each U.S. dollar was worth about 35,500 Turkish lira—a complicated ratio, but one that afforded me the heady thrill of announcing, "A million? No prob!" I spent the week learning, but it wasn't until I passed the souvenir stands outside the ruins of Ephesus that I felt I had hardened myself to the Turkish marketing come-on. There, a young man bearing an armful of dolls and a striking resemblance to Johnny Depp deliberately bumped into me. "Excuse me, madame," he said, his voice warm and rich as ripe olives in sunshine. "You dropped something."

I looked to the ground and then to him. "What did I drop?"

He paused for a moment, searching my face soulfully. "It was my heart," he dripped, but I kept walking. I was finally ready to buy a rug.

So we went to Oba, a veritable rug ranch of low-slung build-ings and grassy courtyards, just down the road from the House of the Virgin Mary. A hawk-browed Turkish man in a double-breasted suit greeted us and gave a lesson about rug craftsman-ship designed to dispel any notion we might have had that a good rug could be purchased on the cheap. He showed us baskets of tobacco leaves, onion skins, and indigo used for dyeing fibers. He showed us the silkworms boiled alive for our textural pleasure—a sacrifice that Double-breasted assured us the worms were only too glad to make. Same went for the young girls in the weaving room, whose hands shuttled and knotted wool with the flutter-ing speed of hummingbirds. Double-breasted promised that the girls got full health coverage, nutritious meals, and a good wage, and that they didn't complain when the small-motor demands of rug weaving forced them to leave the work by their late teens. "It is a privilege and an honor to make something so beautiful," he said, but I couldn't stop the pitying look that swept across my face as I watched a young girl squatting and squinting before an intricate Persian pattern. An equally sympathetic look crossed her face as she saw us herded into the carpet showroom, lambs to the slaughter.

We were led through a series of rooms where vibrant rugs and kilims were layered like sheets, rolled into columns, and tacked to the walls—each room duplicating and expanding upon the previ-ous room's treasures. At the end of the procession was a ballroom-sized showroom where we were offered Turkish apple tea, soda, beer, and wine (American car dealers should reconsider the pop-corn and Coke routine, I thought). While we were served by a long-lashed girl in harem pants, her counterpart—a sulky John Malkovich look-alike in Western clothes—quietly shut the heavy wood door that was our only escape route.

Like a Turkish caravanserai floor show in which a slim-hipped belly dancer preps the crowd for the heftier model and finally for the cartilaginous creature who shakes her extra-wide-load hips to tambourines and thunderous applause, the rug show started slowly. Malkovich and Harem Pants lifted each rug by the ends, walked to the center of the room and let gravity unfurl it, the bright colors of Anatolia, Kars, and Kayseri washing over us. As the pacing built, the rugs started to cover the shining wooden floor, then overlapped one another. Soon we had left our perches on the wooden bench that lined the wall and begun crawling around on the rugs, examining their fine weaves and lustrous textures. The climax arrived with the unfurling of a massive silk Persian of geranium reds and robin's-egg blues. Though we were already breathless, Double-breasted clapped his hands and Malkovich and Harem Pants, moving like choreographed game-show models, picked up either end of the carpet and turned it 180 degrees, shifting the rug's palette to crimson and cobalt. Amazing! we cried. Astonishing! we clapped.

At that, a cluster of salesmen who had been gathering in the room suddenly converged on us and pulled us to separate corners. Three men whisked me into another room. Their leader was a raven-haired fellow with cheap shoes and a wistful expression. His name, Ogun, means "That Day" in Turkish, a fact that was the source of huge laughs for his two squat henchmen, who clearly understood my English but spoke only in Turkish with Ogun. I started to say that I was in the market for a five-by-seven kilim with a lot of red in it, but Ogun shot me a pained look that suggested such a request was as déclassé as demanding that an Old Master painting match my sofa. Instead, he ordered the henchmen to unroll a series of rugs at my feet. When I shook my head at the choices, the henchmen tossed their arms up in disgust, but Ogun had a more courtly approach. With each selection I dismissed, he nodded appreciatively and moved closer to me, as if irresistibly drawn to my aesthetic.

Soon he began dismissing rugs for me—"Can't you see she won't like that? She wants real beauty," he would scold the henchmen. He asked if my husband would like my choice of rug, and I said I didn't have a husband. He shouted in Turkish to the henchmen, who eyed me up and down, and again tossed their hands up in disgust. "They think this is a tragedy," Ogun said, and then sighed toward his cheap shoes, "and so do I." At this point he asked if I had a credit card with me. I said yes. The haggling began.

The rug I selected, or that Ogun had selected for me, was a jewel-toned affair of blacks, pomegranate reds, jade greens, and deep blues. Ogun explained that normally he would start the bidding around $1,000, but since this was the end of the season, and since I had no husband, he would start at $500. I shook my head at the price, and though my blood was racing, I couldn't coax out a counteroffer. Ogun strode away from my side with his hands thrust deep into his pockets, his shoulders hunched. He nodded his head and Henchman No. 1 scurried to the other room. Ogun smiled, puffed out one side of his cheek, and slowly blew out a low whistle of air. A few minutes later, the henchman returned and whispered in Ogun's ear. Ogun told me that Double-breasted had insisted that I leave with a rug today—how did $260 sound?

Well, it sounded pretty good to me, now that my lust for bargaining had flagged. Ogun wasn't a shrewd creep, I thought; he was a fellow connoisseur. Just then, my friend walked in and saw me handing off my credit card.

"What are you doing?" she demanded, and I explained the situation. "No way," she said to Ogun. "Two of 'em for two sixty!"

Quickly, my friend's bad-cop display made me realize I had allowed myself to be swept along too easily. Ogun looked to me. "Two for two hundred and sixty dollars?" he asked, and I nodded. He held his hand to his heart. He walked to the corner of the room and sighed. "We are friends, Laura?" he said, coaxing a small tear to the corner of his eye. "Why do you hurt me like this?" Finally, I understood the theatrics required here.

"Ogun," I said, so forcefully I convinced myself I was truly affronted. "I don't think you're being honest with me." And I snatched back my Visa card.

At that there was a very pregnant pause in which Ogun and the henchmen bored their Turkish eyes at me. They huddled and Henchman No. 2 threw his hands up in the air and pointed at me.

Henchman No. 1 made a spitting noise. Ogun looked over his shoulder. "So you want two rugs?"

"If the price is right," I said. Henchman No. 2 sniffed and gestured again. Ogun came back to my side and put his arm around me, hand to his collarbone in a gesture of sincerity. "My friend, you know that I must make a living?" I clenched my fist around my plastic. He let out a heavy sigh. "My friend, you may have two for four hundred dollars. No lower, please."

"Three hundred," I said.

"Three sixty," he said.

"Three hundred," I said.

"Three twenty-five," he said.

"Sold," I said, and at that there were cheers from the henchmen and from the small crowd from my tour bus that had gathered for the final negotiation. As I handed off my Visa, Ogun took my hand and wrapped it under and over his forearm as though we had been wedded by this exchange of currency. He lovingly folded and packed my rugs in brown paper and then in a nylon case he promised would fit nicely under my plane seat. It did.

Now I come across my two rugs, one in my living room, the other in my bedroom, and I feel a wave of pleasure at my purchases. But the souvenir that pleases me most is a photograph I have of Ogun and me. We are standing in the courtyard of the rug ranch—I have my hands clasped and my head tossed back in laughter; he gazes at the camera with the smallest trace of a smile. We both look so satisfied—as if each of us ripped off the other, just a little bit.

THE DANGERS OF PROVENCE

Peter Mayle

None of us these days can escape those small, brightly colored, and infinitely alluring scraps of propaganda that our more fortunate friends send us when they're on vacation and we're not. Nothing provokes envy and Monday-morning gloom faster than a postcard. And when that postcard is from Provence, slightly wine-stained, redolent with heat and sunlight and tranquillity, it is probably enough to make you kick the cat as you leave to go to the office.

All, however, is not as it seems. Beneath that implausibly blue sky, a number of surprises—never even hinted at in the photograph of the picturesque village or the genial lavender-cutter—lie in wait for the innocent visitor. I believe I've experienced most of them, and these words of caution are the result of personal and occasionally painful research. Be warned. If you venture to Provence, you will encounter some, if not all, of the following local specialties.

Provence has been accurately described as a cold country with more than its fair share of sunshine, and the climate can't seem to make up its mind whether to imitate Alaska or the Sahara. There were days during our first winter when the temperature fell to 15 degrees Fahrenheit; in summer, it can stay at 85-plus for week after rainless week. The local zephyr is the mistral, which has been known to blow at 110 miles an hour, taking hats, spectacles, roof tiles, open shutters, old ladies, and small unsecured animals with it. And there are storms of quite spectacular violence. Provence is the meteorological equivalent of a meal consisting of curry and ice cream.

KAMIKAZE DRIVERS

Your first few hours on the roads of Provence will not be dull. The Provençal motorist, brimming with élan, impatience, and sometimes, it must be said, with half a liter of good red wine, regards driving much as a matador looks on his encounters with a bull— that is, as a challenge to come as close to catastrophe as possible without incurring physical damage. And so you will find, to your alarm, that cars appear to be glued to your exhaust pipe until a sufficiently perilous moment to overtake you presents itself. This will be achieved with centimeters to spare on a blind bend, while the driver conducts a spirited conversation with his passenger that requires at least one hand being off the wheel. (Conversation in Provence cannot take place without manual assistance.) The mistake made by most visitors is to give in to natural impulses and close the eyes as certain disaster looms. If you can resist that, you will probably survive.

ELASTIC CLOCKS

The Provençal attitude toward time is that there is plenty of it. If by chance you should run out of it today, more will be available tomorrow. Or the day after. Or next week.

This admirably relaxed state of mind is, of course, at odds with the curious habit that many visitors bring with them from Paris or London or New York: the exotic practice of punctuality. It's not that this is ignored. Indeed, the important matter of the next rendezvous is often discussed seriously and at great length over two or three drinks. But somehow the arrangement is never quite as precise as you might expect. A day—let's say, Tuesday—will be agreed upon, with much emphatic nodding. This encourages you to suggest that a time on Tuesday should be fixed, and here you begin to sense a certain amiable but firm disinclination to pin down the rendezvous to anything more exact than a tentative commitment to either the morning or the afternoon. As it turns out, even this is optimistic, since nobody comes until Friday. Excuses are performed by the shoulders. Elsewhere in the world, patience is a virtue. In Provence, it's a necessity.

BODILY ASSAULTS (EXTERNAL)

There have been many occasions when a five-minute chat with a Provençal friend has left me feeling as though I've undergone a course of brisk exploratory surgery. Apart from the obligatory mangling handshake—or, with the opposite sex, the double or triple kiss—there is the vigorous kneading of the shoulder, the attack on the breastbone by the tapping of an iron index finger, the friendly clap around the kidneys, the odd glancing blow from the knuckles of a gesticulating hand, and the tweak administered to the cheek by way of a fond farewell.

In other words, conversation is more than a mere exchange of words. It is a bruising physical encounter with a human windmill.

BODILY ASSAULTS (INTERNAL)

One is invited and expected to drink. Provence is awash with locally produced wine, from the modest *ordinaire* to the grand and heady vintages of Châteauneuf-du-Pape, and it would be impolite and unadventurous not to try as many of them as your liver can stand. There are, however, two alcoholic booby-traps that should be approached with extreme caution.

The first is *vin rosé*. It may be a pale, smoky pink or a deeper tint not unlike the blush of a grog-blossom nose, and it looks light, frivolous, and harmless. It tastes delicious, crisp and chilled, the perfect drink for a blindingly hot day. You reach for another glass (or another bottle, as the first one slipped down so pleasantly) and congratulate yourself on avoiding anything too heavy. This is a mistake, since many rosés contain as much as 13 percent alcohol. This, combined with an hour or two in the after-lunch sun, can produce a truly epic hangover.

And then there is pastis, by far the most popular aperitif in Provence. The taste is clean and sharp and refreshing, exactly what one needs to settle the dust and stimulate the palate after a hectic morning in the market. There is no immediate jolt, as the alcohol is masked by the other ingredients, and it is insidiously easy to drink. Only later, when you try unsuccessfully to walk to lunch in a straight line, do you feel the effects of this delightful Provençal invention.

THE LINGERING GUEST

A house in Provence, whether you own it or rent it, is a magnet. No sooner are you installed, in what you hoped would be blissful seclusion, than the phone calls begin. They are from friends, or friends of friends, who are concerned that you might be lonely or bored. By chance, they find themselves free to come down, cheer you up, and entertain you.

What a noble sacrifice! They have made the journey from some distant rain-sodden paradise in the north just to be with you, to share the discomforts of your bucolic existence—the sun, the pool, the endless racket of corks coming out of bottles, the siestas. And their stamina is quite extraordinary. Despite third-degree sunburn, gastric disorders (always blamed on the local water, never the local wine), lack of television, mercilessly long meals, and all the other shortcomings of the simple life, they bravely soldier on. And on. And on. A weekend visit stretches to a week, and then ten days, or longer.

One hero arrived in October and was still with us on New Year's Eve, only leaving when the builders came to knock down his bedroom wall. And still they come, from Easter until Christmas, willing to endure anything that man and nature can throw at them in Provence. I suppose that, like me, they're gluttons for punishment.

HOG HEAVEN: AT THE MEMPHIS WORLD CHAMPIONSHIP BARBECUE COOKING CONTEST

David Kohn

Take a drive around Memphis and you'll see barbecue cookers everywhere—on porches, in yards, under carports, on the terraces of housing projects. Not those spindly Webers made for cooking up a few burgers, but big cylindrical contraptions, sturdy enough to cook a 130-pound hog for the necessary twenty-four hours.

Which explains, more or less, how I found myself in this humid city, in a treeless field on the banks of the Mississippi River, surrounded by groups of well-nourished men using all manner of equipment—five-hundred-gallon propane tanks, converted oil drums, and gigantic rotisserie ovens—to gently cook several tons of pork. I was in the midst of, as one participant called it, "the big 'un": the Memphis in May World Championship Barbecue Cooking Contest.

That night when I undressed, my clothes, down to my underwear and socks, were fragrant with smoke. It had been a good day. I had eaten three heaping barbecue sandwiches, a plate of ribs, and several large helpings of baked beans flavored with chunks of pork fat.

How had I—a Northerner, a Jew, and a sometime vegetarian—ended up here? Eight years ago, as a newly minted college graduate, I applied for fifty newspaper jobs. I was turned down by all but one, the *Anniston Star* in Alabama. To my surprise, I ended up staying in Alabama for two strange, enjoyable years. There I discovered barbecued pork.

For those who don't know, barbecued pork is to the South what the bagel is to New York. And just as Southerners have no idea how to make an edible bagel, Northerners have no clue how to cook barbecue. So my fiancée and I left Brooklyn to make a weekend pilgrimage to Memphis, she to visit friends and see the city, me to eat as much barbecue as possible.

What is it about the taste of pork barbecue that I find so irresistible? It has to do with the cooking itself, because I don't even like pork prepared any other way. There's something about the way barbecued pig just melts off the bone, about the juxtaposition between the meat's almost buttery tenderness and its heft, its substantiality. When barbecuing is done correctly, the smoky flavor harmonizes perfectly with the sweetness of the meat and the spiciness of the sauce. In the end, though, who knows? It's ineffable.

Every May since 1978, Memphis has hosted the World Championship Barbecue Cooking Contest. Equal parts sport, culinary seminar, frat party, and beauty pageant, it is the most prestigious pork barbecue competition in the world (Kansas City, another barbecue stronghold, holds the preeminent beef event). For twenty-one years, competitors have gathered on the banks of the Mississippi, in Tom Lee Park just a few blocks from downtown Memphis, to see who can cook the best rib, shoulder, and hog.

What was once a low-key get-together has, over the years, become a much larger event. That first year, twenty teams battled it out; this year the number was 227. Tens of thousands of spectators now pay $6 apiece simply to soak in the ambiance (competitors' barbecue isn't for sale, and the public must settle for vendors' fare). At stake is a lot of money, this year almost $40,000 in cash prizes. The overall champion takes home $10,000, while top finishers receive as much as $5,000. And winners can expect to reap endorsement deals with meat suppliers and charcoal makers.

To ensure fairness, the contest has organized a complex grading system that uses 450 volunteer judges; each of these palates has been educated at an eight-hour seminar on rating barbecued pork. To increase its profile and encourage participation, Memphis in May has even set up a series of satellite barbecue contests all over the South, fifty-five in all.

Preparation is elaborate. Each team is given a patch of land, where it sets up a booth in which to cook, throw parties, relax, sleep, and, most important, present its work to the judges. These rigs, as they are called, can be lavish; some have running water, electric fans, built-in cookers, and second-floor terraces. It's not uncommon for a team to spend $40,000 or more just putting one together.

When I first arrived, I was, to be honest, disappointed by the magnitude of it all. Memphis in May was clearly no down-home event. Corporate sponsors, including Reynolds and the Piggly Wiggly supermarket chain, had set up promotional trailers. The sponsoring radio station, Froggy 94, had a large tent topped with a giant leering inflated frog, and their sound system blared Top 40. A bungee-jumping concession had set up shop in the center of the park, charging leapers $25 a pop (by Saturday, the price would double). Memphis in May, it appeared, was nothing more than a corporate-sponsored barbecue-flavored street fair.

But as I roamed the park talking to people, I came to realize that underneath this merchandised surface lay something meatier. The contestants, and their contest, occupied a parallel universe outside the domain of Froggy 94—a place devoted to the ideal of the perfectly cooked pig. For them, Memphis in May isn't really about money; even championship squads end up spending more than they win. For many in Tom Lee Park, Memphis in May, and barbecue in general, are an obsession. As one cook told me: "Once you get into the sweet taste of that pork meat, the sauces and everything, it gets better and better as you learn more and more about it."

Most of the participants were born and raised in the South, grew up eating barbecue, and have been cooking it themselves since they were teenagers. One way to understand these contests, in fact, is as a sort of paean to the Dixie where these men were raised. Not that this South—small towns, home-cooked meals, close extended families—doesn't exist anymore. But it's definitely not as prevalent as it once was.

"Everybody round here been barbecuing in their backyard forever, every one of 'em," said Jimmy Blackford, head cook for the Super Swine Sizzlers. A house painter from West Memphis, Arkansas, a small town just across the Mississippi from Memphis, Blackford was one of the few lean men I met at the contest. "Dad, whoever, somebody in your family'd be doing it; you have family reunions, everybody's barbecuin'."

(Here, "everybody" means, for the most part, men. Competitive barbecuing is, in general, a middle-aged male pursuit. "It's still only a guy thing round where we come from," Blackford says. "Guys get into it. It's just the outdoors, the smoke, that kind of thing." Memphis in May is also primarily white, which is surprising given that barbecue is a Southern black staple. Why the absence of blacks? One reason may be the cost of financing a team. But many blacks may also see the contest as a "white" event, not particularly interesting to them, and also not particularly interested in including them.)

In a way, barbecuing is a simple process. More than anything, it requires patience. You fire up some charcoal or wood, throw on some hog meat, and then let it sit there for a long time. Barbecue is not by any stretch of the imagination fast food. Ribs, the quickest part of a hog to barbecue, requires six hours of cooking; a whole hog needs between twenty-two and twenty-four hours. The key to barbecuing well, I was told over and over, is "slow and low." Cooking a hog for hours at a relatively low temperature (somewhere around 225 degrees) liquefies its connective tissue and fat, leaving only tender meat that practically falls from the bone. This method also allows the smoke to penetrate deep into the meat, imbuing it thoroughly with its distinctive flavor.

But beyond this, the field is wide open for innovation, and every cook has an idiosyncratic theory about how to make great barbecue. The range of ideas is astonishing. Among the strategies I heard about, saw, and tasted: smoking the meat before it's cooked;

using syringes to inject it with sauce; injecting it with beer; basting it regularly; closing it up in the cooker and not touching it until it's done; wrapping it in aluminum foil; cooking it on a kind of vertical rotisserie; cooking with hickory wood; cooking with apple wood; cooking with the skin on; cooking with the skin off; laying the hog face up; and laying the hog face down.

Every cook also has distinct ideas about spicing. For flavor, Memphis-style barbecue relies not only on tangy sauce, but on a rub, a mixture of spices kneaded into the pig. Every cook (even those who use store-bought spices straight from the bottle) has an elaborate story about his unique mixture. One man I met sprayed Dr Pepper and root beer on his ribs—with, I can attest, surprisingly good results.

I ate a lot of barbecue at Memphis in May. It was a great time to be a journalist. Many of the teams I talked to invited me to taste their product. And on Saturday I hit the mother lode. For the blind tasting, which is a key element in the final score, each team sent a sample to the judges' tent, a Styrofoam platter heaped with pounds of tender, flavorful pork, more than even the most famished judge could finish. Consequently the judging tent was awash in these platters. Packs of hungry volunteers—and a stray journalist or two—descended on them like hyenas devouring carrion. The platters were identified by number only, and every so often, a buzz would travel through the pack: Such-and-such a number was especially delectable. In minutes, it would be gone, picked clean.

With all this eating, I was getting a gastronomic education. By Saturday, I was beginning to discern the subtle line that divided the uncanny and the merely delicious. I found plenty of connoisseurs happy to tutor me. One of the most articulate was Phil Minyard, a thick-limbed, likable man who has been organizing, judging, and entering barbecue contests for twenty years.

An occupational therapist who lives in Memphis, Minyard was here this year as a competitor, cooking with his wife and son under the name True Blue Barbecue. "You're looking for something that has a little smoke on it," he told me as we sat at a kitchen table under his canopied rig, drinking Pink Penny Pulldown, a kind of gin-flavored lemonade. "You want enough spice so that it's got that burst of taste to it, but the pork itself has a taste, and you don't want to kill it. That's the worst thing you can do. If you wanna do that, just get somebody a bottle of spice and have 'em chug it."

Even more than with most foods, Minyard said, texture is key: "You wanna be able to pull out a nice piece of meat that you can take and mash with your fingers, and a little liquid runs out. You pull the fibers apart, you see angel hairs, little fine treadles. That means it's tender."

Most cooks are just as obsessed with cookers as they are with the process of barbecuing. This is, after all, a mostly male pursuit, so it's not surprising that machinery plays a central role. Many even design and build their own cookers. Cliff Weddington is typical. Like most participants, Weddington, an amiable seventy-two-year-old auctioneer from Tullahoma, Tennessee, grew up in the country, in the sort of place where people tend to tinker with machines.

"These here, they're propane running tanks off an old Coca-Cola truck," Weddington told me, pointing to his two rib-filled furnaces. "Coca-Cola converted from propane to just regular gas, and I had a friend that worked at the plant, he got three of 'em, and I made him one for two of the tanks. They got old lawn mower wheels under 'em. Some of it is scrap metal; some of it I bought the metal. I just started welding." Using his homemade cookers, Mr. Cliff, as he is known, came in fourth (out of eighty-four entries) in the rib category.

This do-it-yourself spirit pervades the whole event. No one here is a culinary school graduate. "We got to cooking ribs around my shop," said Pat Burke, leader of the Tower Rock BBQ team, "and I said, 'You know, I believe we've got the best ribs I've ever tasted.' We decided: Well, we'll come on down to Memphis, and even if we get fiftieth place, it'll be great."

That year Burke won his first overall championship. A legendary barbecuer from Murphysboro, Illinois (a pork-producing area that is more Dixon than Mason, southern Illinois is a barbecue hotbed), Burke, who owns a small construction company, has won three overall MIM championships in the past eight years. In 1994, after winning his second straight championship, Burke retired from the circuit. He returned last year, drawn back, he says, "for the love of barbecue, and the people we met."

I heard sentiments like this more than once. The "circuit," as the nearly year-round series of barbecue contests is known, has created a community of competitive pork cookers. Especially late at night, when the parties have quieted down and at least one person has to stay up tending the meat, people make the rounds. "After midnight, it gets kinda quiet and peaceful," says Marshall Burgess, a longtime competitive barbecuer. "You can walk around and talk to everybody; you don't have all this hassle. You go in and you see how their cookers work, we talk about this and that, how they do this, and how they do that."

The affection extends to the pig. Cooks speak of their hogs with an odd fondness, as if the creature were a partner in the undertaking. Whole hog cooks invariably refer to their charges as "he." "He's a pretty hog," Jimmy Blackford told me as he looked tenderly at his entry. If you think about it, though, this attitude makes sense. Spend twenty-four hours straight with anyone and you'll end up having a personal bond with them.

Perhaps this affinity explains the fact that a large proportion of people involved in the contest, from officials to judges to contestants to spectators, could be described as, er, meaty. Memphis in May is packed with people who don't seem overly concerned about fat grams. At one point, I was talking with John Willingham, the leader of one of the all-time great teams, Willingham's River City Rooters, when he mentioned that he had gotten into competitive barbecuing after his heart attack, when a doctor recommended that he lower his stress level by finding a hobby. I asked him whether eating large amounts of barbecued pork might not be the best therapy for a heart problem. He became indignant.

"That's a mythical thing," he said, gesticulating unsteadily with his beer. "That's wrong. Pork is the other white meat." At this point, Burgess, Willingham's first lieutenant and one of the beefiest men I met all weekend, chimed in. It was, he suggested, a conspiracy: "It's the beef industry trying to put that over. The way we cook it, we render the fat out of the meat as we cook it. It drips on down."

(I had an odd experience with Burgess: As I was talking with him, I realized that something smelled wonderful. After a few minutes, I realized with a start that it was Burgess himself: This large, sweaty, grease-spattered man smelled delicious, exactly like a pungent pork shoulder. He was permeated with the odor of meat, smoke, and spice. It was just wafting out of his pores, and he smelled good enough to eat.)

From Thursday night, when it began, to Saturday morning, Memphis in May often resembled a frat party: loud music blasting from overtaxed speakers, crowds of shirtless guys with beer bellies standing around drinking beer, drunken couples dancing rhythmlessly in public, costume contests featuring hairy men wearing pig snouts, rouge, and dresses. But on Saturday morning, the tenor of the park changed dramatically. Saturday was judgment day, when all the hard work hung in the balance. Everything became quieter, cleaner, and generally more buttoned-up.

Starting at eleven A.M., the judges fanned out to meet the teams and taste their pork. Each judge would rate three teams, and each team would be evaluated by three different judges (in addition to the blind tasting). By dusk, there would be three winners, one for each category: ribs, shoulders, and whole hog. From those three an overall champion would be chosen.

At the Custom Cookers rig, the sense of tension was as palpable as the smell of smoke. The Custom Cookers were a group of seven friends from the suburbs east of Memphis. Most are employed at a Memphis metalworking shop, Custom Projects. Although it included several contest veterans, the team had been together less than a year, and had never before cooked at Memphis in May. The shop's owner bankrolled the team; he and his employees built the rig themselves, at a cost of $40,000. Like many teams, the Custom Cookers built their rig onto a trailer, which allows them to drive easily to contests outside Memphis. Among its features are a second-floor terrace, three built-in cookers, and a soft-ice-cream machine. They entertain customers at the contests, but the enterprise is basically a hobby.

"Five minutes!" an official yelled to the team from the walkway, a warning that judgment was imminent. The Custom Cookers huddled around team member John Maki, who was giving a frantic last-minute pep talk. "We know what to do onsite," said Maki, his voice vibrating with adrenaline. "We're the best!" They put their hands together in the center of the circle and, like football players before a big game, shouted in unison.

They had worked for this. Head cook Ron Haney, who would be the emcee during the judge's visit, had his speech memorized. Everyone was dressed in identical uniforms: black knee-length shorts and short-sleeved white button-down shirts, with first names embroidered above one pocket and "Custom Cookers Barbecue Team" above the other.

The table, placed carefully in the shade under a canopy, was laid out in a manner befitting a four-star restaurant, with real china, brass silverware, and a clean white tablecloth. The yard was spotless, with no sign of the previous night's partying. To add a distinctive touch, a painting of boats in a harbor had been set up on an easel. Appearance—of the rig, the team, and the meat—counts for a sixth of the point total, and in a tight race could make the crucial difference.

And then there was the star of the show: the 115-pound pig, who had been cooking for twenty-two hours and was as ready as he'd ever be for his moment in the spotlight. Surrounded by a garnish of gourds, the glistening whole hog reclined regally in the cooker, calmly awaiting his visitors.

As the judge—trailed by an assistant whose job it was to guide him from booth to booth—came to the gate, the team formed a receiving line to welcome him. Each person greeted him, politely, with a firm handshake and a straightforward gaze. The last person he met was Haney, who led him back to the trailer where the cooker was. As the other members stood silently at predetermined positions around the yard, Haney explained how this particular pig had been cooked to perfection.

Haney had labored over this presentation, running it by team members over and over until everyone was happy with it. He related how he had found the sauce recipe by chance in his grandfather's scrapbook. (When I asked him about this later, he admitted cheerfully to having made it up.) The narrative was designed to impress upon the judge the care and originality with which this pig had been prepared: "We put him in a cellophane bag to sweat him. . . . If you notice it's got little bits of onion in it. . . . Indirect heat . . . We cook him the first six hours at two hundred sixty degrees, and then after that for the next eighteen at two twenty-five . . . score down each side of the backbone to expose the tenderloin, and the smoke can penetrate . . ."

Then the moment of truth. Haney led the judge and his assistant to the carefully shaded table. Maki's wife, Connie, brought each man his meal. This was a Manhattan nouvelle chef's version of barbecue: a plate gilded artfully with bits of meat from various sections of the pig. (During the "onsite," judges don't actually eat that much, since they want to save room for their other visits.) When Haney, a barrel-chested retired fireman, poured his homemade sauce onto the visitors' plates, his hands trembled. The team stood around the table, watching silently while the two men ate. In case the diners were thirsty, each had a glass of ice water garnished with a slice of lemon. In case their hands got too greasy, each had a pink bowl filled with water in which to rinse off. In each bowl was another slice of lemon.

When the judge had finished tasting, he stood to go. He shook hands again with everyone on the team. "It was an honor," he said. When he left, everyone on the team started cheering and clapping to show their enthusiasm. Once he was outside the gate, team members quickly cleared the table and swept out the yard again. They had five minutes before the next judge arrived.

By evening, the judging was done. The Custom Cookers ended up
a respectable eighth in the whole hog division, which was won by
Pat Burke. The Other Team, a rib-cooking squad from outside
Memphis, won the overall championship. When I talked to Haney
later, he was philosophical. "The meat was the best we've done.
You've got to remember this is the toughest competition of all.
That's why I say don't get upset if you don't make the finals."

On Sunday, with the contest over, I was still hungry. Many people had warned me that after I'd experienced a barbecue contest, it
would be impossible to enjoy eating at a barbecue restaurant, even
one in Memphis. "I've gone to some of the known, famous restaurants, and you will throw rocks at 'em after you try this," Terry
Brewer, a veteran judge from Columbus, Mississippi, told me. To
save time and money, she said, barbecue restaurants will cut corners, parboiling their product, or cooking it partially with gas.

I decided to take my chances. My fiancée and I chose Interstate
Barbecue, one of Memphis's many known, famous places. An unremarkable storefront on a rundown shopping strip in a black part
of town, Interstate, so named because it is near an interstate, offered barbecue without frills or ambiance. We ordered a couple of
sandwiches and ate in the car on the way to Graceland.

It was, in a word, delicious. The meat was tender and smoky,
and the sauce added a nice little sting. Maybe it wasn't quite as delicious as the best I'd had at Memphis in May (my personal favorite:
Burke's sublime apple-smoked pork), but it was still delicious. And
it was miles ahead of anything I'd eaten in New York.

Which brings us back east. A few days after we returned home,
we went to a birthday party at a downtown restaurant known for its
barbecue. Maybe, I thought, it will be like Memphis. As soon as I
took my first bite of rib, however, I knew for sure that Memphis was
a distant memory. The meat (what there was of it, anyway—great
swaths of rubbery fat took up most of the territory) was glued to the
bone. To free it, I had to grip firmly with my front teeth and pull like

a ravenous wolf. But why even take the trouble? Slathered with un-subtly sweet sauce, the meat was as tasteless as gruel.

How had this meat been cooked? It wasn't, you can bet, slow and low. I nibbled for a bit, paid my $50 (that's fifteen shoulder sandwiches at Interstate—my new measure for every cost), and went off into the New York night, hungry and disheartened. My fiancée has ruled out moving to Memphis, so I'm making plans to attend judging school.

PHILOSOPHY AU LAIT

David Downie

"I think, therefore I drink," quipped my studious-looking neighbor at the Café des Phares, the so-called philosophy café, whose terrace spills invitingly onto the Place de la Bastille. "One *petite crème* for the *petit* Descartes," chuckled a nearby jokester as the waiter turned to me.

"*Monsieur?*"

I wrung my memory for a clever mot—from Plato perhaps—with which to order my late-Sunday-morning ration of coffee. "An express to raise me out of the Cave of Illusions," quoth I, blushing. Off moved the waiter without batting an eye. As always, the small round tables were packed elbow-to-elbow and enveloped in a blue fog of cigarette smoke. Newspapers hung from sticks. Mirrors quivered with humanity. The archetypal Paris café interior. A beehive formation of latecomers thronged the sidewalk.

Phare means "lighthouse" and no one seems to miss the symbolism of the café's Bastille location. It is the fashionable mothership that, over the last five years, has spawned dozens of philocafés in Paris, the provinces, and abroad (in other European countries, Japan, New York, and even New Jersey). You can, if so inclined, spend Monday evening philosophizing at Le Buci; Wednesday at Le Cluny near the Sorbonne; Thursday at Le Select Montparnasse; Friday at Le Relais Jussieu, Le Pont 9, or Le Rond Point; Saturday at Le Relais des Arts, Le Tarazoute, Le Royal Jussieu, or the Paris-Rome; and Sunday morning at either Le Bastille or Le Café des Phares, facing each other across the famous square.

The concept—an open-mike improvised public debate on philosophical quandaries—is the brainchild of fifty-year-old Marc Sautet, a would-be professor alienated by the French university system. His goal: to make philosophy accessible to everyone, highlight its cathartic and therapeutic value, and earn a living. Looking like a Club Med *Gentil Organisateur*, the perma-tanned, blue-eyed Philosopher King took the Bastille by storm in late 1992. Predictably, he was savaged by the press and mainstream philosophers ("nonsense propagated by a sophist . . ."), few of whom could be troubled to participate in his one and only eleven A.M. Sunday salon. The dogged Parisian Plato, undaunted, published "Un Café pour Socrate" and, perhaps inspired by Lucy and Snoopy, hung his shingle on a philosopher's office at a chic Marais address (300 francs for a personalized philosophizing session). Soon dozens of philo-moderators across the country, some with impressive academic credentials, were leading enthusiastic, if motley, groups of apprentice philosophers.

Sautet's apotheosis is recent, however, dating from December 1996, when he and best-selling philosophy writers Jean-Luc Marion, André Comte-Sponville, and Luc Ferry were guests on Bernard Pivot's TV show *Bouillon de Culture,* an unbelievably influential program that can establish trends overnight. While philosophy has always been a favored subject in France—high school students study it and *baccalauréat* graduation exam questions make front-page news—it suddenly became all the rage, even spawning a movement of radical-chic, telegenic *nouveaux philosophes* like Bernard Henri-Levy—BHL for short—who has begun making philo-movies (including the recent *Le Jour et la Nuit,* widely considered one of cinema history's all-time dogs).

To academics, though, philocafés remain suspect, a plebeian Collège de France (where distinguished professors lecture, free, to the rapt and reverent, most of them retirees). Instead of welcoming the maverick Sautet, France's legions of savants are busy lacerating themselves over the succès de scandale of the philocafé phenomenon. Is it, they ask earnestly, because the Age of Ideology died in 1989 with the fall of the Berlin Wall? Or could it be a manifestation of "collective despair" linked to globalization, waning family values, and unemployment? Or a fin-de-siècle crisis of the spirit, the conjugation of lost religiosity with the approaching Third Millennium? Or a revolution against the Anglo-Saxon values embodied in commercial TV, the movies, and the Internet? Ah, the Internet!

Strangely, no one seems to be asking whether philocafés are popular primarily because they offer good, ribald fun, in keeping with the best Parisian café tradition. But that is exactly what you're in for on a Sunday afternoon at the Café des Phares, the city's liveliest philocafé. The ritual pecking of cheeks and passing of cigarette packs starts at ten A.M., when several dozen regulars show up to make sure they'll find a spot inside, near the bar, where the action is. A hundred or more casual participants ebb and flow between them and the sidewalk terrace, where they hear the debate through loudspeakers. Walkman headsets disappear as notepads and books are flourished—Plato's *Republic,* Heidegger's *Sein und Zeit,* Sartre, Foucault, Camus, the *Larousse Dictionary of Writers,* even the Bible.

At the appointed hour, Sautet rises to his feet, tests the mike, and, in consultation with a roundtable of regulars, sets about finding the theme of the day. It's like a college-town literature workshop and a Quaker meeting rolled into one, with a pinch of karaoke and a splash of pop psych.

"Yesterday it was *Jurassic Park,*" suggests the first speaker, "tomorrow will it be *Homo Sapiens Park?*" This is met by baffled groans.

"Nothing is to be hoped for, everything is to be lived," offers another speaker. More grumbling.

"Could it be that unemployment isn't a problem, but rather a solution?" This, too, is discarded. Too political.

Meanwhile coffee and beer are floating by, and a philocafé regular is squeezing between tables, hawking *Philos,* a monthly newsletter justly celebrated for its turgid, impenetrable prose. "'All roads lead to Rome,'" warbles Sautet's disembodied voice through the mike. "How about considering the real meaning of this ancient saying?"

The question seems genial enough and is accepted as the theme of the day.

"Because of the Paris marathon," begins an eager woman, "it took me two hours to get here this morning, and I thought to myself, Traveling toward an objective is sometimes difficult, so perhaps the hidden meaning in 'All roads lead to Rome' is that if you try hard enough you can reach your goal."

"Rome meaning the seat of all power?" asks someone.

"The Vatican? The Church—a symbol of oppression?" questions a second.

"The incarnation of totalitarian moralism, the first manifestation of religious globalism . . ."

"This evokes the schism of the popes in Avignon, and is antipapal—"

"Nonsense! The quote is much older, it refers to Imperial Rome!"

Soon the debate is rolling along like a drunken steamroller, the mike passing from speaker to speaker—a pipe-smoking prof with studiously wrinkled trousers, a bird-boned sophisticate with an Hermès scarf. "All roads lead to infinity," quips a youngster hidden by the cig and pipe fog. "Rome is finite; therefore the saying isn't valid!"

The permutations of this millennial cliché turn out to be manifold. Roads are about experience and all experience is valid; roads are the ways of the Lord, and they're unknowable. Rome is shorthand for beauty, love, art, and death, and all roads lead to death, preferably via sex. The road to knowledge passes through sin;

Rome is sin. A literate type quotes Montaigne ("By different means we arrive at the same end") while an irreverent wit borrows from Borges ("If you put a monkey at a typewriter for eternity, sooner or later he'll write Shakespeare's entire oeuvre"). Things are beginning to get out of hand. Someone I can't see starts a convoluted philosophical argument, loses his train of thought, stutters and splutters like a noisy mobylette suddenly out of gas. Amid cruel clucking the mike is passed to the next apprentice philosopher.

"All roads lead to sex," says a Rabelaisian man in his thirties, picking up the libidinous subtext abandoned earlier.

"All roads, or just *sex*tions of them?" teases a voice from the peanut gallery. "Errance or Eros?"

"In the dark, all women are beautiful!"

"And all men are desirable!"

A handsome young fellow in a tweedy jacket makes eyes at the soulful-looking young woman across from him. She rewards him with a coy smile and a riffle of her notepad. Several other potential couples chat away, oblivious to the debate. Sautet, the voice of reason, intervenes to put things back on track. My neighbor leans over and says, "Isn't this silly and pretentious?"

Before I can answer, a gaunt intellectual leans over me from the other direction and sniffs, "It lacks rigor, it isn't philosophy at all." Just then a middle-aged woman with a blond bouffant bustles her way by, loaded with groceries from the Boulevard Richard Lenoir outdoor market a hundred yards away. The smell of ripe cheese wafts up as she reaches for the mike. "She's been haggling over chickens and eggs," quips my jocular neighbor, suppressing hilarity. Suddenly a roller-skating teenager crashes into a table and is rescued by her philo-mom.

Finally, an authoritative voice with a distinctly Italian accent takes the mike and thunders, "The lesson so far seems to be that any sentence can lead us all anywhere!" A collective guffaw goes up, and by the time I slip out to do my shopping on the Boulevard Richard Lenoir several couples have been formed, people have laughed, argued, triumphed, and failed, and lots of drinks have been sold. At their worst, philocafés are innocuous (a bit of posing and pretentious philo-babble never hurt anyone), at their best stimulating, fun, and profitable. My waiter beams as I plonk down twenty francs for two coffees. The babble is good for business.

YOUR MONEY'S NO GOOD HERE

Tim Cahill

"They went thataway, Chief."

I kept walking, checking addresses. This was in New York City, on Fifth Avenue, somewhere around Fiftieth Street, and I was looking for an unfamiliar address. My attire, I felt, may have been inappropriate.

"Chief! Hey, Chief. I'm talking to you."

The man was walking behind me, breathing into my neck. "They went thataway, Chief."

I half-turned. The person pursuing me wore a dirty trench coat and a black watch cap. His curly red hair bunched out around his neck in that peculiar seventies style reminiscent of Bozo the Clown.

"Who?" I asked. "Who went where?"

"The buffalo there, Chief." He pointed west on Fiftieth. "They went thataway."

My unique attire had convinced this gentleman that I was a particularly homely and pale-skinned American Indian. He was, I figured, one of those panhandlers who feels that he must entertain you in exchange for a handout. I was carrying a primitive, but unconcealed, weapon on my shoulder. Something you might use to hunt buffalo.

"So," the man said, "you got any spare change for me, Chief?"

Out where I come from—a little town located between the Crow and Blackfeet reservations—you don't call anyone "Chief."

"Yeah," I said. "I got something for you. Just let me get my pack off."

All this happened nearly twenty years ago, and the best way to understand what I'm talking about is to put yourself in my boots. Like this:

For reasons that, to this day, have never been adequately explained, you've been given an assignment to travel out of state and out of country to a place somewhere at the end of the earth and at the beginning of time, where you are expected to make contact with persons living in one of the few pretechnological, preindustrial societies left on the face of the planet. Upon your return, you are to write an article about this peculiar journey and the people you've met. In what ways, the assigning magazine editors want to know, are these folks different from us? In what ways are they similar?

Because you are relatively young and not the most experienced reporter who has ever lived, these editors—the sadistic bastards—expect a report immediately upon your return from this strange sortie into the past.

The editors work in New York City. You live in one of those big square states out in the middle of fly-over country. The airplane tickets they've sent you show a scheduled stop in New York on the return leg. Your instructions are to deplane, cab into the city, meet with the editors, for a few hours, then get the hell out. Cab back to the airport and flee.

You figure this is a big deal in your reportorial career: the first foreign assignment. The editors have never actually seen you, and all the arrangements have been made over the phone. The editors, you suspect, probably wear pinstriped power suits. You yourself don't actually own a suit and feel that these men and women, who have the power to withhold payment, will undoubtedly peg you for a rube.

That's the deal. The question is: What clothes do you pack? Your trip will take you to the high, wind-whipped plains of El Mundo Perdido, the Lost World, the area where Venezuela, Brazil, and Guyana all come together on the map. It will be cold: near freezing some nights. It will be humid and hot in the lowlands. In the mountains, which rise to ten thousand feet, it should rain every day. Or snow. To get where you are going, you will have to walk. For weeks.

So you'll need a backpack. Stuff it full of tropical gear. And for the cold and rain you'll want quick-drying long underwear, fleece pullovers and pants, and top-quality rain gear. Freeze-dried food. Stove. Fuel. Mountain boots. Sleeping bag, mat, tent. Dishes, utensils, first-aid kit, and water-purifying tablets.

The question is: Are you going to take a sport coat, tie, slacks, and tasseled loafers for your meeting with the editors? Stuff this stuff in the bottom of your backpack and hump it over the mountains and through the rain? For one two-hour meeting?

Naaaahhhh.

Which is how, two decades ago, I came to be walking down Fifth Avenue in New York on a November afternoon, wearing a seriously soiled rain jacket and my waffle-stomper boots (still caked with red South American mud). I was carrying a backpack and a set of lightweight preindustrial weapons that consisted of a weathered bow and a long thin woven basket containing twenty arrows. None of the stuff I was carrying fit in an airport locker, and anyway, the weight didn't bother me much. I'd already carried it halfway around the Western Hemisphere.

"You carry spare change in your pack there, Chief?"

The words "spare change" had sent me spinning.

The South American Indian people I'd just met and lived with for weeks didn't use money. Everything was set up on a barter basis. Sometimes, I couldn't help but notice, even barter didn't enter into economic negotiations. Food, especially, was just given away.

Money was not unknown in the small village of Roraima, which lay under the looming shadow of the great coffin-shaped mountain called Roraima Tepui. The place even had a small schoolhouse, and I suspect that now, twenty years later, much has changed. A paved road, I hear, was built several years ago, and it passes nearby. There is likely a dirt road to the village, and the village no doubt sports several small shops, a cantina, and a restaurant.

But back twenty years ago, the people of Roraima lived in wood-poled huts. The floors were dirt. The roofs were thatch. The nearest place money would buy anything was a ten-day walk away. Buy something big and you'd have to carry it ten days on your back. Money wasn't worth the trouble.

The people I was to meet seemed frightened when my group walked into their village one evening when cold sheets of rain were pounding down and lightning made the mountain above explode into view every few minutes. Children stared at us from open windows, peekaboo style, but they weren't playing.

We stood in the mud and hammering rain in the center of the village until a somber, dignified man emerged from one of the huts and asked us, please, to take refuge in the schoolhouse. No one came to see us that night. In the morning, at first light, a delegation from the village asked if they could enter their own schoolhouse. Would we like some eggs for breakfast?

One of my traveling companions, a Venezuelan from Caracas named Pedro Carniciero, thanked the delegation for its hospitality and explained that we were carrying our own food and would be happy to prepare breakfast for all. But our gray freeze-dried eggs were not a big hit with the local gourmands. The same man who had directed us to the schoolhouse said something like:

"Good Lord, gentlemen, you can't possibly be serious," and, switching from Spanish to the local dialect, said something to one of the younger men, who dashed away and returned with real hen's eggs. The yolks were bright orange and the whites bubbled up in the fry pan like meringue. They are still the best eggs I've ever eaten.

The people did not, however, have coffee, and we were able to make several even-up breakfast deals. Pedro, who'd traveled in the area previously, knew that certain trade items would be highly appreciated in the village. In Caracas, we'd stocked up on high-quality cloth. Red was the desired color. We had about a dozen yards of it apiece.

The cloth bought guide services to the top of Roraima Tepui. It bought long walks in the forest with the woman who knew the healing properties of various plants. It bought an invitation to stay in the village, and it bought answers to our many questions. It was heavy red cloth and, to some small degree, it bought us friendship. I used it to buy a bow-and-arrow set from the best of the village hunters. It wasn't as nice as the one he used in the forest—it was his backup bow—and I had it strung over my shoulder that day in New York City when the Bozo-looking man who kept calling me Chief asked if I could spare any change.

As I rummaged through my backpack looking for an appropriate gift, my thoughts were jumbled, in a condition I now recognize: reverse culture shock. It is only recently that I've come across a quote that expresses exactly what I felt in that moment. In 1807, the great king of Tonga, Finau 'Ulukalala, was discussing economics with one of his first European visitors, a man named Will Mariner. "If a man has more yams than he wants," Finau said, "let him exchange some of them away. . . . Certainly money is much handier and more convenient, but then, as it will not spoil by being kept, people will store it up, instead of sharing it out, as a chief ought to do. . . . I understand what it is that makes [Europeans] so selfish. It is this money."

Just so. The only people I ever met who were completely unaware of money—didn't know the stuff existed—were a group of tree-house-dwelling Melanesians who made their homes deep in the swamplands of Irian Jaya. The women wore skirts made of bunched grasses; the men wore leaves wrapped and tied about their penises. It was a place where red cloth was probably even more worthless than money.

The families were segregated—women and children on one side of the tree house, men on the other. Each side cooked on its own fire, which was set on a base of river rocks. I traded hatchets, salt, and fishhooks for access and conversation, though the people, these good Karowai people, freely offered me great globs of their staple food, a gray-blue paste made from the sap of the sago palm. It tasted a bit like watery library paste, only a good deal more bland than that sounds. It was, in fact, this bland: When I fixed everyone a bowl of rice, one young man burst into tears after a single taste. He was crying, I learned eventually, because the rice tasted so good.

I looked to the walls of the tree house while the young man sobbed. There were the bones of two small fish hung up there—the remains, I imagined, of a fine feast. The Karowai didn't accumulate money, nor wealth of any other kind. And even though it was clearly a challenging task to gather enough to eat every day, these people offered me what they had. Every day. What they had was sago sap.

These people, who didn't know what a dollar was worth, were the most generous folks I've ever met in my life. Okay, so they were rumored to be headhunters and cannibals. The fact is, they were highly generous cannibals and headhunters.

Navigating through that culture, and through the moneyless society I first encountered in South America, taught me a little bit about my own selfishness, and about what a chief ought to do.

"Whatcha got in that bag there, Chief?"

I found a few rags and remnants of the leftover red cloth that nobody in Roraima had wanted and gave them to the red-haired spare-change artist.

He stared at them for a moment, then shook them angrily in my face. "The hell am I supposed to do with these, Chief?" he said.

I tapped him gently on the chest with my preindustrial weaponry and told him precisely what he could do with them.

The Bozo panhandler tossed the cloth on the sidewalk and flipped me an especially enthusiastic bird.

"And watch out who you call Chief," I said, which, I think, is very good advice. Call it priceless.

EMBRACED IN SPAIN

Barry Yeoman

There's nothing like the approach of Carnaval to make a guy feel utterly alone. I was in the three-thousand-year-old port city of Cádiz, Spain, walking along a pier that jutted out from the very corner of Europe. But rather than marveling at the ocean crashing against the stone embankment below me, or at the branchless drago trees in the distance, I was struggling against a funk that had enveloped me as fully as the salt air.

The day before, I had been sitting on an airplane, excited about my trip. I imagined alleyways crammed with ancient, crumbling buildings; labyrinthine neighborhoods scented with olives and oranges; sun so intense it would bronze my skin. I couldn't wait to throw myself into a beery, music-drenched pre-Lenten celebration that had been compared favorably to Rio's. And yet, from the moment I arrived in town, I had been confronted by an unexpected disorientation. I couldn't decipher the Gaditano dialect; couldn't navigate an old city where half the intersections were unmarked; couldn't shake off my homesickness. The coming Carnaval, I feared, would only make things worse: I pictured myself, a thirty-seven-year-old American with a tenuous grasp of the language, friendless amid the revelry.

I was walking back from the castle at the end of the pier, seriously considering whether I should catch the next train back to Madrid, when I thought I heard someone call me. I turned around. Sitting on a bench, in a limestone alcove that separated the pier from the gates back into the old city, was a group of twenty-year-olds, maybe a dozen of them, mostly male. I immediately felt drawn to them. They looked so approachable, all smiles and sunglasses and baggy sweatshirts and denim jackets. I liked their easy physical intimacy, so common among Spanish men, the casual way hands rested on knees. I wanted to join them. "*¿Hablan inglés?*" I asked.

Only, those two words took about ten seconds to force past my lips. My stutter, severe in English, had spiraled out of control in Spanish, so that every word became a battle between brain and breath. I pushed the sounds hard through vocal cords locked in spasm, until finally four discrete syllables tumbled out of my mouth. *Ha. Blan. In. Glés.*

When I came up for air, they were laughing. Not nervous chuckles but robust, doubled-over guffaws. I had just become the star of their day's life-comedy. Not in the mood for their mockery, I said, "*Adiós*," and stormed off through the whitewashed gate and back into the old city.

I had gone only a block before I reconsidered. Maybe it was the loneliness I had felt the night before, a terror so visceral that I was on the edge of puking till dawn. Maybe I needed to confront my demons, lest they trail me throughout Carnaval. But something inside me told me to return. So I walked back and looked them straight in the eyes. "I have a problem speaking," I said. "I've had it all my life. I don't like it."

No one laughed. I felt proud of myself. To lighten the mood, I asked if I could photograph them. Suddenly they were beckoning every friend for fifty feet around to join them in the photo, squeezing together tight. They started singing and clapping. I took out my snapshots from home, and everyone crowded around, marveling at my modest white bungalow with its leafy yard. They periodically snickered at the stutter again, but then one would shoot another a look, and the laughter would stop.

That's how I met The Boys. Throughout that afternoon and evening, these childhood friends—a few of them working blue-collar jobs, but most victim to the city's 45 percent unemployment rate—initiated me into life on the wharves and plazas of the city. They offered me hashish and taught me slang. They proffered a fresh-caught sea urchin, its spiny tennis ball–sized body sliced in half, and instructed me to suck out the fluorescent orange guts. By dinnertime, they had decided that no friend of theirs could be without a nickname. So I became El Metralleta, which means "The Machine Gun." It alluded to my stutter, of course, but it was de-rived from one of the Carnaval groups, a singing gangster family that carried *metralletas* made of anchovy cans and colored paper.

That night, late, we reconvened outside the Falla Theater, a pink mosquelike building named after Cádiz's most famous resident, the composer Manuel de Falla. There, a half-dozen groups of teenage balladeers, dressed as sailors and flamenco dancers and disgruntled housepainters, stood in the plaza, taking turns sere-nading the crowd with guitars, drums, and joyous vocal har-monies. Between songs, the musicians jumped up and down, shook hands, chanted one another's names. Then kazoos would sound and another group would start singing. The crowd, pressed in close, cheered and clapped. The Boys were all smiles, soaking in the music and introducing me around. Eight hours into our rela-tionship, I was still a novelty. But my stutter no longer was.

It became clear that it was physically impossible to go twenty-four hours without seeing The Boys. Cádiz, squeezed onto a tiny peninsula, was simply too compact. Over the next few days, faces began distinguishing themselves, and names stuck in my head. Late afternoons we would sit on the city beach, chasing the sun along the edge of a stone wall, asking questions about one an-other's lives. Do I have a car? A wife? Will I write a book about my travels? If I did, I promised, they would all be in it, and it would be called "El Metralleta en Cádiz."

Two of them came into greater focus than the others, best buds who went out of their way to make sure I never felt alone. Silva was dark and robust, with thick eyebrows, two hoop earrings, and a waist-length ponytail. A camera ham who managed to squeeze his way into dozens of my photos, he could also get very serious, asking about racism in America and nodding earnestly at my reports. Chano was a former sailor who worked alongside the American troops in Yugoslavia. He had pale blue eyes, curly blond hair, and a style so gentle that women generally regarded him as the most decent of The Boys. He and his girlfriend planned to get married and move to the Canary Islands in the spring, where they would at least have a chance of finding work.

Chano and Silva warned me to save my energy for Saturday night, when all of Cádiz would get dressed up and flood La Viña, the old fishermen's quarter. So that night, I put on a yellow tasseled face mask and a sailor's cap and set out. The Boys were right. By eleven P.M., I was caught in a white-water torrent of costumed bodies: nuns and monks, monsters, male brides, cave people. Every single cobblestone street was so crowded that I couldn't see much in front of me. I just let myself be pulled in, enjoying the sensuality of the crowd. Then a street would terminate in a plaza, and a makeshift stage would be set up, where Carnaval bands would be singing satirical songs in complex harmony. Now and then I stopped to listen: to the make-believe Mafia family with their *metralletas;* to a troupe of singing basketball players in polyester sweatsuits; to a band of white-winged angels with heaven-blue gowns.

It was three-thirty A.M. before I caught up with The Boys in Plaza San Antonio, a grand commons fronted by a luminous, turreted seventeenth-century church. They were with their girlfriends, dark women in flamenco costumes with heavy lipstick and gaudy false lashes. Silva wore an American Indian headdress with feather earrings and a fringed suede jacket. Chano was done up more elaborately as San Pancracio, the saint who's supposed to bring work to Cádiz. He wore a green satiny robe; a garland of parsley framed his slender face.

My disguise worked. I was able to sneak up on the group without being noticed—and when Silva figured out who I was, I was greeted with cheers and handshakes and the beating of drums. "Metra-lleta!" Bom-bom-bom-bom. "*Metra-lleta!*" Drinks were placed in my hands—whiskey, beer—and singing erupted, and I was instructed on how to do the flamenco hand-clap to Cádiz's unofficial chant: "*Esto es Cai, y aquí hay que mamar*": "This is Cádiz, and here you have to suck."

Chano introduced me to his fiancée, then brought me deeper into the fold with proclamations of lifelong friendship. "You are of Cádiz," he announced, and gave me a wrap-around hug. Then he took a ceramic shot glass hanging by a string around his neck, wrote "*Del Chano de Cai*"—"From Chano of Cádiz"—on it in black marker, and placed it around my neck. "For you," he said. Silva quickly followed by giving me his kazoo, the ubiquitous instrument of Carnaval. And all the while: "Metra-lleta!" Bom-bom-bom-bom. And more alcohol and more hash, and by this point hugs all around.

And constantly there was the introduction of new friends, who would invariably laugh at the stutter before Chano or Silva or someone would tell them to knock it off. All of the core group went out of their way to be patient, even when I lost patience with myself. They made it clear that they had all the time in the world—relax. They had so many questions about America: How much poverty? Do people own guns? And what about crack? What does it look like? Do people smoke it?

Then, without a discernible signal, we were leaving Plaza San Antonio, forming a train to stay together, hands on shoulders. We walked deep into La Viña, to Plaza Cañamaque, a modern concrete square where a makeshift bar sold San Miguels and men peed uninhibitedly behind the parked cars. Silva and a friend put their arms around each other and serenaded me with a Carnaval song. It was dark, and vaguely menacing, and I felt so enveloped by everyone that the surroundings only made it better. "This is one of the best nights of my life," I told Chano, and meant it.

I finally left the plaza at seven-thirty A.M. Walking back along the coast road, I watched daylight break and the Atlantic turn deep denim blue. I sat on the wall overlooking the ocean while two young recorder players (one with a safety pin through his eyebrow and a pierced lip) welcomed the morning with a quiet, tender "Greensleeves."

I left Cádiz for two days the next week and traveled north to where everyone sounded like my high school Spanish teacher. When I returned on Ash Wednesday, Carnaval was still in full swing. I went to La Viña at ten-thirty P.M. to listen to some music, but instead I found The Boys. They were passing time in the most garish part of the district, where rows of illuminated hamburger stands cast a fluorescent glow on the otherwise dark and ancient night.

They were in fine spirits, and I was glad to see them. "I was just in Sevilla province," I told them, with more than my usual level of clarity, having practiced this little speech, "and I learned something very important. You all don't speak Spanish! Up there I understood everything. Everything!" My spirited declaration had the intended effect of altering the dynamic—in particular, raising my coolness quotient a bit.

Chano, Silva, and a taxi driver friend named Melchor crowded around me. They were loaded with questions. How were the Baroque villages? Did I like them more than Cádiz? The conversation bounced hyperactively from subject to subject. Is there work in America? How much does it pay? Would they hire us? Can we stay with you? What's the name of your city's basketball team? The baseball team?

The Durham Bulls, I told them, answering the last question. That piqued their interest. In Cádiz, the hand gesture for "bull" also refers to a man whose wife cheats on him. Chano tried to explain this concept to me. "If I'm Silva's wife, which I'm not, and I"—at this point he dry-humped Melchor—"what does that make Silva?" I ran through my mental dictionary and came up with "cuckold." They liked this a lot. "Cuckold!" they laughed, pointing at each other. "Cuckold!" they called out to every male friend who passed by. "Cuck-o-o-old!" Chano shouted, his hands a megaphone.

Then Chano asked me the English for another slang word, *mariquita*. I was stumped. "*Maricón*," he said, putting an arm around Silva's shoulder. "Man and man, instead of man and woman." A pause. "Which we're not."

"Gay," I said, but I stuttered a lot. Despite Cádiz's reputation for tolerance of homosexuality, I had decided not to discuss my own orientation with The Boys. They had already come far in accepting my foreignness, my stutter, my age. I didn't want to pit my personal realities against the Church's teachings and their own collective machismo.

But Chano was stubborn. About a half-hour later, after I had already forgotten the Spanish word, he asked me in front of the others, "Are you *mariquita?*" When I drew a blank, he pointed rapidly to himself and Silva. "Man and man," he said. Another pause. "Which we're not. You're not, are you?"

Earlier in the evening, I had gone to an Ash Wednesday mass. As we lined up in front of the gilded altar for ashes—"From dust you came, and to dust you shall return"—a woman read a litany of supplications. Her words, her voice, resonated with eerie repetition. Father, forgive us for violence. Father, forgive us for individual and collective sin. Father, forgive us for not following Christ's words in our lives. Father, forgive us for lying.

Forgive us for lying. If I lied in answer to Chano's question, I'd be stepping into a bigger deception than I could live with. "If I said yes, I'm gay, what would your reaction be?" I asked.

"My reaction?" Chano replied. "*Es igual.*" It's equal. Gay, straight. Doesn't matter.

Not fully believing him, I took a deep breath. "Okay," I said. "I am."

I knew at that moment I was potentially changing the entire course of the trip, perhaps casting myself back into the stomach-turning loneliness I experienced on my first night. I was unprepared for the simplicity of their reaction. All three of them, simultaneously, without consulting the others, reached out to shake my hand. I would have felt profound relief if I was not so stunned by what I had just done. "In the United States, if you tell the wrong person you're gay," I started, and Chano made the motion of slitting his own throat.

"Here," he said, "it's no big deal."

And it truly was no big deal to Silva and Melchor. I didn't detect a moment's pause or a smidgen less affection. It was Chano, to my surprise, who had some sorting out to do. He needed to tell me, for the fourth time, that he and Silva weren't a couple. He assured me that he had no problems with having gay friends, as long as they didn't try to feel him up. And then came the biggie. "Man and woman is better," he said.

"Why?" I asked, to which he replied, "Because man and man is anti-natural."

I conjured up every ounce of my thirty-seven-year-old authority. "For you, it's anti-natural," I said. "For me, it's natural."

This seemed to satisfy him. But just to reseal the friendship, I bought the next round of San Miguels.

Nothing more was said. The party resumed. Chano and Silva were delighted with their new word "cuckold." After a while, I set out with my original intention of finding music. I would never have thought the week would take this turn, or that I would quench my loneliness with this unpredictable group of men, who were fascinated by my stutter but mostly shrugged at my sexuality.

Throughout my stay in Cádiz, I thought about redemption. The Boys had started out in my mind as my childhood bullies, the ones who devoted their entire elementary school career to taunting me because of my stutter. So much had changed in ten days. How easy it would have been to let my initial prejudices rob me of what became a treasured relationship. How easy it would have been for The Boys to do the same.

I had romantic plans for the end of my trip, the final blowout weekend of Carnaval. In my fantasy, we'd be together—Silva, Chano, and the rest—and I'd make a speech announcing my departure. "I speak English and you speak all Spanish, but friendship speaks all languages," I'd tell them.

I met up with Chano and two of his friends at four o'clock on Sunday morning, back in Plaza San Antonio. All three were talking quickly, and I couldn't figure out their plans, but they made it clear I'd be part of those plans. The gist was that we were walking to Plaza Mina, a few blocks away. Chano would try to do some business, and if he succeeded, he would take us all to an expensive dance in a waterfront amphitheater. Silva was already there, dancing his butt off. So was Chano's fiancée.

The plaza was a web of revelers—dense knots of people, mostly in costume, connected by well-trafficked pathways lined with lush North African palms. There was drumming, the drinking of Manzanilla, and laughter everywhere. Chano seemed to know everybody. But he couldn't make his sale.

It was evident that the evening was careening rapidly toward anticlimax. I didn't want my last memory of Cádiz to be watching The Boys wistfully sitting outside the dance. So I bailed. I gave my little speech to Chano alone, gave him my sailor's cap and a short sloppy hug, and walked off.

But, as on the day we met, I didn't feel comfortable with my hasty exit. So I returned, and asked him to tell Silva good-bye for me. "I will tell him he's a good friend to you," Chano said. My last words were supposed to be, "Give a hug to Silva for me." But I only got as far as "Give a hug," and Chano pulled me into a strong, tender, not-at-all reticent embrace. As I walked away again, I heard a loud whistle. I turned around and saw Chano for the last time, feverishly waving good-bye.

ITALIAN AFFAIR

Laura Fraser

et's say your husband leaves you. He leaves you the way husbands always leave in bad novels, abruptly, with a trail of lies that are impossible, after all those sweet years, to believe. Let's say that for weeks and then months you can barely eat or sleep or work. You lie in bed while an Italian phrase keeps playing over and over in your head: *Mi hai spaccato il cuore.* You have broken my heart. You have cloven it in two.

The Italian phrase at least takes you out of your English-speaking mind for a moment, out of the ugly present and into another realm of possibility. There is another world out there. Where they take long lunches and drink good coffee and wine and stay up too late after dinner. Where you will not run into your husband at the grocery store and will not have to hear his girlfriend leave a message on the answering machine at the home where you still live. Let's say you have a few friends you can stay with in Italy, and you speak the language well enough. You can go there to forget. And then a fantasy flickers and you think maybe an Italian man might not be such a bad idea, either.

So you book the flight and for the next few weeks you stare at the trim folder and believe it's your ticket to somewhere much farther away than Florence. To forgetfulness, to contentment, to your old self in a new place.

Finally, the day comes when you leave messages on all your machines that you are completely unreachable and you take off for Italy. You arrive in Florence and your dear friend Lucia meets you, walking with you along those narrow cobbled roads to the Piazza della Repubblica for a late-night glass of *spumanti secco,* and you recount, as well as you can in Italian, the details of the breakup. She makes a gesture flicking her fingers under her chin that Italians use to say, economically, Forget him, he wasn't worth it, life goes on, and you'll be better off. She tells you he was a nice, intelligent man but he never had the love of life you have anyway, the sense of *la bella vita.* She uses another swift gesture to tell the waiter to bring another round.

You wander Florence for a few days, taking in the ice cream–colored marble, the terra-cotta, the Brunelleschis, the Botticellis, and the Michelangelos. You walk past markets and boutiques, you bicycle up to Fiesole, and the view everywhere is lovely but you always have the sense that something is following you close behind. Your Italian friends are in love this year and it isn't convenient to stay long at their houses, so you make a plan to get far away from Florence, too.

And so you go to Ischia. Maybe you'll see Naples, Capri, Pompeii, and the Amalfi Coast, too, but your sights are set on Ischia. Something about a volcanic island with natural hot baths and long pebbly beaches sounds about right. Everything will be stucco white and washed with Mediterranean light. Everything else will be far, far away.

From Napoli you take the rickety metro to Pozzuoli, a fishing town destroyed by earthquakes and hastily rebuilt by people who know it is going to crumble again anyway. Everyone in Pozzuoli wants you to spend the night there, to tourist there, and they're sad when you ask only when the next boat leaves for Ischia.

The people you briefly encounter in the bars and shops in Pozzuoli don't know what to call you, a single American woman in your mid-thirties. You are certainly old enough to be a *signora,* and ought to be married. But there you are, *sola,* with no wedding band. *Signorina?* You don't fit.

The eight-year-old girls call you *signora,* because you're older than their mothers. They ask you where you're from, and where your children are hiding. Where is your husband? He left me, you tell them, and they're startled by your response, uncomprehending. You look down at your shoes and say, "He died," because that they can understand. They nod solemnly and wave you off to the ship.

The air is fresh and cool on the top deck, the sun sinking behind the silhouetted island in the distance. Traveling by boat is romantic, pulling you away from shore, leaving a vast emptiness of water between your old life and an entirely new place. But as the engines warm up and the horn sounds and the ship belches black smoke, you realize you can't outdistance your sorrow, it hangs in the wet air and covers your face with salt water.

When the boat pulls up to Ischia's crater-round harbor, it is night. A bus circles the island on a windy road and drops you off seven miles away in the resort town of Forio. There, motorbikes race through the streets, tourist cafés have all-German menus, and souvenir stores sell stuff you would never dream of hauling home. You hate Forio: It is not the charming village you expected, you can't get a good meal anywhere, the red wine is sour, and the only saving grace is the pensione your hippie guidebook recommended, which is peaceful and cheap and clean, with large tropical plants in an open-air stairway and a *signora* who is gracious enough after she grudgingly agrees to include breakfast in the price of the room.

In the morning, after caffe latte and a good roll, Forio isn't nearly so bad, and the *signora* recommends visiting Sant'Angelo, a smaller village three miles away, with plenty of beaches. You climb aboard a bus filled with German pensioners in mismatching floral shorts and T-shirts and pass several of the thermal baths on Ischia, places that offer all manner of soaking and sweating and rubbing, amusement parks for the arthritic. Finally the bus disgorges the last passengers onto a pedestrian-only zone, and noisy, tourist Ischia turns into the lovely Mediterranean haven you were dreaming about.

In Sant'Angelo, you find a boat taxi that takes you even farther away, past the restaurants with sun umbrellas for rent, to a free pebble beach where you can spread out your cloth, lie down, and forget all the advice of American dermatologists for an entire sunny morning. From time to time you swim in the deliciously clear water, reveling in the freedom to swim and swim forever without hitting a wall or smelling chlorine.

Sometime after lunch you spot a building nearby with large palm umbrellas and a sun terrace on top and wonder, since it has no name, whether it's a private club and whether you could go sit under one of those nice big umbrellas yourself. You hesitate, but decide, what the hell, you are a Blond American Divorcée and no one is going to complain if you tie your beach cloth around your waist and go sit on their patio and dry your hair in the sun. So you walk right in, making use of their shower on the way, and order a lemonade.

The waiter, who is tall and dark and, yes, handsome, is all too happy to give you whatever you like. You feel lovely sitting there on the terrace, drying off, and the square-bodied elderly German women doing the sidestroke in the water below feel beautiful, too, which is a nice thing about Ischia.

Then you realize what you really need is a salad and some good bread and a glass of white wine, which is so light on Ischia it might as well be water. After the coffee the waiter shows you to a comfy lounging chair on the terrace, where Germans are sunning themselves in the all and all, and he tells you to have a nice nap. Afterward, he says, you can try the sauna and the *fango*, which after some confused description you realize is a mud mask with apparently special radioactive healing powers.

You go along with the plan: the nap; the sauna, which steams straight out of the volcanic hillside, scented with fennel; the *fango* spread all across your face and shoulders, left to dry and crack in the sun. When the *fango* is done, you have another sauna to rub off all the mud, and your skin is in fact unbelievably soft, and you race into the ocean for a refreshing swim before coming back to a hot pool in a hidden grotto. As the waiter climbs in with you, you begin to dimly realize he is not doing all of this for a better tip.

Finally he sits with you in the sauna and tells you that you have the most beautiful skin he has ever seen, the color of gold, so soft. And your body. What a beautiful body, so nice from so much swimming, so strong, so curvy. *Bella, bella.* He is, of course, saying all the things a Blond American Divorcée is dying to hear, and in soft Italian. But he doesn't seem to have much of anything else to say. Here he is, the Italian lover you fantasized about. He's wild about you, he'll make passionate love to you, and he leaves you absolutely cold. Maybe, you think, you just have no desire for men at all anymore.

So you leave, explaining you have to meet a friend in Forio, and you become just another fish that got away.

The next day you meet an American woman who has lived on Ischia for thirty years, and she and her friend, a fortyish photographer, take you in a '62 Ford to a hidden canyon on the island where mineral water comes pouring down through the rocks like a shower. Afterward, you lie on the beach and drink a couple of beers and have a cheerful conversation and the photographer starts telling you how much he's attracted to you. You swim out to get away and he swims out after you and suggests that you two should spend the night together. He has some really great music you could listen to. Some Carpenters and some Fleetwood Mac. And he has studied yoga and he knows that your energy will be good together. You have the perfect body, he says, you are the perfect woman for me. For a moment you consider going back to the waiter in the sauna the day before. You bide your time until you can politely say you have a phone call to make to the States and return to Forio alone.

Italian lovers, you realize, are as easy to pick up on Ischia as ceramic ashtrays painted with lemons. You go back to the pensione and read a novel and watch the ocean and realize it's just fine to be by yourself. You fall asleep making plans to move on the next day. A mosquito wakes you in the dead of night and you write a twelve-page letter to your ex that you will never send, but putting it all down in a notebook in a pensione on Ischia seems to make it feel better. In the morning, you're ready to explore someplace new, alone.

At breakfast you say *buon giorno* to the *signora* and nod to the gentleman at the table next to you. You notice he is not German and you wonder about him. He looks remarkably like Bob Dylan ten years ago, only less craggy, with shiny brown curls, a beaklike nose, and watery blue eyes. He's wearing a long, soft denim jacket and a tapestry vest and thick silver bracelets.

You're studying your hippie guidebook when he starts asking the *signora* some questions about the island. You join the conversation by asking her a question yourself without making eye contact with the man. When she leaves, you offer him a look at your guidebook. You speak to him in the third person formal, *lei*. You tell him what you know about the island and when he asks, you say you're probably leaving that morning but you're not sure, you still might want to climb the mountain first. He slips into the second person familiar, *tu*. You find out he is from Paris, half-Italian. He teaches art at a university, the philosophy of aesthetics. He first guessed you are German, but your accent is good and he can't tell, and you say you are from San Francisco, which you always say instead of America.

Your brain parts company with your mouth for a moment and you tell him he has a face like Bob Dylan. He seems surprised at what a direct and personal thing that is to say, you American you, and you quickly add "Ten years ago," though it's probably closer to five, and he doesn't really look displeased. Amused. Wasn't it strange, he says, that Bob Dylan just played for the Pope in Bologna? Has he become a Catholic or what? And what's with the hat?

It's always hard to know what religious phase Bob Dylan is in, you say. But the hat was *troppo* cowboy. The day the Stones play "Sympathy for the Devil" for the Pope, he says, I'll become a Papist. You like his sensibility, and he says that if in fact you do climb the mountain instead of leaving that morning, he'd like to come along. You shrug. Why not. Pompeii can wait.

In a few minutes you climb aboard a bus and notice that he, like you, has brought along a beach bag. He leans toward you away from the Germans and asks you your name. "Laura," you say, with the pretty rolling Italian pronunciation. He tells you his lovely French name and you say, in your best formal schoolbook Italian, that it is a pleasure to meet him. He laughs.

The bus takes you to the highest road on the island and from there you walk another couple of miles until the road turns into a small brushy footpath and reaches the summit. Here, you really know you are on the island: water on all sides, Capri just obscured by the clouds. You sit on volcanic rocks overlooking everything and he smokes and says there's no sight he loves more than grapevines with the ocean in the distance. You talk about all the islands you've been to, Stromboli and Sardinia, Crete and Santorini, and find you've both climbed to the top of Formentera, too, the tiny island off Ibiza. You go further afield and talk about Iraq and Egypt, French politics, then Bill Clinton and Paula Jones. American politics are ridiculous, he says. Who cares whether the President propositioned her? At least Kennedy had better taste in women.

We are far too puritanical, you agree.

At Mitterrand's funeral, he says, his mistress was right there with his wife. Much more civilized. The problem with Americans, he says, is they think a little affair will destroy a marriage. How can you be so claustrophobic? It puts far too much pressure on the marriage.

On the way down the mountain, wandering through terraced farms with lemon trees, tomatoes and figs, he asks about your marriage. We're just traveling, he says, you can tell me anything.

You tell him the story in brief, so in love, only married a year and a half when he left, a complicated psychological scenario. Did you have time for affairs? he asks. No, you say. But my husband did. Well, he says, that is all history. That is all behind you now, yes?

And are you married? you ask. "I'm not talking," he answers in English. That answers the question, you say. Okay, he says, he has been married for ten years and has two children. I know better than to ask whether you had time for any affairs, you say, and he smiles; you're learning fast. You wonder to yourself whether you would have an affair with a married man with two children, and decide that in the United States, you would not. Then you figure that's why God made Frenchmen.

You find lunch, and then decide to go to a beach you've heard about, the Sorgeto, where hot water bubbles up from the rocks. After a swim, lying on the pebbles, you realize the rocks on the beach are warm not from the sun but from inside the earth. The farther you dig down into the rocks, the warmer they are. You lie on your stomach to snooze and just when you're drifting off you feel a warm rock placed lightly on the small of your back and all the desire you thought was dead radiates from that rock through your entire body.

In the evening you find the only restaurant in Forio where Italians are eating, and you talk over pesto like old friends. You discreetly go back to the pensione at different times to your separate rooms. Later, when you tiptoe around the open stairway to his room, the eagle-eyed *signora* catches you walking where you have no business walking and you realize you'd better leave in the morning.

So you have the bright idea of escaping these German tourists and going to Procida, a tranquil fishing village nearby, says the hippie guidebook, and the French aesthetics professor is game. After a crowded bus ride and a boat trip you land on Procida, which is charming in its 1950s-Italian-movie style, but the beaches are dirty and the pensione are deserted and the whole place is simply glum. After lunch you return to Ischia, and you suggest Sant'Angelo, and ɔy evening you're back to the whitewashed village with the bright geraniums and fragrant jasmine and oleander. You're hot and tired but still in fairly good traveling spirits and when the hotel with the great view says it's full you ask if there might not be a private room to let somewhere nearby, and there is, with a terrace, and meals are included. You drop your things and rush to the beach to jump in. "*Lava tutto,*" he says. The feel of the water washes away the whole day.

Afterward, in the room, you mention that it's strange to share a room, it's somehow much more intimate than making love. He nods. "We've made a grand progression in a short time," he says, and then he picks up a big white towel and offers to dry your hair. A little later he thinks you are asleep and he traces his fingers down the curve of your back and then he stops and you are desperately trying to come up with the right verb tenses. Imperfect subjunctive: "If you were to stop touching me," and then present conditional, "I would die."

Dinner is on another terrace, and the sun sinks red into the ocean. There are grilled eggplants and arugula salad and roasted potatoes with rosemary and tomato salad and bruschetta and that's just to start. Over a lovely piece of sole he looks out over the view and starts laughing. We have found the perfect place, he says, delighted. "Gorgeous," you say in English, and he likes that word, tasting it like wine.

The next day you stretch out on lava rocks away from all the people as the sun washes over you. "*La vita bellissima,*" he says, and you know that one of the things you have in common is a willingness to believe that life is truly beautiful at times and you should enjoy the pleasure of it completely. You talk about authors and films, Marcel Proust and David Lodge and Marguerite Duras and Martin Scorsese. The names and titles are a shorthand for what you can't express in your incomplete Italian, but it's enough. You are drugged with pleasure, lying on the rocks, going through cycle after cycle of swimming, drying off, eating, making love, swimming, and drying off again. The next morning you ask, "What should we do today?" and he says, "The same thing we did yesterday. In reverse."

At some point it occurs to you that these four days are unique, that their particular beauty can never be repeated, and that probably you will never see him again. And you realize you may never have another lover like him, either. His lovemaking is like a long, languorous Italian meal, full of delightful appetizers and side dishes, a variety of simple, exquisite tastes, finished off by an unfiltered cigarette. "After thirty-six years you decide to take up smoking now?" he asks. You smile and tell him it is all his fault.

When I get back, you say, I'm going to have to find a lover like you.

"*Inutile,*" he says, and laughs. Your only hope is to teach someone. Then he becomes more serious, avuncular. You'll find someone, he says. All you need is a man who is older than you and younger than me. A professor of literature who speaks Italian. There must be some of them in San Francisco.

They're everywhere, you say, like German tourists.

Over dinner, when he's quiet, you ask him if he's thinking about school on Tuesday and he says no, he's thinking about you. *Cara signorina,* he says, his only compliment. You dear woman. In such a short time you know him better than most people do, he says. Then he laughs: You even know about his secret life.

Maybe, he says, we will find each other again some time.

I hope so, you say. You really shouldn't die before you see San Francisco.

The next morning is all business, a bus ride to the port and a ship to Naples where you practice putting distance between each other. In Naples, he helps you find the train station and your ticket and takes you to a very quick, noisy, wonderful Napolitano lunch. He crosses the street to the train station and says send a postcard at Christmas. Then he abruptly says, "I'm abandoning you here," and kisses you on both cheeks, *ciao, ciao. Piacere,* you murmur, a pleasure, and he is gone.

He is gone, but on the train ride back to Florence, the sad feeling of loss that followed you to Italy doesn't return. You are lighter and happier and even, somehow, feel more beautiful. The physical miles of travel, you realize, can't make the pain in your life go away. But you have traveled inside, too, and it has expanded you, let you discover that *la bella vita* always exists alongside what is ugly, and you can at least find it for a time, if you look.

TAMPAX NIGHTMARES

Susan Hack

"Excuse me, where's the nearest place I can buy some Tampax?" I whisper.

I'm in Sana'a, capital of Yemen, about to set off on a two-week November desert drive. My little friend (and I don't mean my travel buddy) has arrived earlier than expected. I've gone down to the front desk of my hotel to see the reception clerk, who, thank God, is a woman.

"Tampax? What's that?" she asks, loud enough for two oil workers checking in next to me to overhear.

"Um, you know, tampons. For when you have your period."

"You mean pads."

"No, not pads, tampons. The ones you insert."

She looks at me, pity in her eyes. "Madam," she confides in a low voice, "in Yemen we do not insert."

Okay, we're not talking rape, death, or dismemberment here, but a Tampax nightmare is one of the worst travel experiences a woman can have. (Men, you may not want to read further.) Tampons inspire insane brand loyalty; one girl's best friend is another girl's leaky sponge. But not only does Yemen not have my preferred brand of tampon, it does not appear to have any tampons at all.

In desperation I ask our guide, Mohammed, a tribesman with a curved dagger in his belt and an automatic pistol in his glove compartment, a man who is prepared to protect us from kidnapping, who will keep us safe against thirst and scorpions in the Empty Quarter, who we've hired to drive us ten hours in a Toyota 4 × 4 to the top of a roadless mountain to a fortress village called Shahara—I ask this white-robed man of the desert to take me to a Sana'a pharmacy.

Ten pharmacies, in fact, none of which have tampons, and whose clerks treat me, when I ask for tampons, as if I'm morally and physically tainted. A true gentleman, Mohammed can see my mounting frustration, but I'm too embarrassed to tell him what I'm looking for. "Whatever is troubling you, chew this," he says kindly, handing me a bouquet of qat. "Qat solves everything."

A mild stimulant, the Yemeni equivalent of a stiff drink, qat's green leaves bind you up, which partly solves another feminine problem: how to shit with dignity in the desert. Squat toilets and rock toilets I'm prepared to handle. And thanks to qat, I don't have to shit much at all. But the prospect of going native when it comes to period control is making me crazy, making me consider curtailing this trip. It's a hot country, Yemen. I've packed lots of white.

For a moment I debate going to the American embassy, to ask the diplomats if they have any tampons, or if they can give me a list of expatriate women residents to whom I can appeal for a sisterly loan. Finally I call the Sheraton, an American-owned hotel chain, and ask the guest relations director where I can buy insertable feminine hygiene products. "I don't use them myself," she says amiably (she is from Pakistan), "but I believe you can buy them in the big department stores here. Try City Market on Az-Zubeiry Street." Mohammed and I get back in the 4 × 4, and I ask him to take me to City Market. It's not so big after all. Zip.

By now I really am desperate, so I give in and buy pads. Not minipads with wings, or even pads with adhesive strips. These ma-

ternity ward–sized pads have string belts. Like the kind Mom used
to use. One word sums up my situation. That word is *yuck*.

Even though we stand on the cusp of the new millennium, we
women continue to deal stoically with this immutable fact of our
biology, this evolutionary hand-me-down, euphemistically called
the curse, my little friend, that time of the month or, as the French
say revealingly, *les Anglais.* Why do we endure this monthly mess,
this cramp- and bad mood–producing event? Some evolutionary
biologists believe periods are the ultimate female weapon in the
battle of the sexes, a red banner telling us when we're fertile, enabling us, unlike the females of any other species, to deny sex and
children to unsatisfactory males. All I can say is, Too bad they
didn't have home-pregnancy tests and early ovulation prediction
kits back in the days of *Australopithecus.*

Ladies, I think you'll agree: Tampax is the greatest invention of
the twentieth century. (The tampon was actually invented by the
ancient Egyptians, who made theirs out of shredded linen and
gum arabic. Tampax, the first mass-produced tampon, came into
being in 1936 after a Denver physician, Earl Haas, patented the idea
of a cotton plug on a string.) Yes, Jonas Salk's polio vaccine has
saved millions, and the cell phone and the personal computer have
brought previously inconceivable levels of convenience to daily
life. But could you survive without tampons? Would you ever leave
home without them?

Astronauts don't (NASA has developed special space feminine
protection), and neither, according to marine experts, should any
woman considering snorkeling or scuba diving in shark-infested
waters. Ditto safari camps, where lions, leopards, and hyenas have
been known to pull women off trails and from their beds.

According to *Advertising Age* magazine, 70 percent of American
women prefer tampons to pads. Unfortunately, that view isn't always shared by women in other countries. In Latin America and
some Islamic nations, many women still think tampons will spoil a
girl's virginity. Feminine hygiene giants Procter & Gamble,
Kimberly-Clark, and Johnson & Johnson are still battling to pene-

trate the former Soviet Union and China, to boost their share of the potential $2 billion global tampon market. Distribution can be problematic in remote or rural parts of Africa and Asia, where popular feminine protection consists of rags or handfuls of dried moss. So if you're traveling anywhere exotic, without twenty-four-hour pharmacies, pack an adequate tampon supply.

Here are some international tampon travel tips. In Japan, buy big sizes; tampons there run small. In France, another popular American tampon, o.b., goes by the brand name Nett (from *net-toyer,* or "to clean"). According to that bible of women's health issues, *Our Bodies, Ourselves for the New Century,* if you're truly, seriously desperate (or put off by pads), homemade tampons made of natural sponges or sterilized cotton will do the trick.

Alas, tampon nightmares don't end there. There's technical failure. Use and abuse. A friend of mine, who understandably wishes to remain anonymous, was about to go on a romantic sailing weekend with a brand new boyfriend and his best friends, a married couple who owned the boat and whom she hadn't met. The "little friend" came along too. She figured she could keep her beau at first base, but silly girl, she flushed a used tampon down the loo. A bunged-up toilet delayed the departure. A plumber was called out to the boat, and after hours of probing, announced to everyone what he'd found. Trip canceled, new friends pissed off, romance ruined.

And what about customs inspections? Ever looked a Syrian border guard in the eye while he unwraps your Tampax from its packaging? "What is this? A cigar?" He unwraps another, trying to solve the mystery of the cardboard tube, cotton package, and that funny little string. "Strange American lady," he seems to say, though in reality he barks: "What are these for and why do you have so many?"

Managing menstruation is not that big a deal. Like Nike says, "Just Do It." But let me tell you about my other worst Tampax nightmare, which happened in Lebanon, in 1983, during a tank battle in downtown Beirut. I was a freelance reporter working out of the offices of the Lebanese newspaper *An Nahar*, and when the shooting started I knew I'd be taking shelter in the basement for a while. Guess who picked this inconvenient time to arrive? This is a real nightmare: convincing a panicky pharmacist shuttering his shop to take time out to rummage around for some boxes of Tampax Super Plus. He's only got Regular and shoves them at me over the cash register. "Take them, take them," he hisses. I quickly decide I can live, shrapnel being the immediate threat, with less than my desired Tampax absorbency. Then I discover there's no toilet in the newspaper's basement, only a printing room. Amid the muffled thump of incoming missiles, a brave female colleague shields me from view while I insert.

For years I thought no one could top this story, until I mentioned it to my friend Johanna, a graphic designer living in Japan. "Tampons, ha! What about diaphragms?" she laughed. "A Sudanese customs guy took mine out of my makeup bag at the airport in Khartoum and waved it in my face. I didn't have the heart to tell him what it was or where it had been."

ON JAPANESE TRAINS

Sallie Tisdale

Somewhere in the controlled anarchy of my weeks in Japan last fall, I found myself in a group hug, in the public arena of a crowded train station. I was traveling to several temples with a shifting crowd of Buddhist friends and acquaintances, most of them Americans with no experience in Japan and only a little conversational Japanese.

We'd been moving from one monastery or temple to the next almost every day, bearing gifts, paying respects, attending ceremonies. We rose at three-thirty or four every morning, joining in temple schedules until after breakfast, and then moved on, by foot, taxi, bus, and train, sometimes all in a day. Mostly, we took trains; when I wasn't in a zendo in Japan, I seemed to be in a station. And after a few weeks in the world of Japanese trains, I felt as though movement itself was my home.

That day in Kanazawa, a busy city in Ishikawa prefecture, we were overcome by giddy exhaustion. We had a long wait at the Kanazawa station—when we weren't moving, we were usually waiting. We piled onto a bench in a heap, a dozen scruffy, coarse Americans out of place in the decorous quiet of Japanese business travelers, and somehow Mikio ended up in the middle. Mikio was raised in Tokyo and Osaka, but is married to an American woman and lives in the United States now.

Mikio has told me more than once that he is "not Japanese" anymore. Japanese who leave the country and live elsewhere for a time are never quite the same, he says. He often has a slightly bewildered expression on his thin face, the look of a man who thinks he's missed an appointment. Even in Kanazawa, Mikio had that look. The American boisterousness and informality he'd gradually grown used to in his new home stood out starkly in his old one. From deep in the tangle of arms and legs, I could hear his plaintive, clipped cry: "We do not touch much!" he yelped, muffled by the bodies of his alarming friends.

Taking trains is inevitable in Japan, unavoidable—but why would you want to avoid it? The trains are a microcosm of the whole country. I have never had a romantic vision of Japan, never felt a particular urge to visit. This trip was purposeful, specific—not exactly about Japan for Japan's sake. But day by day, living in the world of the trains, I found myself delighted. It was like stumbling into an accidental love affair with someone as different from your dreams as a person can be.

We do not touch much, Mikio said, suddenly very Japanese again. I knew in the midst of it how out of place our group hug was in that world, but I puzzled over his words. The Japanese are always together. The Japanese tolerate crowds that Americans, the most space-hungry people in the world, find impossible, but in all this swarming humanity, there is always distance, too. They are never alone and they are never completely together, either. Where there is no privacy, there are many masks.

The Japanese are always together, millions of people on a few small islands, mostly in small houses with small rooms. They crowd the sidewalks, walking rapidly from chore to chore, one demand to the next, in well-dressed, quiet urban mobs. They travel together, lining up politely at bus stops and filling subway platforms in converging flocks.

Even at home, there is little privacy. Many houses have no central heating, and families spend wintertime together in a single small space. Almost every workplace operates as a second family, with attendant obligations and society. Japanese hotels charge by the customer, not the room, and put as many people into each as possible—futons lined up on the sweet-smelling tatami mats with only a few inches between. Many public bathrooms are shared by both genders, men discreetly lined up at urinals and women silently squatting in stalls. In the public bathhouses, strangers crouch together on the tile floors to wash before climbing together into big communal tubs. Many people ride trains in standing-room-only crowds for hours every day, the crucible for all this togetherness.

To say "Japanese trains" is to say a mouthful. There are long-distance and local trains of several kinds, as well as city subways and streetcars. The national system was made private some time ago, and there are now six Japan Rail (usually called JR) companies connected throughout the country. They work together so well that the rider never knows this. From one city to another, you may move from one line to the next, from the hands of one company to the next, without a clue. Fares, rail passes, and tickets are treated as though the companies were one.

Throwing yourself into the hands of the Japanese rail system is like entering the belly of a giant creature—a massive organism where everything happens quickly and by large measures. More than 100,000 people pass through the enormous and ugly Tokyo train station every day—sometimes many more, shoved into place during rush hours by white-gloved, well-groomed handlers. At such times, Mikio says in his precise English, "You are like a water molecule in water. You cannot go where you want to go." He tells me a story of a briefcase that was carried away by closely packed bodies, floating across the car, out of reach, and never falling to the floor.

In every city's rail station, hordes of commuters appear like rivers of lemmings, pouring out of trains, across platforms, and down the long flights of stairs to the next platform, the next train.

They fill the passageways, heading in a single direction, then splitting apart into smaller streams—men, men, men, all in dark suits, white shirts, ties, and uniformly serious expressions; flocks of women in skirted suits; small groupings of beautifully coiffed women in kimonos scooting along in tiny steps; masses of uniformed schoolchildren in pleated skirts and ironed shorts, banging heavy book bags on their thighs; even half-naked sumo wrestlers swaggering along, twice as big as their fellows and exuding an almost American self-consciousness. At any moment, you can be swept without warning against a wall by a crowd appearing from around a corner—a descending, ascending, hurrying crowd. Shoved, not by hands or bodies, but by the sheer force of the group that is suddenly moving in the other direction, so intent on its goal that it can't be resisted.

The Japan travel guides I've seen say little about the trains, this central phenomenon, this complicated cultural ceremony. The most obvious and least helpful piece of advice is that foreigners should buy the "JR Pass," which covers almost every JR train. These passes seem shockingly expensive, until you stand before a price board in Japan and start adding up individual fares. The pass must be bought before you arrive in Japan, and through a travel agent; even then, you're given only a voucher, which must be exchanged inside Japan for the precious pass itself.

This exchange takes place with almost ritual stateliness at one of the many Travel Service Centers, small offices with counters staffed by courteous agents who shake their heads disconsolately at English. Our first day of real train travel after an initial stay at a Nagoya monastery began with this exchange. Three agents huddled over our vouchers and passports, turning pages and opening drawers and going through files for a long time, with much whispered consultation, examining our documents and stamping page after page of mysterious forms.

Finally, each of us held a pass worth hundreds of dollars, and a plastic ruler with a picture of the bullet train on it. This little gift was *omiyage*, small tokens often given by merchants in gratitude for your purchase.

The passes are convenient in more than one way. JR fares are dauntingly complicated, depending on the destination, the type of train, the type of service, and whether or not you're reserving a seat. With a pass, you need never stand in helpless incomprehension before a fare schedule as complicated as an organic chemistry reaction, trying to figure out which ticket to buy and how much to pay. You still need a ticket, but you can get it at the JR office without concern over fares most of the time; it is there, too, where you can get reserved seats and ask for a smoking or nonsmoking car. (The best secret of Japanese train travel I learned last fall was about reservations. They're good to have, but not always possible. Lots of people make reservations they don't keep, and you can sit in a reserved car without a reservation, as long as you're willing to get up if someone holding that seat arrives.)

Reservation or not, you need a ticket, and you must never, ever lose it. There are gates within gates, stations within stations, and you may need more than one ticket per trip and your ticket and pass may be checked several times. If you do not pay enough, you will not be able to exit the platform at your destination. The automatic gate will stay shut, sometimes beeping a warning, and it's off to the "fare adjustment" window—sometimes a complicated machine these days—to pay more.

All of us were still befuddled by jet lag that first day and only beginning to realize what it means to be illiterate. There is a little English on basic signage in the large stations—"Lavatory," "Exit." Nothing more. You cannot solve Japanese, which has more than one written alphabet, by falling back on high school Spanish or Latin. You can only fall back on luck and trust, which are good tools for the traveler, after all.

With train atlas and maps in hand, we headed down the sidewalks of Nagoya, trailing wheeled luggage behind, into the subway, where a dozen identical schoolgirls surrounded three of the men in our group, giggling and having their pictures taken. Then it was onto the train station, and beyond.

No one had warned us about the stairs.

Japanese train stations are miniature cities, tiny worlds. The big stations cover several blocks and may be several stories high or deep. Rough-textured walkways for the blind crisscross the station floors, meeting and splitting at corners in mysterious patterns. Dozens of long concourses and intricately interwoven rail lines are all connected by stairs. Japan is a rough place for wheelchair users. Oh, there's an elevator or two, even an escalator now and then, but far from one another. Mostly, you go up and down stairs, lots of stairs, level after level of stairs, which sometimes seemed to stretch before me late on a tiring day like the Sisyphean hills of bad dreams, hills which must be climbed again and again, without end.

The big stations have entire malls—stores selling groceries, clothes, shoes, books, and all kinds of gifts and souvenirs; restaurants, delicatessens, bakeries, pharmacies, postal stations, and banks, where travelers eat, shop, sleep, wash, make telephone calls, watch television, mail letters, and wait. Everywhere one sees the *gyaru*, or "gals"—underfed, bleached-blond teenage girls in gigantic, awkward shoes and miniskirts, slouching and sneering at passersby.

On the trains, pretty young women in neatly pressed uniforms pace the aisles without cease, pushing carts loaded with beribboned *bento* boxes, ice cream, coffee, tea, whiskey, and gifts; the conductor in his white gloves strolls through, solemnly punching tickets; stations are announced far ahead of time—once, twice, again and again.

In all those days, watching this chaotic harmony, I felt Japan to be a place of secrets commonly held. Japanese lives are stitched in large measure out of duty, obligation, and ambition; our lives are built more on expression and entertainment. Our American identity is so dedicated to the individual—theirs, so dedicated to community. We are snakes and frogs, oil and water.

Our odd group was always watched, usually with discreetly averted eyes—the attention of being pointedly ignored. Now and then we were surrounded by curious schoolchildren, or approached by a single adult. The Japanese are courteous to tourists, curious about foreigners, but they have none of the bonhomie Europeans and Americans share. They don't chat you up. I had the same conversation over and over in Japan, with one polite stranger after another, in hotels, on subway platforms, in restaurants. How do you like Japan? they would ask. Do you know my friend So-and-So, who lives in the United States? I struggled to answer with my few limited phrases. Oh, your Japanese is so good, they would always say, in clear English.

The noise is constant. In a world of careful beauty, there is endless, disconcerting commotion. Incoming trains are signaled with chimes that sound like Swiss music boxes. Announcements are repeated relentlessly: "Please stand behind the white line," a woman's voice says from the speakers each time a train arrives, even if a new train comes every two minutes. The community is forever being brought together, willingly or not, by noise: sharing the news, political candidates' amplified slogans, advertisements, and television shows scattered through public spaces.

The commotion is visual as well, mostly in the form of advertisements of uncertain meaning: Here is a geisha holding a power tool, looking oddly excited; there a phone number for something called the "Human Scale Resort." I stood outside the Nagoya station one day, stopped in my tracks by a television screen on the side of an office building—a television screen the size of a house, blaring its daily shows and commercials to the town.

The trains have little luggage space—a little overhead, sometimes a small cupboard at either end of a car. It is hard for an American to leave a suitcase between train cars, out of sight, but on a Japanese train, the suitcase is truly safe there. On our first travel day out of Nagoya, one of our group left a borrowed $900 video camera sitting on the subway platform; it was waiting in the office when one of us went looking.

One way the Japanese tolerate their lack of physical privacy is by the strange combination of rigid courtesy toward others and silent self-containment. Trains are filled, sometimes to the brim, with people reading, having quiet conversations, working, and, often, sleeping, without disturbing each other—each person acting as though he or she were alone. The Japanese seem able to sleep sitting up and even squatting without moving a muscle, only rocking gently back and forth with the motion of the train. They can sleep standing up, facing a wall, forehead bowed, for hours.

The Japanese have solved the traveler's problem of bags with a complex network of luggage service centers. If you know your schedule in advance, you can have your luggage sent from one station on to another, and carry only a small piece on the train. This was impossible for my group because we were making so many brief stops—arriving in one town by mid-afternoon, leaving for another by the early morning, and needing all of our luggage at every stop. We formed a moving buttress of gaijin—sweaty, large, overloaded Americans passing through stations and train cars the way a sneaker wave moves along a beach, sweeping small items along in its wake. (Everything in Japan is a little too small for Americans. On one bus trip out to the remote Noto Peninsula, a group of women fell into uncontrollable giggles when one of the men got stuck in the miniature toilet and had to be rescued.) On the trains, we struggled with our suitcases and packs, we sat on them, held them on our laps, and apologized over and over again.

The guidebooks I've seen usually suggest that a traveler take the express trains instead of the *futsu*, or local trains. This is good advice if you're only interested in getting to the end of the line, but there is so much to see along the way.

The Shinkansen, or bullet train, is not quite as fast as a bullet but it is fast, and more comfortable than most forms of travel. I never even saw the inside of a "green" (first-class) car, and can only imagine how much better it could be. Bullet trains, these phallically streamlined machines, slide into the station on time to the second, white and gleaming, their aerodynamic cabs angled as sharply as a collie's head. The trains are always on time and they are always clean. The cars have swiveling, padded seats, beverage holders and folding tables, automatically warmed toilet seats, drinking fountains, recycling bins, reader boards rotating endlessly with stock quotes and news, and what I came to think of as the Beautiful Bento Girls on an endless loop from one end of the train to the other. The Shinkansen stops briefly wherever it stops, being more a machinery of time than space—rapidly accelerating and then holding steady, swaying around curves, shooting through tunnels fast enough to pop your ears.

Local rural travel is another world. The trains rock gently through the countryside, flashing past rice paddies, gardens, farms, and the backyards of isolated apartment houses and small developments, where lines of laundry hang and children clamber over playground equipment; past glittering pachinko parlors in the middle of nowhere; over wide viaducts and under arching bridges, down to the sea; through feathery cedar forests and up into the spiky mountains where rough clouds play at the peaks. They click steadily through mountain tunnels and along precarious oceanside tracks, hypnotic, civilized, and seemingly timeless.

To get to the famous monastery Eihei-ji, one of the leading temples of Soto Zen Buddhism, we rode a rickety single-car cogwheel train straight through the farmed countryside and up. A ceiling fan slowly rotated back and forth above us as we sat facing each other on narrow, cracked leather benches. The outside of the train car was painted with cartoon dinosaurs and penguins, chugging steadily up the mountain.

Toward the end of the trip, on the day most of the group was leaving the country, we were surprised to find our rural station crammed with people. It was a bank holiday, and the Japanese do not stay home on holidays. They travel in great crowds and the trains actually run more often rather than less. Suddenly, the neat world of waiting in line and sitting in reserved seats disappeared into a mêlée of polite, communal running and shoving into every available inch. People sat and stood in the aisles, on luggage racks, on the stairs. Our group was dispersed over several cars, and we stood with hundreds of weary, hard-vacationing Japanese for two hours through the countryside, everyone within inches of each other. There was no room to sit or squat, no space for more than one's two feet. And in all those miles, hardly anyone spoke, and no one touched but once. The train rattled hard around a curve and the woman beside me, smiling, tilted forward on high heels, lost her balance. She fell into the waiting arms of four people, who neatly put her back on her feet without a word.

OSCAR NIGHT IN ANGKOR WAT

Jeff Greenwald

ertain sounds must have been ubiquitous and comforting to far-flung travelers of every age. The sound of ice cracking, maybe, or the pealing of bells; a steamship blast, or the whistle of a train. Here in Siem Reap, Cambodia, 125 miles north-northwest of Phnom Penh, it's the prattle of CNN. In every outdoor restaurant and guest house lobby, live Academy Awards nominations coverage (not to mention Penisgate, the Olympics, and Iran) competes with the geckos and frogs, creating a buzz of background noise that satisfies both the cerebral cortex and the reptilian brain. The TV shimmers as I write—a long umbilicus to a distant planet.

Beyond the Diamond Hotel, the Cambodian jungle gleams beneath the full moon. Less than five miles away lies Angkor Wat, where hundreds of sandstone apsaras—celestial maidens, each one subtly different—dance before the moonlit towers of the monument, as they have done for eight centuries. I, meanwhile, labor by the glow of a desk lamp decorated with an illuminated plastic bunny. It's classic Asia kitsch, far from UL approved. After ten minutes, the plastic rabbit is hot enough to fry an Easter egg.

(There's a weird little correspondence here. Earlier, watching the moon rise above the spectacular monument, I realized that from this near-equatorial perspective the earth's satellite appears canted slightly onto its side. As a result, the visual pattern formed by the seas and craters is different from what one sees in the northern latitudes. Instead of a man in the moon, the people of South Asia perceive a rabbit—and, I have to admit, it's a pretty good resemblance.)

Siem Reap seems to have changed little since my last visit here, almost exactly five years ago. The same kids leap and splash in the river, the same women squat by their baskets of pineapples, pawpaws, and tamarinds. I easily relocate my favorite bar, where bottles of Angkor clink beneath a halo of Chinese lanterns. Strange, how a place one visited so briefly and so long ago can seem so instantly familiar.

And it was the same with Angkor Wat. Passing through the western gate, I remembered with absolute clarity the tightly fitted stones of the enormous (and seemingly endless) causeway, the cows grazing by the lotus pond, and the ranks of delicious apsaras with their adolescent breasts, pendant earrings, and Dr. Seuss hairdos.

What's different about this visit is that I'm with John Sanday, the Kathmandu-based architect who lately escorted Prince Charles through the palaces of Patan. Charged with conserving the temple of Preah Khan (one of the main sites within the sprawling Angkor complex), Sanday is an expert on Khmer ruins of the eighth to fourteenth century. This afternoon he led me on a grueling tour of Southeast Asia's most famous ruin, describing the construction and deterioration of Angkor Wat's stonework in great detail.

Cambodia, according to Sanday, has never experienced a major earthquake. The toppled stones and broken lintels that fill the Angkor ruins were not unseated by tremors. More gradual forces brought down those walls: water seepage, salt crystallization, the serpentine invasion of roots. The end result is a rather artful decrepitude, a kind of conspiracy between earth and monument. Stated less poetically, it's like Jeff Goldblum at the end of *The Fly:* a weird hybrid of organic and inorganic elements, monstrous and heartbreaking.

The ruins at Angkor cover an area of seventy-seven square miles. Many are being conserved or restored; some are still overgrown by jungle, just as André Malraux found them in 1923. (Malraux was expelled from Cambodia for looting Angkor's sculpture; he would return years later, as French minister of culture.) The big cheese of these monuments, of course, is Angkor Wat itself: a single gigantic Vishnu temple, built in the early twelfth century by a Hindu king named Suryavarman II.

Even in this day and age, certain monuments have an almost metaphysical power. If you enter Angkor Wat at just the right time—before the tourists arrive, the vendors set up, and the landmine victims arrange themselves along the broad sandstone causeway leading to the central towers—it overwhelms you. It wipes your slate. You forget you ever heard of cloning, or anthrax, or Monica Lewinsky. Something echoes back to you, though you haven't made a sound. Lotuses bloom in the reflecting pool; a breath of incense trails the air; an ankle bracelet rattles behind you. Along the inner gallery walls, exposed to the rising sun, the bas-relief apsaras gesture with seductive smiles. The air seems perfectly still, and your eyes sting in the climbing light. It's vivid to the point of transcendence: you and Angkor Wat, alone at last.

It's like winning the lottery, you think to yourself, or getting stuck in an elevator with Janeane Garofalo.

An airplane whines by, snapping the moment. And when the spell breaks in Cambodia, it stays broken. The beggars and waifs and water sellers filter in, tugging you back into these last stumbling years of the millennium. How impossible it is to imagine the place in its heyday: back in the 1100s, when the vast open courtyards were filled with wooden houses, animals, shops, and cafés. Of those lives, nothing remains; time has annihilated all but the stone. In the harsh sunlight, there is something unsettling about the naked lawns of the Angkor Wat compound. Like so much of Cambodia, it seems inhabited by ghosts.

And here's the rub: Despite the charms of Angkor, Cambodia is not a charming place. The civil war that drove millions of people to the killing fields in the 1970s and 1980s was not an isolated incident. From their earliest records, the Khmer have been a warlike people, obsessed with battle and victory, torture and death. They fought the Vietnamese, the Thais, the Chinese. Sometimes they lost; often they won. The glorious Angkor reservoirs and monuments, Buddhist temples included, were built by captured slaves. Angkor Wat alone represents at least thirty years of hard labor. Knowing this, I admit to a nagging sense of guilt. The Chinese and Burmese use slave labor today; will future generations gawk in admiration of their efforts?

Woke up later than usual on my final morning and joined Sanday for a trip to the Roluos Group, a thirty-minute drive from Siem Reap. These are the oldest monuments at Angkor, built nearly three centuries before Angkor Wat. I loved their grace and simplicity, the beautifully detailed lintels that, carved from a high grade of sandstone, look as if they were finished last month.

More than the ruins, though, I relished the too-short drive into the countryside: past the covered market with its baskets of bananas, past the elegant wooden houses resting on timber stilts, past the dry rice paddies, the lean sweet cows, the farmers' daughters with red welts of therapeutic cupping on their cheeks and foreheads.

Once again, the idyllic appearance of the countryside is belied by Sanday's description of what lies beneath. Much of the region is still seeded with antipersonnel mines, designed to kill or maim. Demining the region is a herculean task; it takes the United Nations teams nearly an hour to sweep each square meter of land. The only metal part of many mines is the detonator, and any bottle cap or bit of foil, however small, will set off the detector. When this happens, the offending area must be probed with long needles, and the cause of the alarm discerned. When an actual mine is discovered, an attempt is made to neutralize the detonator. This is

often impossible. The mines are painstakingly extracted from the
ground, set in a pile, and blown up at the end of the workday.
Sanday has heard several such blasts, which rattle the windows of
his World Monuments Fund office.

What is it with this country? What is the root of its terrible luck?
Sanday suggests that the Khmer—like some equally unfortunate
African nations—are bedeviled by bad karma, locked into a de-
monic cycle of tribal war and self-destruction. (Declarations like
these seem completely convincing here in Asia, where such con-
cepts are not New Age platitudes but the bread and butter of spiritual life.) During my brief visit to central Cambodia, warnings of
local Khmer Rouge activity were updated daily. Mine victims—
many of them children—are everywhere. As recently as last July,
political tensions in Phnom Penh erupted into violence, claiming
more than forty lives. Most telling of all, an entire generation of inhabitants seems to be missing, erased during the black reign of Pol
Pot. Cambodia—like much of Europe after the Second World
War—is a nation of the young and the old.

But there is, of course, the odd note of redemption amid the
decay: the knowledge that renewal, at least on a historical scale, is
inevitable. This is especially evident at Ta Prohm, a magical, lushly
romantic temple that Malraux (in his avatar as minister of culture)
declared should be left in its "natural," overgrown state.

Entering the ruin—with its pale gum trees emerging from
vaulted stone rooftops, root-laced bas-reliefs, and mountains of
broken stone pillars—is like wandering onto the set of an Indiana
Jones film. True chaos has a kind of innate perfection, and
nowhere on earth is it better expressed. Doug Coupland (I think it
was he) once observed that colors in nature never clash. A true
ruin, I realize, displays the same mysterious, unerring aesthetic.
Every element seems in place.

And this is true on several levels. To step into Ta Prohm and explore its narrow passageways is to experience the awed, breathless
rush that the first explorers must have felt when they located the
famed Angkor ruins in the jungle. The place is a maze, full of dan-

gers and surprises: The place looks static, but a loose stone—or hidden Hanuman snake—could kill you. The temple is also a case study, an illustrated textbook of the fate awaiting unrestored monuments.

Most compelling of all, though, is the view of impermanence the ruin provides. At liberty in Ta Prohm, it's easy to imagine one is walking through the remains of Shea Stadium, or of San Francisco's financial district. Bulbuls hoot, and monkeys scream in the trees; the fallen buddhas and apsaras seem like natural denizens of the jungle. Eight hundred years after Ta Prohm's glory days, there is nothing here that did not belong to nature in the first place. At peace in a land of warring camps and minefields, Ta Prohm provides an uncompromising example of the planet's ability to restore itself.

A few days back from Cambodia, I wake to a mild, almost caressing tremor—that slight samba shimmy in the roof beams and walls. The quake is so subtle that my housemate, Chrissie, doesn't even feel it, but by the afternoon it's the talk of Kathmandu.

It makes sense that this southern edge of the Himalaya—the world's youngest, most active mountain chain, rising at the breakneck pace of inches per year—would be rocking constantly, and it amazes me that bloodcurdling tremors are not a daily occurrence. Nepal has already had two devastating earthquakes this century: in 1934 and 1988.

The next one is due, if the royal astrologers are correct, within fifteen days. Their prediction is being taken seriously; the past weeks have seen killer quakes in Afghanistan and Pakistan. Smart expats are assembling their earthquake kits, complete with spare rupees, leather gloves, and Pepto-Bismol. The American embassy has issued a "preparedness" report, advising that bathrooms are the safest place to hide and informing American citizens where the evacuation helicopters will be landing. Getting to them will be the problem; Kathmandu is a hasty erection of bricks, beams, and poorly reinforced concrete, rising amid a squid-ink linguine of power lines.

But as in San Francisco, so it is in Nepal. Dawn brings another Shangri-la morning. The bells ring down at the corner Ganesh shrine; brown-eyed cows parade down the dirt lane outside my gate, unfazed by the schoolgirls who touch them for a quick blessing. To the north, the mountains ripple like meringue. Disaster seems impossibly far away. What, me worry? It'll be like this until the summer monsoon—bees and banana trees, singing birds and snapdragons—even as we're digging ourselves out of Ta Prohm–ish rubble.

Tomorrow is Shiva Ratri: the dark new moon night of Lord Shiva, the great Hindu creator-destroyer. The days following will witness the celebrations of Lhosar, the Tibetan New Year. I'll report back from the K@mandu cybercafé in a couple of weeks—if the place is still standing.

THE LAST TOURIST IN MOZAMBIQUE

Mary Roach

Late one night in 1995, I dialed directory assistance for Maputo, Mozambique, and asked for the fax number for the Office of the President. I sent His Excellency a letter on a piece of *Health* magazine stationery, requesting an interview on the topic of meditation. I had read that President Chissano was a devotee of Transcendental Meditation, so much so that he required his cabinet members and his military recruits to be trained in TM. He even attributed the signing of the peace treaty with the guerrilla group RENAMO in part to the practice of TM in his country. A week later, the president's secretary faxed me back. To my great and giddy disbelief, Chissano had agreed to see me.

If anyone needed help relaxing, it was Joaquim Chissano. For years, guerrilla warfare had consumed his country, flattening tourism and every other industry that had managed to take root in the preceding decades. It was a country of guns and politics, and seemingly little else. Though the civil strife was technically over, the nation was still in shock. It lay like a downed prize-fighter, dazed and bleeding. The infrastructure in the capital had long ago been given up on. Power outages happened nightly, leaving cars and pedestrians to navigate the shelled-out streets by moonlight.

Maputo hadn't been as hard hit as the countryside, but mortar shells had fallen frequently enough to turn the occasional cement sidewalk blocks into sandboxes. Garbage hadn't been collected in weeks; it lined the streets like snowbanks in Wisconsin. Cabs were scarce and dilapidated, their trunks and doors held shut with coat hangers and packing twine. Soldiers were threatening revolt, demanding pay for services no longer needed. The atmosphere was spiked with resentment and discontent. If you ruled Mozambique, you'd meditate too.

This was my first visit to a place that had no tourism, a country that didn't know what to do with me. I had traveled to far-flung places before, but I'd been on eco-travel junkets, where they'd take you to the kind of remote mountain hamlet that "just got electricity last year," yet the pension owner's little boy had a Stimpy sticker on his door. More and more, "untouristed" doesn't mean remote. It means hostile and smelly. Travelers can get to pretty much anywhere they want to. It's the places they don't want to go that are left alone. As far as I could tell, I was pretty much the only foreigner on earth who wanted to be visiting Mozambique.

In return for holding the passenger-side door in place on the rutted drive from the airport, the cabdriver helped me find a room. Pensão Martins was airy and clean, so much so that I was lulled into thinking it was A-OK to drink the tap water. (Back home, weeks later, lab personnel would be trumpeting with glee at the bacteriological rarities found cavorting in my sample. "*Endolimax nana!* It's a first for us!") Because I wasn't meeting the president until the following day, I thought I'd do my usual Third World–interloper thing: a little wandering, a little lunch, a little shopping.

I stopped first at Banco de Moçambique to change money. The lobby was chaos, a human pasta of curling, overlapping lines. I was handed a plastic token and directed to a line. This was apparently the line you waited in to find out the proper line to wait in, which turned out to be longer again by half. I could ascertain no common theme to the plastic tokens being held by the people in my line. Mine was green and said *P*; the woman behind me had a red one with an impala on it. Perhaps they were gifts, a little something to thank us for our patience. I was the only one in my line changing foreign money. Apparently I was the only one changing foreign money in quite some time, for the teller seemed perplexed. Finally he disappeared and returned with a newspaper, which he opened and began reading, as though I had so overtaxed him that he felt the need for a break right then and there. As it turned out, he was looking up the exchange rate. So that was pretty much my morning.

As I walked around the city, it began to seem odd that there had been so many people in the bank. It was hard to see how anyone was making enough money to bother with a savings account, though this wasn't for lack of trying. Tiny business transactions were taking place everywhere, homespun economies springing up from the war's aftermath like weeds from the cracks in a cement sidewalk (a sidewalk someplace other than Maputo).

At the city's natural history museum, a pair of guards motioned me aside to show me some handmade pencil cups covered with strips of zebra and leopard hide—floor scraps from the museum's taxidermy room. (I bought three.) Out in the streets, women and teenage boys manned the intersections, selling whatever they could. A boy was selling individual garlic cloves, the way people sometimes do with cigarettes. When I later chanced upon a youth holding out a box of toothpicks, I wondered if the price he quoted would buy me the box or just a solitary pick. One group of boys was selling potted tropical plants, as though, unable to come up with anything else, they'd turned to the earth itself to make a sale. Vendors would walk alongside me for as much as a block, trying to convince me that I really did need a jar of Cobra Wax Car Polish, a pair of shoulder pads, a Richard Marx cassette. It didn't seem to faze them that I spoke no Portuguese.

The one kind of thing I might have bought, they simply didn't have: Souvenirs, other than the gastrointestinal variety, were nonexistent in Mozambique. Though the islands off the coast had once enjoyed popularity among European sun-seekers, there had been no tourism since the conflict with RENAMO broke out. As the souvenirs had disappeared, so, too, had the smiles that had once been used to sell them. People didn't smile at foreigners here, or look them in the eye.

Not that they didn't look. They looked at my shoulder bag. I had a small leather pouch in which I carried some cash and my passport. People were staring at it so openly and so hungrily that I transferred the contents to a nondescript plastic bag. The menace was palpable, and I'm the sort who's generally oblivious of menace. I used to look with disdain upon the travelers I'd see in Peruvian markets who'd put their backpacks on their fronts, defensively hugging them to their bellies. Peru didn't unnerve me, neither did Moscow nor India. Mozambique did. People were desperate, and their desperation had made them hard.

I took a streetcar to the outskirts of the city, to a large open-air market someone had suggested I visit. Here my discomfort edged toward fear. Here people stared not only at my plastic bag, but at me, as though calculating what they might get for my shoes, or how long their dogs could gnaw on my bones. I transferred my cash from plastic bag to shirt pocket. I stepped off the streetcar into a press of impassive faces. Within minutes, a hand reached for the bills in my shirt. There was no attempt at guile, none of the true pickpocket's finesse. The man had simply seen the money and moved to take it. I turned sharply to block the theft, then took my cash from my pocket and wadded it in my fist. My sunglasses were left in my shirt pocket, however, and they were next to go. This thief, at least, made a stab at technique; he tried to conceal his hand behind a folded newspaper. The result of this was that he could no longer see his target. The hand flailed blindly at my shirt for a moment before locating its quarry. "Hey," I said, and looked at the glasses in his hand. He shrugged and handed them back to me. Good people; bad times.

If only to rid myself of the sweat-logged cash stuck to my palm, I bought some impressive black-and-white porcupine quills from a medicine woman. It was hard for me to imagine the jungles of Mozambique as being home to a gentle woodland creature like the porcupine; however, my image of the Mozambican wilds had undoubtedly been tainted by my earlier visit to the natural history museum. The displays there seemed to have been influenced by the country's enduring climate of violence. Lions and leopards were posed snarling and fang-faced on the backs of their prey, claws tearing pink gashes in taxidermied flesh, rivulets of dried stage blood running down and puddling on the diorama floor. It was the most horrifying museum I've ever seen, and I've been to the South African Police Museum and a Tokyo parasite museum, which displayed a thirty-foot tapeworm recovered intact from a man's intestine.

My quills and I rode the streetcar back, trying to look as if we made sense. I retreated to my hotel, feeling defeated and out of place. In the lobby I found a South African *Cosmopolitan* magazine. A cover line read, "How to Be Shamelessly Shallow." This I did not need to read. War-blighted, impoverished countries are highly effective at making the casual visitor feel shallow and spoiled. I was here on a lark. I felt self-centered and resented. I fell asleep in the afternoon heat.

At four P.M. the phone rang. It was Carlos, the president's personal secretary. "Judy?" He had forgotten my name. He informed me that my interview had been rescheduled, and that a car was coming in five minutes to take me to the presidential palace. Five minutes! *¡Ay, caramba! Endolimax nana!* I spackled the pillow creases on my face and went down to the lobby.

I was met by Carlos himself, a smug miasma of cologne and wealth. The price of his suit could have fed a family of pencil cup makers for months. His rings could have put a fleet of dilapidated cabs on the streets. It's dangerous to go from one end of the economic spectrum to the other so suddenly. One gets the mental bends. Carlos pressed his cheek to mine, European style. Soon a red spot would appear where he'd touched me. I was allergic to his cologne, or maybe just to him.

I was whisked through a series of armed gates and security checkpoints. This was a country in which it was easier to meet the president than it was to cash a traveler's check. Carlos deposited me in an ornately furnished anteroom and disappeared. I could see the president, waiting in the next room behind a lace curtain, like a shy bride awaiting her betrothed.

"Judy." Carlos and his pet musk cloud had returned. "His Excellency the President of Mozambique will see you now."

Joaquim Chissano is small for his title, perhaps five feet five, and unassuming. When I picture African leaders, I picture rotund men in loud fabrics and showy eyewear. Chissano was dressed in a dark blue suit and unremarkable black dress shoes. He wore no jewelry aside from a wedding ring and a tie tack. He radiated calm and modesty. I liked him immediately.

The president spoke with me for over an hour. He explained how meditation had helped him handle the deaths of his brother and father and the stresses of his post. He said that meditation recharges his batteries and has helped him with tension headaches. He said he meditates on the way to work (someone else drives) and during delegation meetings. "If people talk and I don't care what they are saying," he said, "I meditate." Carlos pursed his lips.

Then the president began talking about some yoga postures he had just learned, which he did each day as preparation for meditating. "Six postures, which you can do in one minute." Abruptly, he stood up and took off his suit jacket. "If you like, I can show you."

And so the president and I got down on the beautiful blue Persian carpet. We arched our backs and rolled our heads and released our toxins. The president lay down on his back and stuck his legs straight out above his head. Carlos looked up to see the president's dress shoes waving in the air before him. I lay down and did what the president was doing. My dress flopped onto my face. Carlos examined his cuticles.

The president got up and returned to his seat. His tie was hanging over his shoulder. "There is one more very essential exercise," he said to me. He put his index fingers beside his nostrils. "You blow the air out from one side and close the other like this, then take the air like this. Very fast. Now switch the sides. Out and in and out and in." His eyes rolled up into his head, and he made a sound like workmen sanding walls.

The president was practicing alternate nostril breathing, a sort of rhythmic, snorting hyperventilation that calms the nervous system and alarms guests. When I had regained my bearings sufficiently, I joined in. We sat there making funny nose sounds until Carlos could stand it no more. "I think," he stood up, "that it is soon time for the president to have his dinner."

I hoped that Chissano, my one friend in Mozambique, would invite me to join him, but he did not. Carlos drove me back. I ate dinner in a restaurant that appealed to me because it did not have jarring fluorescent lights, and then I realized that the jarring fluorescent lights were simply out, along with all the others in the city except the president's. In a blackout, I ate pummeled-looking chicken and thought to myself that I had never had a stranger day in my life. The strangest thing about it was that it wasn't a strange day for anyone in it but me. Travel is like that.

INSIDE COLOMBIA

Dawn MacKeen

There was a time when the small, egg-shaped lake didn't exist. And the ducks and geese and swans floating atop it, too. It wasn't that long ago, I am told, but the place looks now as if everything has always been there. The bank of the lake and the way it slopes gently downward. The long blades of grass leaning in unison. The trees hanging heavy and low over the water, as if from thirst. Even the perfectly mowed lawn that we're standing on somehow looks natural.

On the other side of the lake, half covered by untamed vegetation, a billboard reads PROPRIEDAD DE TODOS, with a cut-out picture of a smiling little girl beside it. "Property of all of us." It's a big sign, but it doesn't mean much unless you know the story behind it.

"A drug dealer lives there," the woman I'm with claims, pointing to the walled-in house across the street. She is taking me on a narco-tour of Ciudad Jardín, where I'm staying. "He made this lake. It was public land, but he didn't care. He brought all the birds, the swans, and just put them in there. Then the city took the land back and had a big public ceremony dedicating the land back to the people. After that, the city built the lake next to this one." While the birds live in one of the lakes, an alligator now lives in the other. Town legend has it that one of the neighborhood drug dealers kept it as a pet until he tired of it and released it into the water.

The preternatural lake came with everything else in this Colombian suburb—the construction boom, the insane cash flow, and the drugs. Within walking distance of where I'm standing, three of the Cali cartel's four most powerful men built their homes. At its height, after the demise of Pablo Escobar and his Medellín cartel in 1993, the Cali empire oversaw 80 percent of the world's cocaine trafficking. The low-profile Cali cartel preferred bribery to the open violence of the Medellín cartel, and invested in legitimate businesses like a national chain of discount drugstores, a pharmaceutical laboratory, and a bank. The cartel's chiefs posed as successful businessmen. "One of the houses was so big that my mother thought they were building a new supermarket," says my guide, smiling.

Located just outside Cali, the country's third largest city, Ciudad Jardín is an enclave of grandiose homes, tree-lined streets, sport utility vehicles with black-tinted bulletproof windows (known as Narco Toyotas) and *nuevo*-rich residents. There are so many drug dealers in this little suburb that the rest of the residents have a word for a street without one living on it: *sano,* clean.

"Come, let's continue our tour," she says. We drive down to the end of Gator Lake to the white compound of Miguel Rodríguez, who with his older brother, Gilberto, helped run the Cali cartel. Although he isn't home—he and his brother are in jail—it looks as if someone is. A group of men dressed in dark colors stand around in front of the main entranceway, talking. At the corner a man stands guard in a windowed booth. The compound stretches one and a half blocks, hidden behind a ten-foot-high white wall that presses right up to the walkway.

"My friend lives there," my guide says, pointing to where the massive walls are interrupted by a modest-looking house. "When Rodríguez was buying up all the properties around here, he wanted to buy his, but he didn't want to sell. My friend said if there's going to be a safe place to live in Cali, it's here. Look how many people are guarding this area." We briefly slow down to look at her friend's house, but keep moving. We don't want to linger too long in front of any of the houses. The residents, and their body-guards, probably wouldn't appreciate our narco-tour.

Cali sits deep in a valley, where sugarcane is a major crop, an hour and a half east of the Pacific Ocean, and vendors are scattered along rural roads, selling a sweet juice called *guarapo*, made by squeezing the cane until the liquid pours out. The Cauca River, the second largest in Colombia, snakes through here, over rocks and through the green pastures and the clusters of chewing cows. Coming from the countryside back into the city one day, we pass a dead horse at the edge of our asphalt path, frozen on its side like a kid's plastic toy knocked over by accident.

It is on this drive that the duality of Colombia's existence really hits me. From almost anywhere within the Valle del Cauca, Cali's region and state—above the saccharine fields or high-rises in downtown Cali—you can see the surrounding mountains. They are both the frame for a perfect picture, with their lush and densely vegetated inclines, and a stark reminder of where not to go. The warnings began as soon I arrived: Don't venture to the waterfall at the base of the Farallones range; don't go to the river for rafting (where, to get to the water, locals take you on thrown-together carts down railroad tracks); don't make the four-hour hike up to Pico Loro, Pirate's Peak. There's always some story of someone's daughter who was kidnapped there, or of the farmer's son who was killed, or of the guerrillas who were spotted there the week before. The stories seem almost like superstitions or myths passed down from one person to another of What Happens in the Mountains. Even the way the locals tell the "bad" guys from the "good" guys here in the kidnapping capital of the world, by look-ing at the shoes—guerrillas wear rubber boots, the military lace-up leather—seems unreal.

I have come to Colombia with my boyfriend to meet his family and see where he grew up. Before we left, he had told me that almost everyone in the country has been touched by the ongoing conflict. Now that I'm here, I see how true that is. Extortion/ murder/close-call stories pepper everyday conversation—in fact, they *are* everyday conversation. They weave in and out of your day, little reminders that despite how normal everything seems, it's not. These topics would horrify me back home, but here, they just take on the natural cadence of daily life. The small talk somehow makes the reality of the violence recede.

In the middle of a conversation about salsa queen Celia Cruz's new hit song and whether or not she's sold out, my boyfriend's mom announces that her cousin's two college-age sons will be arriving from Florida to spend the holidays. "They haven't been back for six years. After their father was killed, their mother wanted to take them far away from here."

"What happened?" I ask.

"He was kidnapped by the guerrillas. My husband was helping negotiate his release. They were almost done, all that was left was the 'proof of life.' And when the guerrillas could not provide that, the family started to fear the worst."

"Did they kill him?"

"He had a heart condition and they did not get him help fast enough. After he died, the guerrillas tried to get them to pay a— what is the word, ransom?—to see the body. They still do not know where he is buried."

As the languid, vivid, steamy days pass, from time to time I think about how different things might have been around this family's table. How these cousins, who have become so American, would have grown up in their own country. How my boyfriend's good friend might have been sitting across from me. Several months ago the guerrillas kidnapped him while he was on the way to work. His story is yet unfinished; he is still missing.

For almost forty years, the citizens of Colombia have been trapped in a civil war, which has killed more than 35,000 people in the last decade alone. Colombians are afraid to go into the countryside, afraid to drive down their own roads, afraid of being caught by accident in the violent politics of "change." They have become prisoners in their own city, locked up inside. Better to stay in Cali, they say.

So I stay. My days mainly consist of sitting outside on the porch, passing the time reading until it's time to eat; falling asleep, and then eating again. Although it's December, it's hot here. Very hot. Every so often, gray clouds cover the sky and a short burst of rain falls, but even then, it's warm. Ceiling fans continually churn the thick air while mosquitoes gnaw on ankles, especially those belonging to me.

Fruit weighs down branches all year. The rhythms of salsa, cumbia, and vallenato beat onto the streets; fireworks soar and burst during the day and into the night; and a chorus of unfamiliar birds sing in alternating staccatos, always providing background music. Cali feels simultaneously surreal and too real. When mangoes drop at night, it's not always because they are ready to drop; most of the time, in the backyard of the house where I am staying, the bats make them fall. "They eat the mangoes," someone explains. There's a rustle, a low-flying swoop over my head, and then a return back to the tree. The next morning, the bright orange mangoes are lying on the grass, like Easter eggs ready to be found, with quarter-sized bite marks in their flesh and red ants marching all over their sticky sweetness.

The ants, too, seem like they took a wrong turn off the pages of someone's novel and ended up here. Every time we go in or out of the house we have to step over a freeway of ants. The bug highway stretches parallel to the human road, on the edge of the curb, for the length of five buildings. There are two lanes—one filled with ants carrying large leaves, another going in the opposite direction for the cargoless ants who have already made their delivery. Several in line always seem to be wobbling and zigzagging from carrying too much weight. One afternoon I try to follow them but have to turn back when their trail leads to an impasse at some shrubs. My boyfriend's brother says the ants can tell if it's going to rain, and if it is, they don't work. So on cloudy mornings he checks with the weathermen near the doorstep to know what the day is going to be like. They have been there as long as he can remember.

For all of my boyfriend's almost thirty years, this unofficial war has been going on, the only political situation his generation has known. The violence is inbred, endless; everyone fights everyone else in a vicious circle that goes nowhere. Paramilitary groups, created by the landowners to protect themselves, fight the guerrillas. The guerrillas, demanding redistribution of wealth in a country plagued by vast income disparities, fight the government. The government fights the cartels, the paramilitary groups, the guerrillas, and, of course, its own corrupt self. President Andrés Pastrana's predecessor, Ernesto Samper, allegedly took drug money to finance his election campaign, shattering the faith of his followers and further damaging Colombia's already troubled international image; the United States later revoked his visa. In Samper's zeal to rehabilitate himself and to maintain aid from the United States, his administration declared war on drugs and ended up jailing many of the heads of the Cali cartel, weakening their hold on the drug trade and sending many dealers into hiding. But although Pastrana, who ran on a "Road to Peace" ticket, has a cleaner administration and has made some improvements, the country is still not safe. Mayors are still being killed, poor people are still being butchered in the night, kidnappings are still being arranged, bombs are still going off at police outstations in Cali. Peace eludes this country.

The children of the family I'm staying with tell me that their own father was detained one night while driving home from a business trip. The guerrillas were robbing a tollbooth, supposedly to finance the war; they held him and others for several hours. He didn't know what was going to happen to him until they suddenly left, slipping back into the mountains they came from. Stories like that make it hard to understand why these people sometimes end up defending the guerrillas and sympathizing with their cause.

.   .   .

"There used to be beautiful gardens here," my guide says. We're idling in front of a weathered iron gate. Weeds wind their way at will in front of an empty guard's booth, and dried leaves lie scattered on the once very active driveway to José Santacruz Londono's house. Also known as El Gordo, the Fat Man, Santacruz was the mastermind behind the cartel's trafficking networks. He was caught because of a gastronomic weakness. When he had fled to Bogotá, government officials decided to stake out the best restaurants in town, based on the Sherlock Holmes–like assumption that eventually he would come to one, and caught him. That was years ago; he was released, then was shot down by police in 1996, and now his place is just one of the many empty mansions in Ciudad Jardín. Many of the neighbors are either in jail or dead, like the owner of a three-story lakefront property that has been "under construction" for the last decade or so. He was killed, so it stands suspended in time, almost finished, coated in cement, with spaces for windows but no glass. Parts of Ciudad Jardín feel like an American industrial district, with plenty of empty and abandoned buildings.

In addition to the red and green Christmas lights adorning buildings in the neighborhood, barbed wire and electrical jolts are strung along the top of many of the walls we drive by. Outside one house, foot-long metal spikes project outward; another bears a nativity scene. Below the penitentiary-style walls kids bike down freshly swept streets, adults walk dogs, families load and unload groceries.

When the night comes, we move again to the backyard. We push together tables, and plates of food are prepared and carried outside. Relatives from every corner of the city arrive, bringing homemade cilantro-based salsa to complement the fried yuca and mashed plantain. Others bring themselves and their children, who fight noisy battles and throw each other on the grass. Glasses are raised; there is the clink of a thousand and one *saluds*. Freshly blended fruit juices—*lulo,* mango, guanábana—are sweetened with sugar and served along with the national drink, aguardiente, a potent liquor with a licorice taste.

Evenings stretch into nights, and nights stretch into mornings, and mornings stretch into heat; memories are retraced until the path back to the present fades into a blur. Music, voices, the sounds of the hot night drift and swell. Enjoying oneself, and letting others do so, is how one lives here. "Colombians always make up excuses to celebrate," my boyfriend's cousin tells me one night. On the first day of La Feria, the week-long celebration that is an annual rite for the residents of Cali, thousands of people gather along the tall buildings of downtown to watch La Cabalgata, the horse parade. Anyone who has an equine can enter, even if the rider is dead drunk and manages to stay on the horse only by a miracle. People laugh and point; riders are forced to kiss. Horses, devoid of the gaudy trappings commonly found in American parades, gallop and trot. In a crowd so large you'd think the pope was about to pass through, we stand on the side of the road, doing shots, talking with long-lost friends, buying salt-coated mangoes, nuts, and chips from cart vendors.

Another day, the people celebrate by flying a mile-long inflated condom through the city's byways like a latex kite, commemorating its entry into *The Guinness Book of Records* as the longest love glove ever made.

"Better take the photo from inside, yes?" my guide instructs me. We're driving past another coke dealer's wall and a crowd of bodyguards is standing outside. They turn and look at the car and us. It's the first time she takes a serious tone, so I take a picture without looking into the camera, snapping it from just above the dashboard. Looking back, I wonder what the hell I was doing, blithely taking pictures of armed men as if they were safely fixed to tracks on the sidewalk.

We move on to a safer area, to the homes of the lesser-ranking drug dealers, the *traquetos,* those second or third down the line in the great cocaine chain. "Do you see the marble?" she asks, motioning to a pink-and-white home with strawberry-ice-cream-swirled facade. "That's how you know if a *traqueto* lives there." The other mark of a *traqueto,* I learn, is lavishly designed gates.

The gate that marks the entrance to a vacation home once owned by a *traqueto* in Popayan exactly fits her description; it's like an upright horseshoe, worn by the most cherished of hooves, with its elaborate iron twists and turns. Behind it a fern-lined stone pathway leads to a brick house with Spanish tiles. A fountain trickles outside. Two hammocks slouch between the wooden posts on the porch. It's only when we're parking our car, after a one-and-a-half-hour drive to this colonial city known for its religious fervor, that I notice the separate building and the guard tower.

"That's where the bodyguards used to walk," one of the workers tells us as we're unloading our luggage for our three-day stay at the place, which is now owned by a friend of my boyfriend's family. The house itself is a square, with the middle carved out for a courtyard and the bedrooms surrounding it. Outside, fifteen dogs—puppies, adults, mutts, purebreds—faithfully follow a twelve-year-old girl who lives with her parents on the property. Whenever we catch a glimpse of a tail or the scent of a canine, we know the girl cannot be far away.

At night, when the mountain climate of Popayan forces us all under blankets, near the warmth of the fireplace, we learn about the previous owner and the house he built. As the caretaker talks, a bat flies overhead, drops down to several inches above our heads, forcing us to duck, and then fumbles around, bumping into things for fifteen minutes as it tries to find a way out of the room. The former owner was a small-time drug dealer in the Cali cartel, we're told. He was ruthless to those who crossed him, kind to those who worked his land. Like other drug dealers who designed their homes with secret compartments—behind bars, walls, cupboards—this one created an out as well.

"Go up the stairs and find the bookcase," the caretaker says. We get up and start toward that part of the house. The bookcase is wholesome-looking, made of lacquered wood, and appears stationary, as if it is built into the wall. But when we push on it, it opens up to reveal a hidden compartment, squeezed like a teenager's attic room between the roof and the dining room below. Several of us start knocking on the hardwood floors and walls, listening for hollow sounds, pulling up floor rugs and pushing back paintings.

"Do you think there are bodies buried on the grounds?" I ask. They all look at me as if I've seen one too many American-made Mafia films. But later we find out about what *was* under the ground: a tunnel. Down the gravel road, a house stands where the drug dealer used to spend most of his time. It is more secluded, farther from the entrance to the premises and the main road. We learn from a neighbor that he used to sleep there because he felt safer.

When we drive to the second house the next day, I finally understand why. From the bathroom in this house, the neighbor tells us, he would just have to flick a lever that moved the sink to reveal a small tunnel to a room, complete with a bed and separate bathroom, that lay at least seven feet under the ground next to the house. In an emergency, he could take another tunnel that stretched the length of two football fields, under the farmland, to a place where he could exit and get away. Although the sink contraption is no longer there, the small tunnel is, and so is the room—it is box-shaped and used for storage now, stuffed with wood, dust, and the frame of his bed. But the main tunnel is no longer there. The current owners, who are not the owners of the main house, have used its foundation to build a big lake. Paddleboats are anchored in one corner and ducks swim along the top, making the only ripples on the water, save for the occasional gust of wind or the landing of a small bug. The reservoir of water looks so natural, as if it has always been there.

I left Colombia the same way I entered it—not sure about many things, not even about what's under the ground I walked on. I don't know why the beautiful mountain roads are so dangerous, why so many people are dying. I don't understand, and I don't think many Colombians do either.

FADE INTO BLUE

Amanda Jones

It had been forty-eight days since she'd met him and twenty-nine days since she'd last seen him. How good is the memory? She remembered waking up that morning thinking, oh God, the place wasn't what she'd expected, and the men, the colonialists, were barbarians. Coming here was a mistake.

Still, here she was in this strange and twisted place. A country overrun by gun-toting expats who still called the natives savages and shot them dead if they got in their way. It was a gray place, and these white men were gnarled and decrepit. They leered and lolled and became florid-faced too soon. There was a feeling of carelessness. They were there for the money, which grew on the trees as coffee beans and tea leaves.

She'd been taken to a party where the whole town appeared hell-bent on shooting someone or drinking themselves into oblivion. Her host was a young man brimming with an old man's failures. You'll be staying with me, he told her, swaying from side to side and poking his overripe face too close to hers, hand scuttling up her arm, crablike. You'll sleep in this guy's room. The guy, no, he's rock climbing. He won't mind, he'll find somewhere else to stay. Oh, she thought, feeling strange. She fell to sleep that night with the smell of the unknown rock climber filling her head. It was intriguing.

Yeah, the host said the next morning, if you come to my work, I'll send a bloke to take you walking. Although I'll be buggered if I know why you wanna walk, there're nothing but trees out there.

She went to his coffee factory. The place was oppressive. Gray corrugated iron belching flames and blackness and debris into the shrouded highland morning. A honk and a native man scurrying, head down, to open the gates. No white person would open a gate in this place. Life without respect. She sensed that there would be trouble on this island soon. These foreigners had it coming.

Inside, there were stocky black men behind heavy doors, lifting and bulging and dragging and stoking. And storm fencing, lots of it, and another group of men huddled around a dying fire. Huddled as if it were cold when it was sweltering hot. More foreboding.

And then the office, separated from the black men by barbs and bars. There were cigarette butts and dirt and a fluorescent pall, sputtering and ghoulish. She noticed the empty vodka bottles, the safe, the yellowed papers, and the filthy typewriter. She stood in a corner and watched a white man hit a native in the face for removing a pen from a desk. She drifted into the next room. Introductions were made. A boy—no, a young man—stood up and stepped into the squalor.

Later, she thought about how some events in life are inescapable. An unforeseen lasso is tossed, dragging us off our intended course, toward destiny. She thought about the magnetism between some people. How when we pass them in the street we recognize it and smile, feeling the pull but passing even before the smile is gone. When we see someone across a room and we feel the shadow of loss when they turn and leave, glancing back as they go. Is there a scientific explanation for this?

The man stood there drenched in blue light—at least that's how he appeared to her. It was the kind of blue that artists use to depict dream scenes. She saw him with shock and perfect recognition, a vivid jigsaw piece mistakenly mixed into a gloomy puzzle.

And then he smiled, and his face broke open. Beautiful teeth on a beautiful face. But a tired face, a heavy face, a burdened smile. She studied him. Fair-skinned. Brown hair that hadn't been tended to in days. Blue eyes beneath perfect eyebrows and long dark lashes. A jaw from some superhero caricature, cleft and all. This was the rock-climbing man. The one who had slept at the factory because she'd taken his room.

He told her he would be the one to take her hiking; and she felt some ridiculous lift in spirits. He turned to show her the way they would go on a map pinned to the wall, but she stared at his fore-arm instead. Then she felt stupid and walked outside. For God's sake, look where they were and who he was. There must be some-thing terribly wrong with any man who chose to live and work here in this private hell.

As they drove to the mountain she asked him about his life. He was ex-SAS, special-service military. That had been his job. Skilled in rescuing and killing. He was probably very good at it, because he wouldn't talk about it much. He was here managing the coffee factory, he said, because his heart had been broken in his home-land. His skills didn't stretch to protecting his own heart.

They walked uphill for a long way on a muddy path that tricked her with its altitude and tangled roots and flimsy shrubbery. He was very quick, this skilled man. As they walked he began to tell her long stories. About how many times sadness had brushed her fingers through his hair. About the science of staying alive. About life and death and the small difference between the two. And about the scaffolding that had crumbled when the love blew away.

As he talked, she saw the scenes he was describing in her mind. She saw him jumping from planes, hanging from bridges, diving in dark rivers, riding silvery horses, loving transient women.

She was fiercely drawn to him. As he talked, she wondered again what it is, this link between people. Does the heart strike at the same moment? Are the thoughts painted with the same palette? Do we recognize them from another time the mind cannot remember but the soul can?

When she was clumsy and tripped on the trail, he was behind her. She had her camera in hand and felt her foot slide over the edge but could do nothing to save herself. I'm falling, she cried, half in jest, and a firm hand caught her under the arm. It did not pull her up, just stayed there until she steadied herself. Her skin felt polished where the grip had been.

They talked about many things but not the manifest attraction between them. He looked at her often, and those blue eyes made her beautiful when they settled on her.

What did he see? Probably he saw a woman who never wore a watch. A woman to whom time meant constraint. Tall, long arms, thin shoulders. Her hair was fair and long, and very often tangled. Her affliction was that of a wandering spirit, keeping her on the road. Farther and farther away each time, in search of sights unseen and stories she would likely never tell. She was never without a tribal amulet around her neck. She believed in their power. She had been places most white people have no desire to go and seen things most couldn't imagine. It made it hard to talk about her life. She liked people but never minded being alone. She was a photographer and a writer, and guarded her freedom like a lioness does her cubs, instinctively savage the moment it was threatened.

That night, she was invited to another awful party. She kept wishing he was there. It annoyed her, that kind of wishing. She'd be talking to someone and her attention would glide away into the parallel world of replay and elaboration. He didn't come, he hated those parties, preferring to remain around the perpetually dying fire with the dark-skinned men with their trusting smiles and fearsome eyes.

On the fifth day, she woke early with the gong from the prison next door. Her ticket said she was to leave that day, but she knew she would stay. She was glad no one asked why; she didn't want to answer the question if she *enjoyed* this place or was staying for him, the beautiful, mysterious man who inhabited her vision.

She hiked alone with him again, through bush with no path, with grabbing branches and soggy soil, past cobwebs as big as houses. They reached the waterfall he had promised her, where the water churned out of the mountainside and hammered at their feet. He sat on a rock and did not see the waterfall. She sat on another rock and stared at the waterfall but saw only him. Though the sun was high and hot, he looked pale and chilled. Something crowded out his sun. She knew there was no use in asking. She'd have to wait.

They came across a village where naked children showed her how to use a slingshot. They walked back through the musky dusk, talking about chaos, time, chemistry. He turned, slid his fingers through hers, and said, You make me happy. Simply that.

He would work all night, and he asked if she would come to the loathsome factory to keep him company for a while. Of course, she said. They sat and drank port and looked at a world map, picking countries they wanted to go to, telling tales of strange people in peculiar places. They found they had similar interests, similar minds, different lives.

When the night was almost over, he leaned forward in his seat and the structure of his face shifted. His eyes lay mute under those arched brows and his mouth stretched across a thousand unsaid words. I am going to tell you something no one else knows, he said. I shouldn't, but I need to tell someone. You must never mention it again. I will tell you why I am really here. The alcohol in her brain responded to the flattery and not to the gravity. It was raining outside. Tell me.

This island, he began, is divided, and not by those who belong here. On the other half there is oppression, genocide, political intimidation. An invading force tolerated and supported by the West. I am a soldier, a good soldier, and soldiers must fight for what is right. The natives need help. There is a rebel force. I've been there before. I'm going back across the border into the jungle—for a long time. Yes, there is a chance I might die. A very real chance. The invading army kills people like me. His eyes dug into her. Do you think I am an idealist?

And so there it was. His shadow. His withheld truth.

They talked idealistically about how idealism was the only way change happened in the world. They talked until the brown men had finished burning the beans and the sky was seamlessly dark. It was four A.M. and the hours had passed quickly. He laughed for the very first time and it was a colorful, natural laugh.

The days, as all days, were numbered. They went to a tribal dance where the beauty was monumental and the colors ethereal. She saw it through the lens of her camera and was intoxicated. Behind that lens she changed into something that had a right to pry and to capture. She was greedy, and time went upward in long streams of smoke, and existence became paint and sweat and glistening skin and the smell of pig fat. She tried not to think about what he had told her and he pretended she knew nothing.

One night, the rain fell in steel sheets and they took refuge in the empty house of a friend. The houseboy lit a fire, they cooked and drank, lying on the floor. He stroked her hair, slowly, carefully. They found a book of the Chinese zodiac. She was born in the year of the tiger and he the snake. It did not portend well for the future.

He took her many miles on his motorbike. She pressed against him on the back, feeling the wind, burying her face in the nape of his neck. They crawled below the earth to a subterranean chamber, where the tough native boys with them sang a gentle song by candlelight and threw stretched shadows on the far wall. She closed her eyes. There would be many indelible memories.

He showed her, patiently and seriously, how to make a harness out of two lengths of cord. How to make a harness and then glide easily down a cliff. He took her to villages and to rain forests. He stood by as she bargained in markets, advising on things he didn't care much about. He taught her how to shoot an arrow with a longbow. He tied a rope around her and coaxed her up a cliff when she asked to go rock climbing. He muted his cry when she loosened a rock and it fell on him from above. He taught her how to hold and load a gun. How to shoot and not be shot.

He drove her to the airport when she finally left the highlands and flew to the coast. She had another week. She didn't need to ask; she knew he would come.

That night she was without him. She met people who were tanned and soft-spoken from days shaded by bougainvillea on shimmering black sand. She felt loud and uncontained beside them, still strung high from rock climbs, motorbikes, and caves. She went to bed in the fading heat and did not sleep.

He arrived the next morning. They put on tanks and dived down to skeletal wrecks, war boats and fighter planes, their skin brushing underwater.

The days evaporated. There was no discussion of where he was going or what she was going back to. They lay on the bed, their breath touching. It seemed like a waste of time to close their eyes, so they stayed awake until the light crept over the sea, telling stories. When she did fall asleep, she dreamed in blue.

Everything was heightened. The colors in the air, the music, the smells, the words, the feelings. Time was burdened with an exquisite tension. And it finally ran out.

He took her to the airport and they didn't speak. He gave her a talisman; she gave him some words she had written. She committed his smell and face and voice to memory and turned to the plane. When she turned back, she saw a blue light shining through the window.

NAVIGATING NAIROBI

Alicia Rebensdorf

The puddle is formidable. I've already trekked a block to scout a crossing, and it's beginning to defeat the purpose. My shirt sticks to my back and the wet hems of my pants swat my bare ankles. Car horns, *matatu* music, and vendors shout, a cacophony barely audible over the rain banging in my ears. I'm on the corner of Moi and Kenyatta Avenues at three-fifteen P.M. in the rainy season. Nairobi is at its crescendo.

I've been in Kenya long enough to know that the afternoon showers are one of only two things in Africa that are punctual. The other was not my lunch date. I had planned to be back at my hotel by the time the rain hit. It comes fast and hard, and smears the city gray. Dirt spreads from unfinished sidewalks and rivers run brown down the undrained streets. As I try to navigate a way across the murky moats, I count unclogged drains as No. 23 of the things I take for granted back home. Rain falls fat like the drips off awnings and I search for some temporary shelter.

The sidewalks are already crammed tight with those waiting out the storm under awnings. The women bright with their dark skin and deep colors. Lanky men in suits. Teenagers in jeans and

American T-shirts. Either having adapted to Nairobi's overpopulation or never having a need for personal space in the first place, they press close. A woman's round hip hugs a businessman's thigh, a baggy-jeaned boy is squeezed tight to a grandmother's bags. I squish between an older man with a Chevron cap and an umbrella vendor. I pull my wet shirt loose, concerned it might betray the rectangular outline of my passport hidden in my bra. No. 24.

The older man smells like urine and body odor; his elbow is bony. The umbrella man courts me and other pedestrians with his song. *"Umbrrrrelli! Umbrrrrelli! Shilingi kidogo, umbrrrelli."* His *rrr's* are round and buttery, his *lli's* a click of the tongue; each of his words ends with a swing. I look at the striped umbrellas, which look exactly like the umbrellas of the four other vendors on this block and the five on the block before this. He catches my glance and mistakes it for interest.

"Very good. Good price for pretty *mazungu* like you."

"Asante lakini sihitaji umbrelli."

"Oh, you speak Swahili. Very good. Do you have a boyfriend?"

I flash him my brass fake engagement ring and push back farther into the group. I squeeze next to a young woman with straightened hair. My breast presses against her arm. I've grown accustomed to Kenyan men asking about my availability, but it still makes me feel shitty.

I stand there, wet and squished, listening to the rain pelt the city. Cars continue driving on the asphalt islands at freeway speeds, ignoring, as usual, any puddles or people. Horns wail over the rain, scolding those pedestrians bold enough to cross their route. The *umbrelli* hawkers croon and the muffled bass of music thumps not too far away. I still smell the older man, and his odor mingles with the waft of curry from an Indian café around the corner.

On my left is a line of people waiting for a *matatu*. Privately run buses and minivans, *matatus* are Nairobi's most effective transportation system. In Swahili, *matatu* means "three," and although that may be the number of people *matatus* were designed to carry, the drivers seem to interpret it as meaning three people per seat.

Crammed tight, the *matatus* careen around Nairobi's roads, reading traffic signals as suggestions rather than orders and using their horns more than their brakes. If there is an antipode to Africans' great patience, it can surely be found behind the wheel of African cars. People who wait hours in lines and months for mail suddenly can't pause seconds for another car to pass.

The rumble of blaring speakers and vibrating metal alerts me to the arrival of a *matatu*. I can barely make out the familiar rap beat over the booming bass, the music hiked to a volume that neither the speakers nor the automobile was designed to withstand. Between the bass, the potholes, and the lack of shocks, the *matatu* bounces down the road, catching as much air as it does asphalt. I stand back as the *matatu* swerves toward the curb. I am fortunate in being shielded by a large woman who is less fortunate. Her generous hips catch the brunt of the puddle, her floral skirt made dark and muddy. The brightly painted *matatu* is similarly stained. Mud obscures its chartreuse coat and splatters the steamed-up windows, plates of glass made pointless on each side. The driver leans on the horn, and people scurry out of the small minivan. It is quickly reloaded and pushes its way back into traffic.

Occasionally people look at me, the white girl in the crowd, but I keep my eyes forward, pretending not to notice. My body casual, I act comfortable, inconspicuous, as if I belong in this mass. In truth, I have never felt so obvious; I feel as though I am standing naked in front of class. The young woman adjusts her stance and her thigh is now pressed against my own. She does not say a thing, but I can imagine what she thinks of this *mazungu* next to her. Paranoid, I feel her unspoken judgments and assumptions crowd me: rich, spoiled, egocentric, colonialist, slutty white chick horny for black dick. I feel claustrophobic, squeezed too tight. I want to fight the crowd off, elbow my way into some room so I can stand on my own.

The rain lets up a little. Through the cars and crowds, I can just see across the street where two skittish tourists scurry to their destination. Costumed in their safari shorts and fanny packs, they act as if they are on the Serengeti, perked ears turning to every noise. A crippled man sitting on the corner with only one leg and a disfigured arm reaches out to them. His stump is visible through torn pants, the mangled arm curled in on itself. They stare and scoot away.

I look at the young woman beside me. Her lipstick is faded pink; her dark brown skin is flawless. I don't want her to think I am like the tourists. I push on them all of the assumptions I fight off myself. I am different. I have to convince her that I am the exception. The noise of the rain and horns and vendors is too loud; she cannot hear my silent pleas. What I am unable to say aloud, I try to say through body language. I make my shoulders loose and my arms limp. I let the crowd squeeze me like a rag doll, as if this will distinguish me from the tourists and make our common pigment less evident. As if my skin pressed against the black woman's arm will compel the colors to bleed, hers tinting mine just the least bit darker.

A small child wanders down the street. His dark skin is ashy and his gray ragged clothes look as if they were once bright. His eyes and stomach are large, his limbs small; snot gathers thick under his nose and runs down his chin. He spots me in the crowd. Evidently my body language is not quite the color camouflage I hoped it to be. One of his hands extends to me, palm up, while the other hand wraps tightly around a glue bottle. Glue is the drug of choice for Nairobi's street children. Cheap and quick, it numbs the hunger and deadens the minds of the children who use it. This boy looks about four. I've seen younger.

He stands there for a while, head tilted up, demanding eye contact. I ignore him. After about a minute, he tugs on my wet shirt. "*Mazungu*, please money."

Reluctantly, I return eye contact. "*Pole, sina pesa*," I lie.

He remains where he is, hand still out, as I stare into the street. I may be accustomed to this, but I am not immune to it. I may look past the dirt, and weather, and noises, and crowds, and cripples, and smells, and stares, but I still see them. I may avoid those eyes pleading up at me, those eyes like a dog's at the dinner table, but I still feel them.

Beneath my slack shoulders and self-righteous denials, I know I am more like those crowding judgments and timid tourists than I am like the people I touch. I cling to trite distinctions for a sense of superiority and to validate my right to be here, but all it really does is make me another white who claims to be an exception, another arrogant American with a cool stance and slightly strutting walk.

The boy waits for me to change my mind. The crowd waits for the rain to stop. The pedestrians wait for the cars to stop. The vendors wait for anyone to buy. The cripple waits for one unhardened heart. Kenya waits for long-promised aid, health care, hope, justice. No, I will never be used to this. I do not have the patience. I am sick of waiting for the streets to drain and the lines to shorten and the phones to work and the water to be hot and the frustration to ease. I cannot wait anymore. I push my way past the boy and out of the crowd.

The *matatu* seems to have displaced some of the water in the curb and I renew my search for a crossing. I watch one man make a leap to the other side. His gray suit makes it across safely. I figure he has found a spot and follow his lead. The sensation of water splashing up my calves reminds me that his legs are longer than mine. Kenyans may be known for their running, but there is something to be said for their long jumps too. My sandals squish with water as I run to safety on the other side of the street. Here, there are tin-roofed shacks where merchants peddle colorful *kenga* cloths and dubbed tapes. I dash past them, their stereos competing with the rain on their roofs, their reds and yellows struggling to be seen through the dust and mud.

Nairobi consumes my senses, each of its parts fighting for my attention. Its colors deafen and its streets bang in my head. I'm almost to my hotel, but for just a second, I stop. From here, the rain beating on the tin roofs sounds like a song. For just a second, all I can hear is steel drums celebrating the afternoon.

OUT OF AFRICA

Wendy Belcher

Travel writers are romantics. We like to believe that our feelings and experiences are so personal, so intense, that their meaning cannot be conveyed by other people's language. When I sat down to write my first book about Africa, published in 1988, I believed that I was writing only what I had experienced, what had happened to me. Now I realize that I was doing nothing of the kind, and that the experiences I conceived of as mine were themselves, in deep and sometimes untraceable ways, shaped by other people's language.

I found this out when I recently decided to browse the first sentences of travel books about Africa. I have always been interested in first lines—the way they are maps at a frontier. What would my fellow writers' first sentences tell me?

I started by looking at the travel books about Africa that I owned. To my surprise this small sample revealed striking similarities. I set off for the research library at the University of California at Los Angeles, one of the preeminent collections of Africana in the world, and spent the day doing an informal shelf search in the DT section ("DT" is the Library of Congress designation for

African materials). The travel books there backed up my hunch. Intrigued, I prowled through several used-book stores and the local superbookstore, rapidly pulling and shelving dozens of books. I then dragged a friend to a travel bookstore and asked her how much she would give me if I could predict the topic of the first sentences of their books about Africa. "Nothing," she said wisely, and even I was surprised when I was right four out of five times. Most travel books about Africa open with the author alone, carried along by some vehicle, looking down over some landscape and feeling anxious.

If I were a critic, rather than a practitioner of the genre, I could start right in with a long essay on this finding. I can't do this, however, because I am distracted by my dismay. To be an utterly "conventional" writer, open your book about Africa with yourself arriving. Let me admit it, then: I am guilty as charged.

My first book opens with me on an airplane at an airport in Africa. I express feelings of anxiety and doubt, and then view the city through the window of a taxi. Only one part of my opening can I claim as unique; certainly it is not the confusion at the airport, nor the haggling with porters at the airport, nor the taxi ride away from the airport. If I wanted to, I could approximate my opening by cutting and pasting lines from other books by foreigners about Africa, right down to the mention of the conveyor belt. Voilà. My plot, if not my phrasing.

This uncomfortable observation must be underlined by noting that I haven't even looked at the remaining pages of these travel books. What other similarities might I have found if I had addressed more than opening lines and paragraphs?

The question remains to be asked: How is it possible that our books open with such common objects (vehicles), images (vistas), and emotions (vexation)? Is it simply that our experiences were so similar? Even if we were to state that, for the sake of argument, all non-Africans' experiences in Africa are exactly the same, why do we structure our telling of these experiences in the same way? For instance, why didn't I start my book in the middle of my journey and use flashbacks? Why didn't I write my book as a series of character sketches? Why didn't I cluster various experiences by topic instead of chronology? Why didn't I set any part of the book in the United States?

Simply put, because that's not how travel books about Africa are written. That is, when I write I am subject to conventions of which I am not consciously aware. In fact, I was quite proud of the opening of my first book precisely because I thought it was unique. But even I, who grew up in Africa and therefore was not so subject to the travel form, started my autobiography in the standard manner of travel books about Africa—with the heat, the hubbub, and a rickety vehicle. I started my book on Africa just as hundreds of others had.

Don't just take my word for it, though. Let me show you how the openings of travel books about Africa are so similar as to be almost redundant.

Almost invariably books of this genre start with airplanes or ships; those written before the 1940s favor ships. Even after airplanes and cars came into wide use, ships continued to open many such books. Consider three opening lines, given in order from oldest to the most recent:

On the 6th December, 1856, I embarked, with my wife, on board the Royal Mail Screw Steamer *Ireland* (Lyons McLeod, *Travels in Eastern Africa*, 1860).

They were still dancing when, just before dawn on October 19th, 1930, the Azay le Rideau came into harbour at Djibouti (Evelyn Waugh, *Remote People*, 1931).

Side by side we stand in silence by the ship's rails (Dorothy Oliver, *Four Wheels Across Africa*, 1980).

Since the 1930s, the airplane has been a solid favorite. Crack any recent travel book about Africa and you have an excellent chance of finding the author in the first or second sentence on an airplane, in an airport, or driving to the airport. Consider these first sentences:

> The plane got into Kinshasa at three in the morning (Alex Shoumatoff, *In Southern Light*, 1986).

> Our plane landed at daybreak (Karl Eskelund, *While God Slept*, 1961).

> As I boarded the plane for my second return home . . . (Rosa Claudette Anderson, *River Face Homeward*, 1966).

> We touched down at noon (Dervla Murphy, *Cameroon with Egbert*, 1990).

If the book does not open with an airplane or a ship, it very likely starts with some other form of transportation: a train or train station, an automobile, such as a Land Rover or a taxi, a motorcycle, or occasionally, draft animals such as camels or oxen.

Perhaps my point will seem obvious. Books about Africa tend to open with getting there. Travel is about transportation, after all. Since Europe and America do lie some distance from Africa, isn't it sensible to have planes and ships? Doesn't it make a kind of literary sense to start a book about places distant to the reader with vessels of one sort or another? Even if the place is not distant from the author?

Let me put my observation in a different way.

Only one of the books I came across, and I flipped through more than two hundred, opens with the form of transportation most common in Africa and to Africans: oneself. That is, walking. The one exception I found refers so indirectly to walking that it hardly seems worth mentioning (L. M. Nesbitt, *Hell-hole of Creation*, 1935).

Even books about hiking through Africa do not start with the narrator on foot. The only book I could find that genuinely starts

with someone on foot is not a travel book. It is a novel by Maria
Thomas, an American writer who lived and worked in Africa for
twelve years and whose death in 1989 has only made what little
work of hers we have seem all the more compelling. I include it
not as an exception (which of course it cannot be since it exists outside the genre) but as a critical comment. Her novel *Antonia Saw
the Oryx First* (1987) starts, "Like an African, the white doctor came
to work on foot."

This is the power of fiction: It can say in eleven words and one
image what I will only belabor in explaining. Maria Thomas opens
with a white person walking on African soil. Not sailing, not riding, not flying, not above—walking. And that walking is not in a
wilderness or on safari. Her doctor is in the midst of. She is in a city
and surrounded by people. And, not for the first time—this is no
arrival scene. Perhaps Maria Thomas had also noted all the machines. I like to think so. As she points out a few lines later, "No one
white ever walked in Africa."

I understand why authors don't want to start their books with
walking. The problem is that walking is too, well, pedestrian. It is
commonplace, and it does not provide the opportunity to do what
any travel writer worth her salt is trying to do—give you the big
picture. The walker sees only details, the rider sees the world. In
fact, the point of opening with the foreigner inside or astride some
vehicle seems to be to provide a vista. The oval pane of the airplane window, the trapezoid pane of the car window, the railing of
a ship, all furnish a frame through which we see an entirety: Africa.
In my sample of airplane-initiated books, six start with aerial
views. I list a few of these here, despite their length, to show you
how powerful such an opening is.

Seen from the air west of Cape Verde, at the Westernmost
point of Africa, in Senegal, the ocean sunrise, clear red-blue,
turns an ominous yellow, and the sun itself is shrouded,
ghostly, in this dust of the northeast trade wind of the dry
season, known as harmattan, that blows across the great
Sahara desert (Peter Matthiessen, *African Silences*, 1991).

The plane flew low over the Mauritanian desert. One could pick out the routes of ancient dried-up rivers cut into the eternity of mountainous, uninhabitable rock. But at this height it all looked reassuringly small, like a child's excavations on a beach. . . . It rapidly became dark, and soon only a ribbon of pink separated the blackness of the sky from the blueness of the haze over the earth, into which we descended as though into an abyss (Mark Hudson, *Our Grandmothers' Drums*, 1989).

From the window of the small plane, I looked down and saw the wooded savanna where I would live for the next year. The landscape was dotted with Senufo villages, like models we might have built in grade school geography, tiny and seemingly perfect. . . . Just outside each village, clearly visible from the air, was a dense circle of trees—the sacred grove. . . . The groves had been there long before airplanes were invented, and the thick vegetation had hidden what was inside from curious eyes like mine. Although I peered down, it felt like cheating (Carol Spindel, *In the Shadow of the Sacred Grove*, 1989).

The lyricism of these descriptions proves the acsthetic power of the aerial view. But notice how apt the phrase "deus ex machina" is for these openings. The foreigner, citizen of privilege, descends via a sky crane "as though into an abyss." On the one level, such a description of a plane descending into night reflects the eerie beauty of the experience. On another level, Africa is being described as it always has been by Westerners, as a dark, unfathomable place that swallows what is human. Carol Spindel seems most aware of the inherent power of the view from above, calling it a form of "cheating." She acknowledges that she sees Africa as most Africans never do, "from the air." One other writer addresses the issue in her first sentence, but not so directly in terms of power: Elspeth Huxley admits in *Four Guineas* (1954) that the "most illuminating" way to travel in Africa is by bus and bicycle but that for reasons of "haste and comfort" she traveled by car and plane instead.

The vista ("a distant view through or along an avenue or opening," says *Webster's*) is not limited to books that begin with an airplane. "Through the window I see" is common to car openings as well. Furthermore, many of the travel books that open on ships open on their decks, with the narrator looking over the railing at the African shore.

Distance enfolds. It allows, even forces, summary. Traditions in logic and literature teach us to proceed from the general to the specific. Pan the horizon and then zoom in. But I think something else is at work here as well: Describing the big picture establishes the authority of the narrator. The view from above, from outside, gives one the right to speak: I have seen the whole. Or, more subtly, it appeals to the reader for admiration or sympathy: Do you see the immensity of the thing that I must cope with alone? How my small self is pitted against a continent?

The appeal of the vista opening is so strong that it's used even when there is no transportation. The overview does not need a vehicle to be expressed. The window of a hotel can supply a vista; panoramas can be had from hilltops.

In other words, what we have in the aerial or littoral opening is a convention of travel writing as common as the transportation convention: the outsider looking down over the landscape, mostly through some protective barrier.

This protective barrier can be multilayered: the body of a vehicle, the height of a hotel or hill or airplane, the length of the sea. Anything that separates outside from inside while insulating.

This barrier interests me. It hints at something. It connects to the other thing I have noticed about the openings of travel books about Africa: their persistent mood, or perhaps "tone" would be a better word. The tone is negative. Expressions of disappointment, anxiety, and uneasiness abound. Mary Kingsley tells us in *Travels in West Africa* (1898) that everything people told her about Africa could be categorized under these headings:

The disagreeables of West Africa.
The diseases of West Africa.

The things you must take to West Africa.
The things you find most handy in West Africa.
The worst possible things you can do in West Africa.

It would appear that the sum of our knowledge about Africa can still be so listed. Many non-Africans open their travel writings with the expectation of trouble:

Right from the start I know that nothing about this trip is going to go as planned (Thomas A. Bass, *Camping with the Prince*, 1990).

Five minutes after my plane touched down at El Fasher airport I knew that something was wrong (Michael Asher, *A Desert Dies*, 1986).

Why did I ever go to West Africa and why am I sailing again tonight? This long coastline of evil reputation seldom gives any white exile supreme happiness, and for some is still the "white man's grave" (Lawrence G. Green, *Under a Sky Like Flame*, 1954).

I walked out of my cabin and across the deck . . . [and looked at the] sullen and livid sky. . . . I was disappointed. Was this dismal air, this overcast sky, portentous for my journey? (Robert Browne, *Beyond the Cape of Hope*, 1965).

Or they open in the middle of trouble:

We were completely lost (H. E. Symons, *Two Roads to Africa*, 1939).

The station at Beira was bedlam . . . (Sacha Carnegie, *Red Dust of Africa*, 1959).

Water squirted through two empty rivet holes wetting my feet, and seeped between flimsy plates each time the metal dinghy slapped the merest swell on the broad and profound face of the Zaire . . . (Paul Hyland, *The Black Heart*, 1988).

I was sicker than hell (Roger Courtney, *African Argosy*, 1953).

I have arrived, the author lets us know, in a place where things do not work out, where I am not in control, where the likelihood is that whatever can go wrong, will. Thus, the barrier of the vehicle, the distance of the vista, do hint at something. Most non-Africans feel that Africa is something that you need to protect yourself from. They indicate that traveling to Africa is to expose yourself, to descend "as though into an abyss." Even while describing the lure of travel, the beauty of a landscape, they manage to insert the opposite: fear and loathing.

So another convention in travel books about Africa is revulsion. Perhaps this first line says it best: "I arrived in Laive already . . . sick of Africa, wanting out" (George Packer, *The Village of Waiting*, 1988).

I don't want to complain. Any foreigner abroad can be forgiven for expressing apprehension at the start of a journey. Anxiety is the heartbeat of travel. And it's a modernist convention to use angst as the motor of narrative. But it must be pointed out that these types of openings are not common in travel books about, say, Provence. Or as common in travel books about China or Argentina. You do not get descriptions of the place of arrival as a "grave," a "murky blackness," or "bedlam." You do not get descriptions of the author as sick, tired, or bored.

Why is it that they abound in non-Africans' books about Africa? What are we so afraid of? What do we imagine that Africa threatens us with? And on what do we base this fear, since many of us have never been to Africa? In the face of this overwhelming redundancy of transportation, landscapes, and anxiety, can we really argue that we are writing exactly what happened to us? Isn't it more likely that we have shaped our experiences to fit the conventions? Or that our experiences themselves are the result of our reading?

Of course, some travel books about Africa do not start with any of these conventions. Hemingway opens *Green Hills of Africa* (1935) with a description of waiting in a blind for game. (I thought I would find more hunting openings, given the popularity of safari literature as a travel form, but I didn't.) Waugh starts *A Tourist in Africa* (1960) with the necessity of wintering abroad. Two or three books open with the map of Africa spread out before the author. Two or three start by talking about other books about Africa. (Galbraith Welch notes another similarity among books about Africa in his *The Jet Lighthouse* [1960]: "A book reviewer once estimated that over one half of the books which have been written about Africa contain the phrase which Pliny copied from the Greeks to the effect that from Africa something new was always coming.") Beryl Markham waits until the third paragraph of *West with the Night* to mention an airplane and until the sixth to mention vistas. But there aren't many exceptions, and many of those I found had simply delayed their conventional openings. That is, vehicles and vistas and vexations open the *second* chapter instead of the first. The first chapter the authors spend, instead, talking about what inspired them to go to Africa. They back up a step in the journey.

Which brings me to the observation I have made before. It is not so much what our books start with as what they don't start with. For instance, wouldn't you think we'd sometimes open with people, particularly people from the place we have traveled to?

Travel books about other places do. Jonathan Raban opens his book *Arabia: A Journey Through the Labyrinth* with a miscommunication between an Arab man and a white British prostitute. The first line describes the Arab man; the street interaction that follows shows that the woman imagines him to be wealthy, despite all appearances to the contrary, simply because he is Arab. The man does not understand what she wants and, in an attempt to guess, finally pulls out some matches. She curses him and leaves. Raban never once mentions himself.

Other kinds of nonfiction books about Africa do sometimes open with local people. Journalists who report on the continent for national newspapers like the *Los Angeles Times* or the *Washington Post* regularly publish expanded versions of their articles in book form, unabashed to title their books *The Africans* or simply *Africa*. To their credit, though, both David Lamb and Blaine Harden open with descriptions of Africans, although only one of these introductory men has a name and expressed ideas.

Otherwise, I found only one travel book that opens with an African, and that African not so carefully detailed as Raban's Arab. This is it:

The witch doctor curses (Rory Nugent, *Drums Along the Congo*, 1993).

Over two hundred books and this is the sole example of an African in a first line. Whether this African is an improvement on none at all, I will leave to your judgment. I can increase the count to two if I include a preface from Negley Farson's *Behind God's Back* (1941) in which the author introduces himself along with an African. This is the extent of the introduction: "Another man and I waited to be picked up from a railway station." It should be noted, however, that the African goes nameless and has a "sullen face."

Don't you think, too, that travel books about Africa would sometimes open with villages, where most Africans live? Again, I could only find one, by a former Peace Corps volunteer. Susan Lowerre's *Under the Neem Tree* (1991) opens with a vista of Walli Jalla, a small village on the banks of a tributary of the Senegal River. The next closest thing to this kind of opening is being treated to views of wild landscapes or views of the city available on the way to the hotel.

No travel books I found started in the midst of a mosque or a marriage or a meal, to name just a few of the myriad facets of everyday life in Africa.

I don't except myself from this critical observation. The Africa book I am currently writing doesn't start with Africans either. And perhaps starting with African people or cultures would be dishonest, a denial of what our books are really about. Our endless fascination with other cultures often amounts to little else than this: what they tell us, through imagined difference, about us. We start with ourselves (rather than with Africans) because our books are ultimately about ourselves. We tend to start at the beginning (arriving), go to the middle (surviving), and then end (leaving) because our readers live outside Africa. We detail landscapes from a protective distance to underline our readerly status as spectators rather than participants. And we are afraid because we have been told in a thousand ways that Africa is a place that will kill us.

None of us sat down to write what we had read about Africa, but that's what we did. Our endlessly similar opening lines put the lie to our romantic image of ourselves as artists creating as no one else can or would. We are, all of us, derivative.

So you see how it goes. Books create books. And thus, because we read, books about Africa create Africa. Millions of Africans can attest that no book is needed to know the land you live on, the people you live with, the religion you practice—in short, to know what it is to grow up in a place. And, perhaps, if you do not read, if you have never been to school, if you do not listen to the radio or watch television, if you are not Muslim or Christian, if your oral traditions are intact, you can know Africa apart from what has been written about it.

But the very fact that you are reading this essay indicates that you don't and, in a way, can't know Africa apart from your reading. Again, I should know, for neither can I—and I grew up there. The Africa known by those without books or beyond the long shadow that books cast is a totally different Africa from the one I know. Or will ever know.

I have one more confession to make.

My first book is about returning to the African country where I grew up. My first sentences fit every convention of non-Africans' book openings. Still, I could argue that I only wrote what happened to me. So what, I could say, if non-Africans' autobiographies use the travel form so much that the two forms have become synonymous, ourselves forever arriving? That doesn't mean my experience wasn't real.

But this would be dishonest. Gauguin and I are alike. Just as he painted some of his pictures of Tahiti before he arrived, I wrote the opening lines of my first book before I went back to Africa.

The very first sentence came to me while I was living in Seattle. It arrived in my head fully written. It's true that it was based on my memories of living in Accra as a child. Still, it was not what happened to me; it was what I imagined would happen to me. When I got off the plane I didn't think, "Here I am." I thought, "Yes, it is how I imagined it would be, how I wrote it to be."

You could say that I went back to see if what I had written was true. This is the circle of reading and writing and experience. No one knows where it leaves off. Or where it begins.

These are the first lines of my first book:

A wave of wet heat swept over me. It pushed by, pungent with asphalt and ocean and greenness. I swayed and clutched the metal railing. Its coolness did nothing to mute this sensation: the warm air was amniotic fluid, and in it I was moving back into something both forgotten and deeply known. Looking up as I descended the steps, I could see the terminal across the shimmering airstrip (Wendy Belcher, *Honey from the Lion*, 1988).

THE MAN WHO LOVED BOOKS IN TURKEY

Lisa Michaels

Last spring, when setting out for two months in Turkey, my husband and I had no trouble making a quick selection of T-shirts and toiletries. But when it came to picking books, we paused, weighing each one, literally, in our hands. Packing reading material for a long vacation on the cheap is like packing for travel in a light aircraft: That dead weight will come to haunt you. My husband solves the problem by choosing thick volumes that promise weeks of reliable pleasure: *David Copperfield*, say. I, on the other hand, want to bring a good helping of the smorgasbord I have back home, an array sufficient to give me the illusion of whimsy. I recognize that rueful expression my husband wears when we plan a weekend out of town and I rush around assembling a foot-high stack of books—more printed matter than I could get through in a lazy week at home. Time after time, he's watched me lug most of it back unread.

This time, I couldn't afford to overpack: Our trip was to be done without porters or rented cars. Whatever I chose, I would carry on my back. In the end, I set out for Istanbul with ten pounds of books, among them Coleman Barks's translations of Rumi (I planned to visit the mystic's tomb); *Innocents Abroad;* Mary Lee Settle's *Turkish Reflections;* and a couple of things that had been recommended to me—Dale Peck's *The Law of Enclosures; Out of Egypt* by André Aciman.

This was a healthy stack, but by the time I reached southern Turkey a month later, I had finished them all. It was a relief, then, when I saw, in a seaport town on the Aegean, the sign "Used Books, Libros." I followed the arrow down a cobbled street and came to a tiny bookshop, not much bigger than a walk-in closet. The stone floor sloped to one side and the walls were fixed with rickety shelves. No one was in attendance, only a cat carefully shredding a well-shredded chair, so I started browsing. The English-language titles were dust-smeared and covered one wall: Barbara Taylor Bradford novels, lots of Agatha Christie, a small section of out-of-date guidebooks—*Europe on $5 a Day*—made quaint by inflation. They were mostly standard fare, yet here and there were a few surprises: Isherwood's *Christopher and His Kind, The Virgin Suicides* by Jeffrey Eugenides.

It was an alphabetized discard pile, a whole inventory delivered by vacationers. Each volume held the story of a person who had passed through the town: a social worker who devoured this Patricia Cornwell mystery in one of the cafés above the harbor, glad to have no responsibility for the plot; a man who read Lord Kinross's *The Ottoman Centuries* in a dingy pension near the market, the bed exhausted and he wide awake.

For the most part these volumes told a tale of people bent on light reading—mysteries and bodice-rippers and Louis L'Amour westerns. It's easy to feel scorn for such books, for their failure to drape anything artful over the bare machinery of their plots. But they bear you along and spit you out, and then—here's the lovely thing—you can throw them away. Like sample shampoo bottles or slips of hotel soap, they're perfect for traveling: You won't mind leaving them behind. That was the trouble with my plan, trying to patch up the holes in my literary education while on holiday. I ended up with books I felt obliged to cart home again.

No surprise then that I had passed up the mysteries and was considering a copy of Conrad's *Nostromo* when the owner appeared through a side door. He was a large, doleful man whose head nearly brushed the ceiling.

"Is this any good?" I held up the Conrad.

"Excellent," he said, in deep tones.

"Anything else you might recommend?"

The bookseller didn't even glance at his stock. "No, it's all trash. Business is no good." He gave me a bare look. "Have you read E. O. Wilson?"

I hadn't, but I had known someone who revered the old ant specialist, and the bookseller took this as encouragement. He went to a table at the front of the shop, brushed the dozing cat to the floor, and came back with a well-thumbed copy of the *Times Literary Supplement*. "This is also quite good," he said, pointing to a review of some other ecologist's tome. He dropped the paper to his side. "Do you like Tom Wolfe? Saul Bellow?"

"Well . . ." I hadn't time to answer.

"Have you read Graham Swift's *Last Orders?* I heard he stole the plot from Faulkner."

Poor fellow. I had another month to go, at most, without a good book. But he was as hungry as the spiders that strung webs in the corners of his shop: He had to wait for what might come to him.

Grudgingly, I pulled a novel from my bag: William Maxwell's *The Folded Leaf.* "Can I trade this?"

"Of course," he said. "But do you have anything else?" He peered into my satchel.

"This I'm keeping," I said, closing the flap on a copy of *The Executioner's Song*. My husband had just finished it, and I'd read it before, but it was a book I wanted for the bookshelf back home.

"Is that Norman Mailer?" The bookseller's eyes had lit up.

"Yes," I said. "But I don't want to part with it."

"Mailer—he wrote the book on Oswald?"

"The very one."

"And another . . ." He riffled through his mental card file, then raised a triumphant finger in the air. "*Army of the Night?*"

He went on like this for the better part of an hour, until the late-afternoon light in the doorway beckoned me out. "Look, can I have the *Nostromo* for this?" I asked, holding up the Maxwell.

"All right," the bookseller said, and we exchanged offerings. "But tell me, is the Mailer as good as they say?"

I had nearly reached the sill. "It's terrific."

"And when are you leaving Antalya? Perhaps I could borrow it."

"Tomorrow," I said. "Early." I was glad it was the truth.

The bookseller stood in the doorway, looking deflated, as I set off down the street. Just then I was glad to escape, but later I would feel guilty for not leaving him the novel or at least chatting longer, starved as the man was for literature and literary conversation. It was his stack of book reviews that made me reconsider: It seemed unfair that a man with such keen tastes had to subsist on essays about books he might never read—all appetizers and never a meal. Perhaps it's a small courtesy to leave vacation reading in your wake, no matter what it costs you, to sail through a strange country, discarding books for those following or left behind, your bag getting lighter as you go.

THE MEANING OF GDAŃSK

Jan Morris

I stand at the end of a deserted peninsula, in a city with a lost name, and see lying in the harbor a warship that isn't there. Everyone who comes to the city sees that phantom vessel, and hears the blast of a broadside that sounded nearly sixty years ago: for this is the former Danzig, in the extinct Polish Corridor, and the vessel is the long-sunk German battleship *Schleswig-Holstein*, whose bombardment of the vanished barracks of the Westerplatte peninsula began the Second World War.

The city is called Gdańsk now, but I grew up with Danzig, and can't get out of the habit. Long ago in my school atlases it was always called Danzig, and sometimes had a little plan all its own, in a corner of the map of Central Europe, to show that it was a place peculiar to itself—a Free City, in fact, under the sovereignty of the League of Nations, within the strip of Polish territory that separated East Prussia from the rest of Germany. Danzig was a fateful place, and when it mutated into Gdańsk, that proved fateful too: It was here that the Soviet empire first began to crumble before the superior convictions of democracy, and the hero Lech Wałęsa of

Solidarity lives here to this day, like the knight of an old fairy tale, behind the high hedges of a suburban villa.

There are not many places in the world where the history of our time seems more immediate. And it is history clarified by hallucination, where things are a little more exact than they ought to be; legendary champions live on bus routes and insubstantial battleships kill soldiers long since dead.

The prime Gdańsk illusion is central Gdańsk itself—Old Danzig, that is, which was for centuries one of the great seaports of the Hanseatic League and a lordly center of Baltic commerce, culture and diplomacy. Teutonic Knights in chain mail—Polish kings in ermined robes—cloaked merchants from Gotland or Riga—traders in amber or Arctic sealskins—eminent astronomers and illustrious sculptors—these were the sort of people who haunted the memories of the place, and the streets of the city were tall-gabled and sprinkled with spires.

For years Danzig was the biggest city in eastern Europe. Sometimes Polish, sometimes German, briefly French, it remained a revered old seaport of the Baltic until—crash!—in 1945 the Red Army, driving the Wehrmacht out of Poland, demolished the whole place by bomb and gunfire. Old Danzig was almost entirely destroyed, probably more completely than any other European city. Within the circuit of its medieval walls, with its quays and warehouses beside the Motlawa River, nothing was left but rubble. It is one of the miracles of our century that fifty years later we can walk those very same streets, among the same tall-gabled houses, beneath the towers and steeples of Danzig's ancient churches, as though nothing at all has happened.

I suppose the reconstruction of Old Danzig—as it was—is the single most spectacular rebuilding job ever, one honorable memorial of Communist rule in Poland. I defy any ill-informed stranger to guess that this marvelous city is not in its original incarnation. Proud and mellow stand the houses of those ancient merchants in their stately ranks, apparently worn a bit by age and weather but instinct with centuries of consequence, and above them stands the mighty red hulk of the Church of Our Lady, one of the largest brick churches in the world, like a very declaration of sacred permanence. Seven town gates of Gdańsk still look down, as they always did, upon the water traffic of the river, and a constant bustle of shoppers, tourists, and buskers enlivens the elegant square called the Long Market, for so long the prime mercantile exchange of the Baltic Sea.

I could hardly believe it all. I could hardly credit that the Restauracja Tawerna, where they served me boiled eel and potatoes as though they had been serving them without a break since the fifteenth century, fifty years ago was no more than a pile of rubble. It was almost inconceivable to me that the venerable roofed crane on the riverfront, a famous municipal symbol since the Middle Ages, was only a synthetic substitute, or that the beautiful Baroque mansions of Mariacka Street, with their elegant stone terraces and flourishes of sculpted stone, were really no older than I was myself. Very few people in Gdańsk today can remember Old Danzig as it originally was, before tragedy destroyed it and bold hearts built it up again.

Occasionally reality does impinge. The thoroughly authentic traffic of the modern city whirls around the ring roads, beyond the Torture House and the Great Armory's florid turrets. From the tower of the Town Hall you can see the massed derricks of the modern docks, away at the mouth of the Vistula. The Old Polish Post Office really is the actual post office that Günter Grass immortalized in *The Tin Drum,* and the royal gate that was always the city's ceremonial entrance is one of the very few old structures that did not need rebuilding.

Besides, a city is an animate object, and Gdańsk has never been exterminated. An old man stands in the Long Market, selling starfishes and amber from a tray just as his forebears doubtless did five or six centuries ago. A young man rides by on a bicycle, inexplicably loaded down with bits of old cardboard as he might ride a pony heavy with firewood from the forest. There is an immemorial smell of ropes and tar along the quays, and a generic shrieking of gulls. Coveys of feral cats scurry about in holes under the river footbridge, spat upon by naughty boys and fed by a cadaverous man in spectacles and leather jacket. Two young soldiers in the traditional capes and triangular hats of the Polish army sit on a bench by the water licking ice creams.

In short, from time to time I am reminded that although the fabric of the city may be deceptively new, the life it lives is the same robustly organic life it has lived for a thousand years. This is very good for me, because sometimes during my stay in Gdańsk I began to feel that the sham and the genuine were disturbingly confused here, past and present all mixed up, the very conception of old and new made meaningless. I was beginning to feel that I really had seen that German battleship belching shells upon the peninsula of Westerplatte, and that perhaps Gdańsk really was Danzig all the time.

But that old man selling starfish, and those two fine young sergeants licking ice creams, looking just as Polish soldiers have always looked, brought me back to the real thing.

In a shop on the Motlawa embankment I saw an old model of a paddle steamer, circa 1890 I would guess. The ship was called *Luirpold,* was brightly painted in the red and white Danzigian colors and bravely flew the crown and double white cross of the Gdańsk ensign. I bought it at once. They packed it up for me in a comical contraption made of several shoeboxes taped together, and with hilarious care and hazard I carried it away with me to Copenhagen, to London, and home to Wales.

Now it sits on a windowsill in my library, looking complacently exotic against a background of damp Welsh pastures. It is more than just a model to me, more than just an old Polish pleasure steamer, and it has voyaged much farther than the mere voyage from Gdańsk to Llanystumdwy. Think what storms of history that old ship has paddled through! The bombardments and the invasions, the bombings and the street fighting—fire and cold and terror and oppression! I don't know whose windowsill it stood upon when the wars came to Danzig, or when the commissars took over Gdańsk, but I like to see its grand old ensign flying here now, to remind me always—as its home port did—that truth rides above hallucination, and always wins in the end.

HOW ZURICH INVENTED THE MODERN WORLD

Carlos Fuentes

In 1950 I was twenty-one years old and arrived for the first time in Switzerland to pursue studies both at the University of Geneva and at the Institut Universitaire des Hautes Etudes Internationales. I was employed at the Mexican Mission to the International Labour Organization (ILO) and served as secretary to the Mexican Member of the International Law Commission. All of this gave my arrival in Switzerland a very formal tone. Geneva was, as always, an international city. I made friends with foreign students, foreign diplomats, and foreign journalists. I met a beautiful young Swiss student and fell in love with her, but our clandestine meetings were interrupted (A) by my expulsion from the very strict pension where I was staying on the Rue Emile Young, and (B) by her parents' commandment that their daughter should not consort with a young man from a country of dark, uncivilized people, who probably ate human flesh.

I consoled myself, the day that my girlfriend told me it was all over, by going to a cinema on the Place du Molard to see Carol Reed's famous film *The Third Man*, which was then the greatest movie attraction in the world. It starred one of the most beautiful women ever seen on the screen, Alida Valli, a perfect mask of icy sensuality and flaming, vengeful, diamond-clear eyes. But most important, it was acted by Orson Welles, whose *Citizen Kane* I had seen as a child in New York and which impressed me forever—to this very day—as the greatest sound film Hollywood has ever made. Its formal beauty, the audacity of the lighting, camera angles, and illumination of significant detail, all converged in the telling of the great American story: money, how to make it and how to keep it; happiness, how to search for it and never find it; power, how to attain it and how to lose it. Kane was both the American dream and its reverse, the American nightmare. Now, at the Molard cinema, Welles appeared in the shadows of the Vienna sewers as the cynical dealer in crime, Harry Lime, a little Caesar, a pygmy Kane of the postwar underworld, who justified his criminal activities with a phrase that became universally famous and that directly affected Switzerland.

Italy, said Harry Lime–Orson Welles, has had the Medicis, assassinations, and corruption, and produced Michelangelo. Switzerland has had peace, order, and lots of cows, and produced the cuckoo clock.

I do not recall how this line was taken by the audience in the Geneva movie house. I know that I moved from the strictly watched pension to a bohemian garret on the Place du Bourg-de-Four and, with a Dutch fellow student, began exploring the underside of cuckoo land, the nightlife of Geneva. It was, indeed, full of sub–Harry Limes in seamy cabarets, prostitutes with bleached hair and little dogs sitting in eternal attendance at the Canonica coffeehouse, and a couple of beautiful dancers my Dutch friend and I promptly made friends with. I was quite happy until, on demanding a Saturday evening with my dancer, she gave me the following reply: "*Non, pas samedi. C'est le jour de mon mari.*" Oh, the ghost of Calvin; where even seductive dancers are no more than animated, Puritan cuckoo clocks. Was Harry Lime right after all?

I had read Joseph Conrad's *Under Western Eyes* before coming to Geneva, and clearly envisioned that city as a center of political intrigue, swarming with Russian exiles and fearful anarchists. Yet even in the tragic, hothouse atmosphere described by Conrad, there was a resemblance to cuckoo land in the words Sophia Antonovna addresses to the protagonist, Razumov, "Remember, Razumov, that women, children, and revolutionaries hate irony." Could she have added, "And so do the Swiss"? As a Mexican, I hated generalizations about my country or any other. All I could do, rereading Conrad in Geneva, was to repeat with him, "There are phantoms of the living as well as of the dead."

Then, in the summer of 1950, I was invited by some old and dear German-Mexican friends to visit them in Zurich. I had never seen the city and had a preconceived idea that it was the very crown of that Swiss prosperity that so harshly contrasted with the other Europe I had been witnessing in the spring of the same year: London still on ration coupons for basic necessities, Vienna occupied by the four powers, bombed-out Cologne, Italy without heating, third-class carriages bursting with shabbily dressed people carrying suitcases tied together with string, children picking up cigarette butts on the streets of Genoa, Naples, Milan . . .

It was a beautiful city, this Zurich. The balmy June days held a whiff of dying spring and nascent summer and it was difficult to separate the lake from the sky, as if the waters had become pure air, and the firmament another mirror of the lake. It was impossible to resist the sense of tranquillity, dignity, and reserve that set off the physical beauty of the surroundings, and one wondered: Where are all the gnomes? Where is the gold hidden? Is this the city where the Nibelungen become visible, wearing top hats and frock coats, as in a George Grosz caricature?

I must admit that my potential irony, well founded on the shores of Lake Leman, came apart one evening when my friends invited me to dinner at the Baur au Lac hotel on the lakeside. The summer restaurant was a floating terrace on the water. You reached it by a gangplank, and it was lighted by paper lanterns and flickering candles. As I unfolded my stiff white napkin amid the soothing tinkle of silver and glass, I raised my eyes and saw the group dining at the next table. Three ladies sat there with a man in his seventies. This man was as stiff and elegant as the napkins and tablecloths, dressed in double-breasted white serge and immaculate shirt and tie. His long, delicate fingers sliced a cold pheasant, almost with daintiness. Yet even in eating he seemed to me unbending, with a ramrod-back, military bearing. His aged face showed "a growing fatigue," but the pride with which his lips and jaws were set sought desperately to hide the fact. His eyes twinkled with "the fiery play of fancy."

As the carnival lights of that summer's night in Zurich played with a fire of their own on the features I now recognized, Thomas Mann's face was a theater of implicit quiet emotions. He ate and let the ladies do the talking; he was, in my fascinated eyes, the creator of times and spaces where solitude gives birth to "beauty unfamiliar and perilous," but also to the perverse and the illicit.

How right I was. I could not have imagined that evening of my youthful, distanced encounter with a writer who had shaped the minds of my generation. From *Buddenbrooks* to the great novellas to *The Magic Mountain,* Thomas Mann had been the securest post of our Latin American literary attachment to Europe. Because if Joyce was Ireland and the English language, and Proust, France and the French language, Mann was more than Germany and the German language. As young readers of Musil, Broch, Schnitzler, Kafka, Joseph Roth, or Lernet-Holenia, we knew that "the German language" was more than Germany; it was the language of Berlin and Vienna and Prague and Zurich, and even Venice, as well. Yet it was Mann who brought them all together as a European language because it was founded on the imagination of Europe, something more than its component parts. Mann was already, in our young Latin American eyes, what Jacques Derrida would one day call "the Europe which is what has been promised in the name of Europe." Seeing Mann that night, and seeing him dining on the lake in Zurich, instantly fused in my mind the two spiritual spaces, Europe and Zurich. Thanks to that meeting-without-a-meeting, which was nevertheless a meeting-within-a-meeting, I crowned Zurich the capital of Europe that very night.

I was curious, I was impertinent. Dare I approach Thomas
Mann—I, a twenty-one-year-old Mexican student with a lot of
reading behind me, true, but with all the gaucherie of one still ig-
norant of social and intellectual sophistication? Susan Sontag, in a
memorable piece, has recalled how she, even younger than I, entered the inner sanctum of Thomas Mann's house in Los Angeles
in the 1940s, and found precious little to say, but much to observe.
I had nothing to say but, like Sontag, a lot to observe.

There he was the next morning, at the Dolder where he was
staying, dressed all in white, dignified and even a bit rigid, but with
the eyes more alert and wide-ranging than the night before.
Several young men were playing tennis on the court but he was
watching only one of them, as if this young man had been the
Elected, the Apollo of the courts. He was, indeed, a beautiful
youth, no more than twenty, perhaps twenty-one, my own age.
Mann could not take his eyes off him and I could not take my eyes
off Mann. This was incredible. I was watching a scene from *Death
in Venice*, only thirty-eight years later, when Mann was no longer
thirty-seven (his age on writing the masterful novella of homosex-
ual desire) but seventy-five, much older than the smitten
Aschenbach pining over young Tadzio on the Lido.

Yet the situation was astoundingly, famously, painfully, the
same. The dignified man of letters, the Nobel Prize author, the
septuagenarian Mann could not hide, from me or anyone else,
the passionate yearning for the twenty-year-old boy playing tennis
on the courts of the Dolder Hotel that fine June morning of 1950
in Zurich. His daughter Erika—as I later learned—came along,
seemed to chide him, forced him to abandon his passionate out-
post and go back with her to the humdrum life, not only of the
hotel, but of the immensely disciplined man whose Dionysian
urges were forever controlled by the Apollonian dictate to enjoy
life only if you can give form to it. For Mann, I saw that morning,
artistic form came before forbidden flesh, true beauty was in art,
not in the aging, formless, eventually rotting carcass of passing
pleasures. It was a dramatic, unforgettable moment, a true com-

mentary on the life and work of Thomas Mann, this arrival of his daughter Erika obviously chiding him for his erotic weaknesses, gently pulling him back, not to the order of the cuckoo land, but to the order of the spirit, of literature, of artistic form, where Thomas Mann could have his cake and eat it too—where he could be the master, not the toy, of his emotions.

I sat down to lunch with my German-Mexican friends at the Dolder. The young man who served us at table was the same one whom Mann had been admiring that morning. He had not had time to bathe and smelt slightly of a healthy, sportive sweat. The maître d'hôtel called him—"Franz!"—and he rushed to another table.

So there was a mystery in Zurich; there was more than cuckoo clocks. There was irony. There was rebellion. There was the Café Voltaire and the birth of Dada, right in the middle of the bloodiest war ever fought on European soil. There was Tristan Tzara thumbing his nose at rationalism: "Thought comes from the mouth." There was Francis Picabia making art out of nuts and bolts. There was Zurich telling the blood-drenched, decaying, hypocritical world that sanctioned death in the trenches in the name of a higher rationality: "All that we see is false." From that simple premise, uttered at the Café Voltaire in Zurich by the monocled Tzara, sprang the whole revolution of sight and sound and dream and humor and skepticism that actually buried the smugness of nineteenth-century Europe but could not avoid the barbarism to come. Was Europe not yet or could it ever be "what had been promised in the name of Europe"? Was it to be only Treblinka and Dachau? Yes, if we assume that all that came to Zurich and then flowed from Zurich—Tzara and the Surrealists, Hans Richter and Luis Buñuel, Picasso and Ernst, Arp and Man Ray—was not "what had been promised in the name of Europe." But it was. What was always promised in the name of Europe was the critique of Europe, the warning of Europe against herself, her own arrogance, complacency, and surprised confusion when the blows finally fell. It was the warning of the Zurich artists in 1916. It should be the warning once more, as the phantoms of racism, xenophobia, anti-Semitism, anti-Islamism, rear their heads anew and remind us of Conrad's words in *Under Western Eyes:* "There are phantoms of the living as well as of the dead."

Who had seen these phantoms, painted them, given them corporeal horror? Was it not yet another citizen of Zurich, Fuseli, the greatest of the pre-Romantic painters, who had already embodied, since the eighteenth century, all the themes of the dark night of the Romantic soul, as described by Mario Praz in his celebrated book *The Romantic Agony:* Fuseli and La Belle Dame Sans Merci, Fuseli and the beauty of the Medusa, Fuseli and the Metamorphoses of Satan, Fuseli and André Gide's warning that not believing in the Devil means giving him all the advantages of surprising us? Does not the baptismal font of Romanticism—the beauty of the horrible—come from the Zuricher Fuseli? The gloom shattered by unattainable light; the joy of crime that became Harry Lime's anti-cuckoo trademark; the Fatal Man and the Fatal Woman who have entranced our impossible imagination from Salome to Greta Garbo and from Lord Byron to James Dean . . .

Zurich as an urn of archetypes for the modern world? Why not, if we take this broad look? Did not James Joyce sing bawdy songs at the Café Terrasse that played on words with the annunciatory glee of the forthcoming *Ulysses?* Did not Lenin constantly attend the Café Odéon prior to his departure to Russia in the famous sealed car? Did the two ever meet, only in Tom Stoppard's play, or in Samuel Beckett's true recollection? Did not all of these ghosts walk on the waters of Lake Zurich?

And yet, for me, dazzling as the art of Fuseli and the pranks of Dada might be, tensely opposite—and apposite—as the Zurich life and work of James Joyce and Vladimir Lenin might be, it is always Mann, Thomas Mann, the good European, the true European, the contradictory European, the critical European, who always comes back to my mind and emotion as the figure whom I most associate with Zurich.

How many times was he there? How can we separate Mann from Zurich? What a long life there, coming and going from his villa at Küsnacht to those in Erlenbach and Kilchberg, the places of work and repose and daily life. But then there are also the Zurich highlights in the life of Mann. The 1921 visit where he dares to raise his lecture fee to one thousand marks. The 1926 reading to students from "Disorder and Early Sorrow." The joyous 1936 celebration of his sixty years, choosing Zurich not as a foreign place but as "a homeland for a German of my kind," "an ancient seat of German culture" "where the Germanic fuses into the European." The troubled visit of 1937, at the edge of the Nazi night and fog, preparing *Lotte in Weimar* as a desperate attempt at a new *Aufklarung*, shrugging off Gerhart Hauptmann's refusal to meet him with a philosophical attendance for "other times," struggling to keep his son Klaus off drugs, "a world where moral effort . . . is a thankless business."

And then the return after the war, the innocent activity, as though age and fatigue were of no consequence, the hotel room at the Baur au Lac constantly invaded by mail, requests for interviews, the tiny pebbles of glory in the boots of the great man, amounting, finally, to an insufferable burden. And the repose of beauty in a yearned-for youth, the awaiting for "a single word from the boy and the knowledge that nothing, nothing can empower old age to love again . . ." And when, on August 15, 1955, "the throne became vacant," I looked back on that distant, chance encounter in the Zurich summer of 1950 and wrote:

Thomas Mann had managed, out of his solitude, to find the affinity he sought between the personal destiny of the author and that of his contemporaries in general. Through him, I had imagined that the products of his solitude and this affinity were named art (created by one) and civilization (created by all). He looks so sure, in *Death in Venice*, of the tasks imposed upon him by his own ego and the European soul that, as I, paralyzed with admiration, saw him there that night in Zurich, I dared not conceive of such an affinity in our own Latin American culture, where the extreme demands of a ravaged, often voiceless continent often kill the voice of the self and make a hollow political monster of the voice of the society, or kill it, giving birth to a pitiful, sentimental dwarf.

Yet, as I recalled my passionate reading of everything he wrote, from *The Blood of the Walsungs* to *Dr. Faustus*, I could not help but feel that, in spite of the vast difference between his culture and ours, in both of them—Europe, Latin America; Zurich, Mexico City—literature in the end asserted itself through a relationship between the visible and the invisible worlds of a narrative; nation and narration. A novel, said Mann, should gather up the threads of many human destinies in the warp of a single idea; the I, the You, and the We were only separate and dried up because of a lack of imagination.

And then, as the 1950s wandered into the 1960s, we became aware of another Zuricher, Max Frisch, and *I'm Not Stiller;* we became aware of Friedrich Dürrenmatt and *The Visit;* we even realized that Jean-Luc Godard was Swiss, and that the proverbial cuckoo was as dead as the equally proverbial duck; Harry Lime left the sewers and became fat and complacent, announcing wine before its time. But even he, Welles, had suffered the fate of Kane: self-indulgent but tragic, perhaps he left shreds of his immense talent in the hands of the hard, tragic, merciless Swiss writers such as Frisch and Dürrenmatt, those whom Harry Lime had thought no more than clockmakers.

I have two endings for my tale of Zurich. One is closer to my own age and culture. It is the image of the Spanish writer Jorge Semprún, a Republican and Communist sent at age fifteen to the Nazi concentration camp of Buchenwald, who, on being released by Allied troops in 1945, fails to recognize himself in the emaciated youth rescued from death and will not speak of his ordeal until his face tells him he can talk again. What Semprún does in his notable book, *L'écriture ou la vie,* is to wait patiently until a full life is restored to him, even if it takes decades (which it does), before speaking of the horror of the camp. Then, one day in Zurich, he dares to enter a bookshop for the first time since his liberation several years before, and catches his own glance in the bookshop window. Zurich has given him back his face. He has no need to recount the horror. Recovering his face has told us all there is to know. The life of Zurich surrounds him.

But the other ending is closer to my own memory. It happened that night in 1950 when, unbeknownst to him, I left Thomas Mann sipping his demitasse as midnight approached and the floating restaurant at the Baur au Lac bobbed slightly and the Chinese lanterns quietly flickered out.

I shall always thank that night in Zurich for silently teaching me that, in literature, you know only what you imagine.

STORMING *THE BEACH*

Rolf Potts

DAY SIX: JANUARY 22—STORMING *THE BEACH* AT PHI PHI LEH (PRELUDE)

It is three o'clock in the morning, and Lomudi Beach is possibly the only stretch of sand on Phi Phi Don island that is completely deserted. The only buildings here are small, sagging bamboo-and-thatch dwellings that probably housed Thai fishermen before the onslaught of sun-starved Europeans and North Americans turned those fishermen into bellboys and T-shirt hawkers. The high-tide line here yields a sodden crust of garbage—plastic water bottles, rubber sandals, cigarette butts—but this detritus is only evidence of the boaters, snorkelers, and sun-burned masses who haunt the other parts of the island. Devoid of dive shops, pineapple vendors, and running water, Lomudi is quiet and empty.

Given the current development trends in this part of Thailand, Lomudi will probably sport a disco and an airport within a couple of months.

I hear the rhythmic thump of a longtail boat somewhere in the darkness, and I realize that my moment is at hand. Gathering up a sealed plastic bag of supplies, I wade out into the shallow waters to meet the rickety wooden craft that will take me across a small stretch of the Andaman Sea to the forbidden shores of Phi Phi Don's sister island—the majestic, cliff-girded Phi Phi Leh.

Phi Phi Leh is not forbidden because of ancient tribal rituals, secret nuclear tests, or hidden pirate treasure. Phi Phi Leh is forbidden because it is the current filming location of a Leonardo DiCaprio movie called *The Beach*. My sole mission on this dim night is to swim ashore and infiltrate the set. I am not a gossip journalist, a Leo-obsessed film nut, or a paparazzo. I am a backpacker. The primary motivation for my mission is not an obsession with Hollywood, but simply a vague yearning for adventure. I wish I could put this yearning into more precise terms, but I can't. All I can say is that adventure is hard to come by these days.

Admittedly, I have a daunting task before me. In the wake of ongoing environmental protests, Leo's purported fear of terrorism, and the obligatory packs of screaming pubescent females, security on Phi Phi Leh has reached paramilitary proportions. Thus, I have given up on the notion of a frontal assault. Instead, I plan to swim ashore via Loh Samah Bay, change into dry khakis and a casual shirt, and—under cover of darkness—hike across the island to the filming location.

I'm not sure what will happen if I make it that far, but—summary execution excepted—I am prepared to deal cheerfully with whatever fate awaits me. This attitude has much less to do with optimism than with the simple fact that—after one week of obsessive preparation—I don't really have a plan.

DAY ONE: JANUARY 17—DICAPRITATION

Thai Air flight 211 from Bangkok to Phuket has been taxiing around for the last twenty minutes, and there seems to be no end in sight. The European package tourists in the seats around me are getting fidgety, but this is only because they have not set foot on actual soil since Stockholm or Frankfurt. I, on the other hand, have been in Thailand for two weeks, and I've already faced the numbing horrors of Bangkok traffic. There, amid the creeping tangle of automobiles, buses, tuk-tuks, humidity, and fumes, one is left with two psychological options: a bodhisattva's patience, or homicidal insanity. Patience won out (barely) for me, and I am taking this present delay in stride.

In my lap sits a pile of notes and clippings about the movie production—most of it from Thai tabloid newspapers. Considering that culling hard facts from tabloid gossip is a challenge akin to discerning fate from sheep intestines, my mind frequently strays as I dig through the information.

I wonder, for instance, what would happen if Leonardo DiCaprio's teenage fans here were able to overwhelm his bodyguards. In every part of Asia I've visited, I've noticed how young girls act in the presence of their pop heroes, and it's somewhat unsettling. At one level, there is a screamy, swoony, Elvis–on–*Ed Sullivan* innocence to it all—but at a deeper level, I sense a desperation.

After all, not only is this part of Asia a survivalist bazaar society (where patiently standing in line is not part of the manners code), it also runs on a patriarchal system, where young girls simply have fewer options in life. If Leo's bodyguards ever fail him, I wouldn't be at all surprised by a frenzied display of grim, no-future pathos— a spectacle that, by comparison, would make punk-rock nihilism seem like a gentle tenet from the Sermon on the Mount. I keep getting this picture in my head of the handsome blond movie star being lovingly, worshipfully torn to pieces—of adolescent girls brawling over ragged bits of spleen and femur.

Several months before I came to Thailand, I read the Alex Garland novel on which the movie is based. In the story, a strange man presents the main character (a young English traveler named Richard) with a map that leads to an unspoiled beach utopia hidden in a national park in the Gulf of Thailand. The *Lord of the Flies*–style moral degeneration that results after Richard's arrival on the beach made for a thoroughly engrossing read.

After finishing the book, I toyed with the idea of emulating the plot—of finding some like-minded travelers, hiring a fishing boat into the restricted national park islands, and seeking out an un-spoiled paradise. I ultimately discarded this notion, however, when I discovered that tabloid obsession with the film had already ren-dered my idea unoriginal.

When I arrived in Thailand and the tabloid hype still hadn't let up, a new idea struck me: Why not live *The Beach* in reverse? Instead of seeking out a secret, untouched island, why not explore the most scrutinized island in all of Thailand? Why not try wash-ing ashore on the movie set itself?

The pure novelty of this notion has led me to this very point: seat 47K, Thai Air flight 211, which has now finally begun to accel-erate down the runway. As the plane lifts off the ground and banks for its southward turn, a view of Bangkok fills my window.

Below, urban Thailand spreads out around the Chao Phraya River in symmetrical brown-gray grids that, from this altitude, look like the outer armor from a 1970s sci-fi movie spaceship. For an instant, the earth looks artificial and foreign, as if it's been taken over by aliens.

The aliens, of course, are us.

DAY TWO: JANUARY 18—THE HOKEY POKEY

Although historically influenced by traders from China, Portugal, Malaysia, and India, the beach villages of Phuket island now seem to belong to northern Europe as much as anyplace. Western tourists abound, prices are steep, and miniature golf is readily available.

Since the cast and crew of *The Beach* sleep in Phuket, I came here with the intention of scouting out some information before I set off for Phi Phi Leh. Now that I've arrived, however, I'm a bit stumped: Just how am I supposed to scout out information? Mostly I've just been walking around and talking with other trav-elers, which is not much different from what I did on Khao San Road in Bangkok.

But talking with other wanderers is telling in and of itself, since nobody in the backpacker crowd wants to admit even the slightest interest in DiCaprio or the filming of the movie. Instead, nearly everyone I've met talks about their own travels in wistful terms eerily similar to those of the characters in Garland's book. It would be difficult to characterize the nuances from each of my beach-front and street-café conversations this afternoon, but I can easily summarize:

Phuket, it is generally agreed, is a tourist shithole, best reserved for anthropological studies of fat German men who wear Speedos. For the ghost of Phuket past, try the islands of Malaysia or Cambodia. Laos, incidentally, is still charming and unspoiled, like rural Thailand in the eighties. The hill-tribe trekking around Sapa in Vietnam is as full of wonder and surprise as Chiang Mai treks were a decade ago. Goa and Koh Phangan still can't live up to their early-nineties legacy; rumor crowns Central America the new cutting edge of rave. Sulawesi is, part and parcel, Bali ten years ago.

Granted, I have condensed what I heard—but for all the talk, you would think that paradise expired some time around 1989.

I am currently staying at the $5-a-night On On Hotel in Phuket City, where a few interior scenes for *The Beach* will be shot in March. Since it is an official movie location, I had secretly hoped it would be brimming with an eccentric array of film groupies, secu-rity personnel, and rampaging Leo-worshippers. Instead, the open-air lobby is filled with moths, mopeds, and old Thai men playing chess.

Earlier this evening, I spent a couple of hours here chatting and sipping Mekong whiskey with Ann and Todd, a young couple from Maryland. Our conversation started when I heard Ann quoting a book review of *The Beach* from Phuket's English-language news-paper, which described backpack travelers as "uniformly ill-clad . . . all bearing Lonely Planet guidebooks and wandering from one shabby guest house to the next in search of banana pancakes, tawdry tie-dyes and other trash particularly their own." Since we agreed we prefer the Whitmanesque stereotype of backpack travel—pocketless of a dime, purchasing the pick of the earth, and whatnot—this led to a discussion of what actually distinguishes backpack travelers from tourists.

On the surface, it's a simple distinction: Tourists leave home to escape the world, while travelers leave home to experience the world. Tourists, Ann added wittily, are merely doing the hokey pokey: putting their right foot in and taking their right foot out; calling themselves world travelers while experiencing very little. Todd and I agreed that this was a brilliant analogy, but after a few more drinks we began to wonder where backpack travelers fit into the same paradigm. This proved to be a problem.

Do travelers, unlike tourists, keep their right foot in a little longer and shake it all about? Do travelers actually go so far as to do the hokey pokey and turn themselves around—thus gaining a more authentic experience? Is that what it's all about?

The effects of alcohol pretty much eliminated serious reflection at the time, but now that my buzz is gone I can only conclude that the hokey pokey—whether done well or poorly—is still just the hokey pokey. Or, to put it another way: Regardless of one's budget, itinerary, and choice of luggage, the act of travel is still, in its essence, a consumer experience.

Do we travel so that we can arrive where we started and know the place for the first time—or do we travel so that we can arrive where we started having earned the right to take T. S. Eliot out of context?

The fact that it's too late to know the difference makes my little mission to Phi Phi Leh less quirky than it sounds.

DAY THREE: JANUARY 19—LORD OF THE LIES

Except for the fact that I met the producer of *The Beach* and somehow ended up stealing his Italian-leather screenplay binder, today hasn't been all that eventful. Mostly I've just been rereading Garland's novel. Tomorrow I leave for Phi Phi Don.

This morning's *Bangkok Post* featured a press statement from DiCaprio, who declared his love of Thailand, his affection for the Thai people, and his sincere concern for the local ecology.

The ecology comment comes on the heels of an environmental controversy that has been brewing since last fall, when 20th Century–Fox announced it was going to plant a hundred coconut palm trees on the Phi Phi Leh movie set. The reasoning, apparently, was that Phi Phi Leh didn't quite meet the Hollywood standards of what an island in Thailand should look like.

The months following the coconut palm announcement have been fraught with protests, promises, legal action, threatened legal action, publicity stunts, and rumor. Thai environmental activists claimed the palms would disrupt the island's ecosystem; 20th Century–Fox responded by reducing the number of trees to sixty. When activists derided this as a meaningless gesture, 20th Century–Fox (perhaps misunderstanding the difference between environmentalism and landscape maintenance) paid a $138,000 damage deposit to the Thai Royal Forest Department and planted the trees anyway. Now environmentalists are claiming that producers flouted their earlier compromise and brazenly planted no less than seventy-three trees at topsoil depths up to a meter deeper than had previously been agreed.

While the precise facts of this controversy would require a Warren Commission reunion, the fact remains that 20th Century–Fox's actions are a drop in the environmental bucket compared to the large-scale tourist development that has besieged Southeast Asia's islands over the last decade.

Garland alludes to this phenomenon in his novel: "Set up in Bali, Koh Phangan, Koh Tao, Boracay, and the hordes are bound to follow. There's no way you can keep it out of the Lonely Planet, and once that happens, it's countdown to doomsday."

Countdown to doomsday. Kind of makes a person wonder if Garland was aware of the irony when he sold his novel's film rights to a media entity that makes Lonely Planet look like an obscure pamphlet publisher based in the back of someone's Vanagon.

Protests aside, the real environmental impact of the filming won't be determined until after the movie appears in theaters and half a million starstruck teenagers in places like Nebraska and New

Brunswick simultaneously decide that they, too, are going to buy a ticket to Thailand to seek out the last paradise on earth. In a perfect world, I never would have had to sneak onto the verandah of the Cape Panwha Resort Hotel and skulk around while the cast and crew of *The Beach* ate dinner.

Unfortunately, my more prosaic efforts at intelligence gathering (wandering around town, sending e-mails to friends of friends) had yielded little. Playing spy for a few hours was the only way to accurately gauge what I was up against.

Since I am the type of person who would rather hike eight extra miles than try to charm a park ranger into accepting a bribe, I was not filled with confidence as I took a motorcycle taxi out to Cape Panwha earlier this evening. I'd read on the Internet that the resort had hired extra security guards, and I was not looking forward to schmoozing my way past them.

Miraculously, despite my patchy beard, motorcycle-tossed hair, and sweat-salted backpacker attire, none of the hotel personnel gave me a second glance as I strolled past the reception desk and into the verandah area. I immediately spotted the cast sitting at a long table across from the restrooms. Leo was not among them, but I could tell from a glance that each person there vaguely corresponded to a character in the novel. Somebody in casting had done a good job.

Overcoming an innate, juvenile sense of dread, I moved to an empty table overlooking the swimming pool and ordered a Manhattan. I had never ordered a Manhattan before in my life—but since it cost more than my hotel room, I figured it probably contained lots of alcohol. I felt extremely out of place, and I needed something to calm my nerves.

I sipped my drink and tried to act aloof. It was easy to tell the film people from the other hotel guests. The movie folks ate and drank and laughed; everyone else peered around silently. I'm sure that half the people there were waiting around on the off chance that Leo would walk through. I also suspect that—with the possible exception of a chubby little Japanese girl who kept standing up in her chair to gawk over at the cast—those exact same people would pretend not to notice if Leo actually showed up.

By the time Andrew MacDonald arrived and sat down at the table next to me, I'd washed my Manhattan down with a couple of Heinekens. My anxiety was mostly gone, and the only reason I hadn't sauntered over to schmooze with the cast was that it simply seemed like a stupid idea. Instead, I'd chosen the more conservative option of sitting around and doing nothing. I took the appearance of MacDonald—the film's producer—as a good sign.

Aside from DiCaprio, MacDonald was the only person from the movie whom I could have recognized on sight. From one table away, he looked even younger and skinnier than he did in newspaper photos. Sitting there—gangly, boyish, pink-toed in his Birkenstocks—he looked like someone sullenly waiting to be picked last for a game of kickball.

Figuring it was the night's best chance, I feigned courage and walked up to him. "Excuse me," I said, "you're the producer, right?"

"I'm sorry, that's someone else you're thinking of," he replied, looking everywhere but at me.

"No," I told him, "you're Andrew MacDonald."

MacDonald seemed to cringe as he looked up at me. I wasn't sure if he always looked like that, or if he expected me to sucker-punch him. Either way, I took it as my cue to keep talking.

I decided to take a neutral, vaguely journalistic approach. "I was wondering if I might interview some of your actors or spend some time on the set of your movie," I said to him. "Is that possible?"

"It's a closed set," he said wearily.

"What about the actors—do you mind if I chat with them a bit?"

"We're not allowing interviews."

"I don't necessarily want to talk to Leo; anyone will do."

MacDonald took out a pen and wrote a phone number down on a napkin. "This is the number for Sarah Clark. She's a publicist. You'll have to go through her if you want to do any interviews. But at most you'll probably just get an interview with me." He didn't look too thrilled by this possibility.

"So are you saying that there's no chance I can get onto the set, even if I swim there?" I said this as a half-joke, hoping it might scare up some clues on how to get past the security cordon around Phi Phi Lch.

"No chance on the island. You can apply as an extra, but that won't be until next month in Phuket and Krabi."

"I was once an extra in a movie called *Dr. Giggles*, but that was like seven years ago."

This utterly irrelevant trivia nugget seemed to disarm MacDonald a bit. "*Dr. Giggles?*" he said, smirking.

"Yeah, are you familiar with it?"

"No, I'm not. Sorry." He stared off at the pool, sighed, then absently checked his watch. "It's been a long day," he said, almost apologetically.

I didn't bother him when he stood up to go.

The events that transpired as I tried to leave the verandah make so little sense that they are somewhat difficult to recount.

First, I had a problem paying my bill, since the hotel staff assumed that I was with the movie crew. When I asked the waitress for my check, she just frowned and walked off. When she hadn't returned after ten minutes, I tracked her down to the cash register.

"I need to pay my bill," I told her. I figured it would be bad manners to scam drinks after having already interrupted the producer's dinner.

The waitress gave me another strange look, then pushed a piece of paper in front of me. "Just write your room number," she said.

"Can I pay now in cash?" I'm not sure why I was being so insistently ethical; one Manhattan and two Heinekens pale in the face of a $40 million film budget.

The waitress shrugged, and I gave her the money. I turned to leave, and as I was passing the reception desk, the waitress came running after me.

"Your friend forgot this," she said, handing me a yellow cloth satchel.

There in the lobby of the Cape Panwha Resort Hotel, the word "friend" caught me off guard. I couldn't possibly imagine who she was talking about.

I opened the cloth satchel and took out a black Il Bisonte binder. Embossed into the leather cover were the words "THE BEACH." And, in the lower right-hand corner: "ANDREW MACDONALD."

Putting the binder back into the satchel, I thanked the waitress and—just moments after my valorous display of Sunday school ethics over the drink tab—walked out the front door.

I spent the motorcycle taxi ride back into Phuket City trying to think of practical justifications for making off with Andrew MacDonald's screenplay binder. Since the binder was empty, I couldn't really think of any beyond using it as a kind of Hail Mary collateral if things got ugly when I invaded the film set.

Considering that the phone number MacDonald gave me turned out to belong to a confused Thai family in Yala Province, the personally embossed keepsake was the closest thing I had to an asset.

Sitting in my hotel, I imagine myself on the shores of Phi Phi Leh, lashed to one of the illegally planted coconut palms and bleeding from the ears: I am being flogged with rubber hoses by a gang of vigilante set designers, dolly grips, and script supervisors. For the sake of reverie, they are all female, vixenlike, and dressed in bikinis.

MacDonald swaggers over. He is wielding a scimitar and has somehow managed to grow a pencil-thin mustache since I last saw him.

"Closed set!" he bellows, fiercely raising the blade above his head.

About to lose consciousness, I muster one last ounce of energy. "I have your personally embossed Il Bisonte Italian leather screenplay binder, MacDonald," I sneer. "Kill me, and you'll never find out where I've hidden it."

A look of horror washes across the producer's face. "Not my

personally embossed Il Bisonte Italian leather screenplay binder!" he screams, dropping the scimitar to the sand.

With a sudden look of resolve, he turns to the bikini-clad lynch mob. "Untie the intruder," he commands, "and tell that DiCaprio schmuck that his services are no longer needed." He turns back to me with a flourish. "I think we've found our new leading man."

A bit overdone, as reveries go—but I'll just blame that on the movies.

They seem to make a convenient scapegoat.

DAY FIVE: JANUARY 21—HEART OF DORKNESS

I'm starting my second day on Phi Phi Don island, but (for reasons that will become obvious) I didn't write anything yesterday—Day Four—so I'll try to cover both days in this dispatch.

To put it succinctly: Things have gone sour in a way that I had not expected.

From a tactical standpoint, my mission is progressing nicely. The soaring cliffs of Phi Phi Leh stand just two and a half miles across the sea from my roost on Long Beach. A few casual conversations with some Phi Phi Leh dive-tour operators have provided enough physiographical clues for me to devise a landing strategy. I even found a deserted beach (Lomudi) where I can make a quiet departure in the dead of night.

The problem, however, is that I'm having trouble explaining why I want to go to Phi Phi Leh in the first place.

I arrived here yesterday morning to discover that all the affordable lodging on Long Beach had been sold out. Welcoming the ascetic novelty of sleeping on the beach itself, I left my backpack with a friendly restaurant manager and set off to scope things out.

Technically, the island of Phi Phi Don is part of the same national marine park system that protects Phi Phi Leh from permanent tourist development. A person could never tell by looking, however, as an unbroken progression of bungalows and beach resorts lines the entire southeastern seaboard. Ton Sai—an old Thai

Muslim village on the isthmus that connects the two halves of the island—is clotted with luxury hotels, dive shops, restaurants, souvenir peddlers, and discos. The only evidence of Muslim heritage is that some of the women selling cigarettes and Pringles wear veils.

When I met a Danish pair on the longtail taxi-boat from Ton Sai back to Long Beach, I was immediately struck by their similarity to a couple of characters in *The Beach*. In Alex Garland's novel (and, I am certain, in the movie script), Richard travels to the beach utopia in the company of Etienne and Françoise, a young French couple he meets on Khao San Road. Granted, Jan and Maarta aren't French, but they certainly seemed graceful, companionable, and adventurous enough to merit a comparison. When I discovered that they, too, were being forced to sleep on the beach that night, I took this as a sign that I should invite them along for my adventure.

I pitched the idea over a pad thai dinner on Long Beach. Since they were both familiar with the novel, I skipped straight into my plans to rent a boat and steal over to Phi Phi Leh. When I saw how this idea entertained them, I backtracked a bit and told them about my experience with Andrew MacDonald the day before. By the time I got to my fantasy about the bikini-clad lynch mob, I had the Danes in stitches.

"You Americans have wonderful thoughts," Jan said between gasps for air.

I saw this as my chance. "Why don't you two join me?"

"Yes," Jan said, still laughing, "why don't we join you?"

"Perfect," I said. "This is too perfect. Let's find a boat and leave tonight."

The Danes stopped laughing. "Are you serious?" Maarta asked.

"I am one hundred percent completely serious. Let's leave tonight."

"But we thought you were telling, kind of, a joke."

This threw me a little. "Would you rather leave tomorrow?"

Jan and Maarta exchanged a raised-eyebrow look, which I took to mean either "This guy is really daring" or "This guy is a total dork." Judging from the exchange that ensued, I'd put money on the latter.

"If you really want to go to the movie," Jan said, "why don't you just wait until they finish on Phi Phi Leh and go to work as an extra when they film in Phuket or Krabi?"

"That's not the point," I insisted. "The adventure is in going to a place where you aren't supposed to go. The charm is in living the novel backwards—going to an exclusive and secretive beach that also happens to be famous."

"The island is guarded like an army," Maarta said. "You'll never make it."

"Even if you do," Jan said, "what will you do when you get there?"

By this point, I felt like whipping out the novel and showing Jan and Maarta that they were saying the wrong lines. The issue was getting unnecessarily complicated. In the story, Françoise and Etienne were much more agreeable.

"I don't know what I'll do when I get there," I said. "Walk onto the set, I guess. You know, see what happens when I violate their community. Like in the book."

Jan and Maarta conferred for a moment in Danish, then turned back to me.

"Why are you doing this?" Maarta asked, with a tone of concern.

Since I thought I'd already answered that question, all I could do was stammer. Ultimately I changed the subject—to the relief, I think, of everyone present.

As I saw it, the reason why I'm doing this should have been obvious.

Or, even more accurately, the reason why I'm doing this should be irrelevant.

Now that I've had time to think about it, I'd say the motivation behind my mission has a lot to do with traveler's angst. I know I'm not the only one who feels it.

In his 1975 essay "The Loss of the Creature," Walker Percy attributes traveler's angst to the idea that our various destinations have been "appropriated by the symbolic complex which has already formed in the sightseer's mind."

In other words, the angst originates not in watching fat, Speedo-wearing German men defile once-pristine beaches; the angst comes from our own media-driven notions of how those beaches should be in the first place. We cannot hike the Himalayas without drawing comparisons to the IMAX film we saw last summer; we cannot taste wine on the Seine without recalling a funny scene from an old Meg Ryan movie; we cannot get lost in a South American jungle without thinking of the Gabriel García Márquez novel we read in college. It is the expectation itself that steals a bit of authenticity from the destinations we seek out.

Even the unexpected comes with its own set of expectations: In Garland's novel, Richard interprets what he sees at his beach utopia through the language of the Vietnam War movies he saw as a teenager.

Percy attempts to explain this phenomenon in his essay. "The highest point," he writes, "the term of the sightseer's satisfaction, is not the sovereign discovery of the thing before him; it is rather the measuring up of the thing to the criterion of the pre-formed symbolic complex."

The challenge this poses for the discerning traveler is that—here at the cusp of the next millennium—the mass media have not only monopolized the symbolic complex of wonder and beauty, they have recently upped the ante by an extra seventy-three coconut palms.

Thus, by storming *The Beach* at Phi Phi Leh, I hope to travel behind the curtain, to break out of the confines of the consumer experience by attempting to break in to the creation of the consumer experience.

I guess I could say that my mission is part of a greater struggle for individuality in the information age—an attempt to live outside the realm of who I'm supposed to be.

At least, that's what I would have told the Danes yesterday, had I had my wits about me.

Today I managed to avoid the Danes entirely. After sneaking a shower at a poolside changing room in Ton Sai, I set off to find a boat that would take me to Phi Phi Leh. Since stealth is an important consideration in my mission, choosing the right boat was a painfully difficult process.

Actually, choosing a boat wasn't really a choice at all, since my only realistic option was to hire out one of the longtail boats that transport people and goods among the islands. Considering that these boats cut through the water as gracefully as bulldozers (none of them have mufflers), my only real option was in finding a driver who sympathized with my cause and wouldn't try to cheat me.

Just before dinner, I found a seemingly earnest boat driver who agreed to take me to Phi Phi Leh for 2,500 baht. We leave in a few hours.

It is already well after dark, and I have stashed my backpack under one of the old fishing huts here at Lomudi. I have sealed some dry clothes, my passport, and a few traveler's checks into my plastic swimming bag. Andrew MacDonald's Italian leather screenplay binder, I'm afraid, was too heavy and will have to stay behind.

I pace the shoreline, killing time before the arrival of the longtail boat. Tiny bits of phosphorescence glow, star-blue, at the edge of the waves, just as they do in the book.

DAY SIX: JANUARY 22—STORMING *THE BEACH* AT PHI PHI LEH, CONTINUED

It occurs to me that I don't know the name of the small, sun-browned Thai man who sits astern from me in the darkness. I hate to write him off as a minor character—"Boat Driver No. 1"—so I have been thinking of him as Jimmy. He just seems like someone who should be named Jimmy: trustworthy, average, unassuming. Even in the dark, he wears a wide-brimmed cloth cap.

Neither of us has spoken since I waded out and climbed into the longtail back at Lomudi. Both of us know we are breaking the law—that Phi Phi Leh is patrolled by police speedboats for the duration of the movie shoot. I am hoping that our drop-off site at Loh Samah Bay (instead of Maya Bay, where the film set is located) isn't patrolled very closely at three-thirty in the morning.

Unlike most of the longtail operators I met in Ton Sai, Jimmy is a quiet, introspective man. When we were negotiating the trip yesterday afternoon, he nodded silently as I took out a dive-shop map of Phi Phi Leh and told him where I wanted to go. At first I thought he couldn't speak any English, but he cut me short when I tried to use my Thai phrase book on him. "Three in the morning, okay," he'd said. "I know Loh Saman Bay." I suspect he is working to support a wife and kids somewhere.

Twenty-five hundred baht—about $70—is no small sum, but I have written it off as an inevitability. Edmund Hillary had to hire Sherpas; I had to hire Jimmy. Perhaps in an effort to accommodate me—or, just as likely, in an effort to conceal me—Jimmy has spread a rattan mat out on the ribbed wooden floor of the boat. Lying on the mat, clutching my plastic bag, all I can see is the bright wash of stars above me. Oddly, the thumping rattle of the outboard motor makes the stars seem closer, like a glittering music video that hovers just over the boat.

My thoughts drift as the boat pushes through the water. I think about my first week in Thailand, when I was quick-dosing on an antimalaria drug called Lariam. Mild psychosis is a side effect of the drug, and—sure enough—on my second day of taking the pills I punched my fist through the door of my hotel room on Khao San Road. It was certainly one of the more violent acts of my adult life, and to this day I have trouble making sense of it. I don't know why I did it; all I remember was how I felt in the moments before security arrived to kick me out of the hotel. I felt not dread or shock, as one might expect, but rather a bemused, incongruous sense of wonder. Leonardo DiCaprio must feel the same way each morning when he wakes up and walks into a world that is staring at him.

"What the hell," I remember thinking to myself, "has happened to me?"

After about twenty minutes, Jimmy suddenly cuts the outboard motor. The silence leaves my ears ringing. I sit up on the mat uncertainly. "Are we there?" I whisper. The boat rocks as Jimmy crawls up to join me on the mat. He pushes his face right up in front of mine, and I see that he is holding his finger to his lips. He rests a hand on my shoulder and peers past the bow into the darkness.

We sit this way for about ten minutes. Strangely, I am not nearly as nervous as I was on the verandah of the Cape Panwha Resort Hotel. Swimming and hiking are tangible activities—far more cut-and-dried than schmoozing people and coaxing information out of them.

But swimming and hiking are not the only obstacles that re-main: Jimmy curses softly and moves back to the stern of the long-tail. Only then do I hear it: the sound of an approaching speedboat. Before long, our wooden boat is awash in the beam of a spotlight. I try to hide myself under the rattan mat, but it's useless.

Embarrassed more than anything, I lie awkwardly in the bot-tom of the longtail while Jimmy and someone on the speedboat yell back and forth in Thai. I absently note that the sealing oil on the hull boards has a pleasant, cedary scent.

Surprisingly, Jimmy yells in his apologetic tone for only a couple of minutes before the speedboat cuts its spotlight and leaves. "Okay," he says.

"It's okay?" I look out from my hiding place.

"Okay," Jimmy says.

I crawl out and move to the stern next to Jimmy. He rests his hand on my shoulder. "Okay?" he says for the third time. I give him the thumbs-up; he starts up the outboard and turns our boat 180 degrees. It's a couple of beats before I realize that we are headed back for Phi Phi Don.

"Isn't this where we just came from?" I ask, pointing my finger ahead into the darkness.

"Okay!" Jimmy says.

It takes me a good five minutes to undo the knot on my plastic swim bag. I'm not particularly proud of what I'm about to do, but I feel like I've come too far to give up now. I crawl back over to Jimmy and I shove the traveler's checks underneath his nose.

"Baksheesh," I say, gesturing back at where we last saw the speed-boat. Actually, I'm not even sure if "baksheesh" is the correct word for "bribe" in this part of the world. I feel a little doltish as I say it, like I'm trying to speak Spanish by throwing out English phrases in a Speedy Gonzalez voice.

Jimmy puts his hand on my shoulder in what I now take as a wiz-ened parental gesture. He looks down sympathetically at my trav-eler's checks. "Boat man, okay," he says. "Eye-land man, maybe okay. Movie man: no. Movie man not okay." He gently pushes my checks away.

"Yes! Okay!" I say, still waving the traveler's checks, but he just shakes his head.

The very trustworthiness that led me to hire Jimmy is now backfiring. Jimmy knows that, even if I manage to bribe my way past the various levels of Thai security on the island, a film crew with a $40 million budget will be less than impressed with my pres-ence. Jimmy is simply trying to save me the money and stress of going through this whole ordeal.

I have no way to convince him that that very ordeal is exactly what I want to experience. Which Speedy Gonzalez catch-phrases could make Jimmy grasp the pitch and moment that drive this en-terprise? What can I say that will make Jimmy appreciate the intri-cate, shadowlike ironies of travel culture? How can Jimmy come to understand a moral world where it's somehow vital to avoid eating at McDonald's in Manila, virtuous to intentionally bypass the *Mona Lisa* while at the Louvre, and noble to sleep in a ditch in Africa?

How can I convince him that this "mission" is not merely an-other variation of the hokey pokey?

My tongue is ineffectual in its pivots; Phi Phi Leh recedes in the darkness behind us.

We go through strange rituals to prove things to ourselves.

As we near our trash-encrusted starting point, I insist that Jimmy cut the engine early, so I can jump out of the longtail and swim the last two hundred meters back to the abandoned fishing village.

Since simple epiphany doesn't screen well in the test markets, I will tell people that I swam those two hundred meters with a defiant sense of triumph. I will tell them that each small step wading ashore was a giant leap for mankind. I will tell them that I walked through the Valley of the Shadow of Death, and that I feared no evil—for the Valley of the Shadow of Death will soon feature guided tours and a snack bar.

CONQUERING HALF DOME

Don George

ometimes we know a journey will be a grand adventure; the three-week expedition I made a few springs ago along Pakistan's avalanche-laden Karakoram Highway to enchanted Hunza comes to mind. Other times we know it will be a little one; on a business trip to Paris this January I was content with stumbling onto a wonderful ancient restaurant and a precious new park I'd never known about.

But sometimes our trips surprise us.

I recently returned from a five-day family excursion to Yosemite. It was supposed to be a little camping lark, but it turned out to be a much grander—and much more terrifying—adventure than I'd ever imagined.

The trip seemed innocuous enough: Our plan was to drive to Yosemite on a Saturday, spend the next three days camping and hiking to the top of Half Dome, then hike back to our car and drive home on the fifth day. This would require three days of four to six hours of hiking. The only moderately troublesome part would be the final ascent of Half Dome, that iconic granite thumb that juts almost nine thousand feet over the meadows and waterfalls and lesser crags of California's Yosemite Valley. But I had seen pictures of the cable-framed walkway that leads to the top of the mountain, and it didn't look too difficult. My wife and I felt confident that our eight-year-old son and twelve-year-old daughter could handle it.

So off we went. We made the winding drive from the San Francisco Bay area to Yosemite National Park in about four hours. It was a splendid day, all cotton-candy clouds against a county-fair sky. Eating carrots and apple slices in the car, we sped through the suburbs and into parched golden hills, and before we knew it we were off the main highway and passing hand-painted signs advertising red onions, fresh-picked tomatoes, almonds, peaches, and nectarines. Our eyes lingered on the weather-beaten stands, where we could see shiny red mounds of tomatoes and green mountains of watermelons, but we pressed on.

We reached Yosemite as the sun was setting, picked up our trail permit, pitched our tent, cooked a quick camp supper, and went to bed. Our plan was to get up early, hike more than halfway up—to the highest source of water on the Half Dome trail—and then camp, thereby minimizing the distance we would have to cover the next day before making our assault on the peak. If you're young and strong, or old and foolhardy, you can hike from Yosemite Valley to the top of Half Dome and back in a day. On previous trips to Yosemite we had met people who had done just that; they would leave at daybreak and plan to get back around dusk. But we wanted to take it easy on ourselves. We had also built in an extra day so that if for any reason we couldn't make Half Dome the first time, we would have a second chance, so we weren't in any hurry.

The next day took longer than we had planned, as it invariably does. By the time we had gotten the kids rousted and had packed up our tents and ground covers and cooking gear, it was about ten A.M. and the sun was high and hot in the sky.

We set off along the John Muir Trail, winding into the rocks and pines. The first section of this trail is still a little like Disneyland, and you pass people in flip-flops and even occasionally high heels,

sweating and puffing and swigging fresh-off-the-supermarket-shelf
bottles of Crystal Geyser. After about a half-hour's stroll you reach
a picturesque bridge with a fantastic foaming view of the Merced
River cascading over the rocks; here you find a neat wooden bathroom, and a water fountain that is the last source of water that
doesn't have to be filtered. The flip-flops and high heels turn back
with a grateful sigh at this point, and the few people you do pass
hereafter on the trail exchange friendly nods and greetings and the
smug satisfaction of getting into the real Yosemite.

Then you walk and you walk and you walk, stepping heavily
over rocks, kicking up clouds of dirt that settle on your legs and
socks and boots. Occasionally you'll be cooled by a shower of
water trickling from high rocks right onto the trail, or by a breeze
blowing unexpectedly when you turn a corner. But for the most
part you step and mop your brow and swat at mosquitoes in the
patches of shade and take swigs of water, careful to roll the water
in your mouth as your long-ago football coach taught you, until
you're surprised by a dazzling quilt of purple flowers, or a tum-
bling far-off torrent shining white and silver and blue in the sun,
and you stop and munch slowly on Balance bars and dried apples
and nectarines and notice how the sunlight waterfalls through the
branches of the trees.

After four hours we reached the halfway point at Little Yosemite
Valley. It's a popular camping spot, with loosely demarcated camping areas—framed by fallen tree trunks, with rock-outlined fire circles and tree stumps for tables and stools—plus a resident ranger,
an outhouse, and easily accessible water in the form of the Merced
River fast-flowing by. We hadn't really prepared for the trip physically, and were already grimy and sweaty and exhausted. On top of
that, we had received conflicting information about where exactly
the last source of water on the trail would be, so rather than press
further up, we decided to stop there for the night. Tomorrow we
would rise early and climb Half Dome.

We had planned to get up at six and be on the trail by eight.
Again, reality intruded, and we got up at eight and set out for

Half Dome around nine-thirty. This was not wise. We had never hiked this trail before and didn't know how long it would take or what obstacles it would present; besides, we'd been told that the best time to climb Half Dome is the morning, since clouds tend to come in by the afternoon. Weather changes quickly in the mountains, and you don't want to be anywhere near the summit when the clouds come in, rangers had said. The mountain is a magnet for lightning. All Half Dome hikers are explicitly told that if they see rain clouds on the horizon, they shouldn't attempt the ascent. Lightning strikes the dome at least once a month—and at least a few careless people every year. Even the cables that run up the final eight hundred feet of the slope are lightning magnets.

So we wound up through the trees as fast as we could. We passed through deep-shadowed, pine-needled stretches of forest path like places in a fairy tale, and we emerged onto sun-blasted stretches of rock that offered amazing views of the surrounding peaks—and of Half Dome towering into the sky.

We reached the base of Half Dome, after a final, extremely arduous half-hour zigzag trek up a series of massive steps cut out of the stone, at about one P.M. Clouds were massing to the east and to the west, but we pressed on. A motley pile of gloves left by previous climbers lay at the spot where the cable walkway began. We chose gloves we liked, grabbed hold of the cables, and began to haul ourselves up.

This is when our little lark turned into a grand adventure.

In the pictures we had seen before the trip, the cable route didn't look all that daunting. Basically, they showed a gangplank-like walkway, with thick steel cables running along the sides, that stretched up the slope of the mountain. In the pictures, hikers with day packs strode confidently up the slope as if they were out for a Sunday stroll.

Somehow the pictures hadn't prepared me for the reality. The cables are set about four feet off the ground and are about three feet apart. As a further aid to climbers, wooden planks connected to the posts that support the cables are set across the mountain path at an interval of about every four to five feet. This is not as comforting as it sounds.

I'd read before the trip that the path slopes up at an angle of about sixty degrees. I had pictured that angle and had mentally traced a line along the living room wall. That doesn't seem too steep, I had said to myself.

Beware estimates made in the comfort of your living room. From the plushness of my couch, with a soothing cup of steaming tea in my hand, sixty degrees hadn't seemed too steep—but in the sheer, slippery, life-on-the-line wildness of Yosemite, it seemed *real* steep. I looked at the cables, and I looked at the sloping pate of the mountain, and I thought, This is a really stupid way to die. Why, I continued, am I consciously choosing to risk my life like this? What's the point? All it would take would be one slip, a hand loosened from the cables. I could already see myself sliding down the face of Half Dome, grabbing frantically at the smooth surface, thudding-scraping-bumping along the rock until, if I was really lucky, I managed to grab a bloody finger-stub handhold on the rock face or, if I wasn't really lucky, I just slipped off the face of the rock, with all the assembled climbers gasping and screaming and my wife and kids yelling, not knowing what to do, how to prevent my fall, and then there would be a brief flight before bone-crushing oblivion. Hopefully, I thought, I will pass out before contact and die relatively peacefully.

All this flashed through my mind as I stood at the base of the cables. "What are we waiting for?" my daughter asked impatiently.

"We're waiting until we grow wings," I wanted to say.

But she was ready—ah, youth, that hath no fear—and began to scramble up the slope. And then my wife went. And then my son started—a little apprehensively, being eight years old and all. But he was on his way. None of them seemed to understand that what we were doing was inherently suicidal!

Still, they were gone, and there really was nothing to do but grab hold of the cables and start to pull myself up this suddenly stupid and hateful mountain. The whole thing seemed so absurd—dying to prove what point? Hadn't I evolved beyond this kind of macho risk-taking decades ago?

Somehow the fact that all kinds of people, from baseball-capped teens to silver-haired seniors, had scrambled up that day and were now headed down the very walkway I was staring up, and that numerous others were on the face of the mountain, in mid-ascent, a dozen yards above me, scrambling up even as I quaked—somehow this was of no comfort.

I was scared. I wasn't exactly convinced I was going to die—I thought I had a chance of making it alive—but I felt I was consciously subjecting myself to an experience that could actually kill me. This was my idea of a vacation? What ever happened to full-service beach resorts and little cocktails with bright paper parasols?

But we started. My first few steps were leaden. My hiking boots kept slipping; my arms, which hadn't done anything all day, suddenly felt dead tired and couldn't haul up the dead weight of my body. In a classic case of self-fulfilling prophecy, I kept slipping and sliding, just as I'd thought I would. I was utterly miserable.

One thing you should never do—or at least one thing *I* should never do—when climbing Half Dome is look around at the view. The view is what can kill you. You stop and brush your brow with your sleeve and your eyes steal a look to the left and whoa! It's a long, long way down. Your view drops right off the side of the cliff to green trees the size of matchsticks, and postage-stamp meadows. You don't want to see this and you definitely don't want to think about it. I swayed and held on to the cables and stayed frozen, letting other climbers brush by me, until the dizziness and the wave-swells in my stomach stopped. My mouth was drier than I could ever remember it being before. My arms ached.

After about fifteen wooden planks, my son and I paused. My wife, Kuniko, looked down from a perch a few posts ahead. "How are you feeling, Jeremy? Do you want to keep going, or do you want to stop?"

Say you want to stop, Jeremy, I prayed. For the love of God, tell her you want to stop!

He was undecided. I was probably green in the face. "How are you doing, honey?" Kuniko asked, concern creasing her face.

"I don't know," I said.

We looked around and saw bulbous black clouds blowing swiftly in. "Maybe we should head down," Kuniko said.

Yes! Yes! a little voice inside me said.

"I want to keep going!" Jenny said.

"No, I think we should head down," Kuniko said.

"I think so, too," I said, whining with as much authority as I could muster. "I don't like the look of those clouds."

So, much to Jenny's loud disappointment, we slid down—which was almost as terrifying as hauling up, except that now your body was helping gravity pull you to your death.

At one point I really did completely slip—my feet just went out from under me, I landed with a sacroiliac-smacking thud, and before I knew what was happening I began to slide down the face of the mountain. Luckily I managed to stomp the sole of one boot squarely against the iron post that supported the cable, thus stopping my fall. Mortality had never seemed nearer.

I lay on the side of the mountain for a few minutes, trying to slow my heart, waiting for my arms to stop shaking.

"Are you all right?" people asked as they stepped gingerly by me.

Then I said to myself, Just go down slowly, one by one, and I did. And suddenly I was at the bottom, stepping off the last plank onto level rock, and I was sitting down and sluggishly taking off my gloves and Jenny was asking, "Dad, are you okay?"

The hike back to camp seemed about ten times longer than the morning's walk. My head was black-clouded with doubts and fears about attempting the climb again the next day. What a stupid way to die, I kept thinking. But at the same time I felt that I had to do it.

The kids were going to do it, everyone was doing it—I couldn't say, Gee, I think I'll just stay down here and watch.

I tossed and turned for hours that night, thinking about that blasted slippery-slope cable walkway. I knew the problem was virtually all mental, that I was psyching myself into failure. It didn't matter. I couldn't magically find the switch in my mind.

After a fractured sleep we woke up and retraced our path of the previous day. I wish I could say that everything had changed, that I had come to peace with the idea of climbing Half Dome and had found a deep pool of confidence in myself, but I hadn't. I had made up my mind to climb Half Dome, but I was fundamentally unsettled about it.

Still, everything seemed a little more propitious this time. We got an earlier start and so we were passed by only a handful of day hikers, which felt good. The sky was a broad expanse of blue, with only a few puffs of white here and there. I was hiking strongly, and we covered the same territory in about an hour less than the previous day. We reached the arduous rock steps at about ten-thirty and were at the glove-heaped base of Half Dome by eleven. We paused to take some deep swigs of water and eat energy bars, and then we were ready.

Jeremy and Jenny set off first, fearlessly. Kuniko and I had decided that I would go up next, so that if I slipped, she might be able to help me. I swapped the thick leather gloves I had used the day before for lighter cloth gloves that permitted more feeling in my fingers. That seemed to help some.

I knew my problem was all mental, but that knowledge wasn't helping much. The climb was still terrifying. But this time I thought: If you just focus on each step, you'll be okay. Don't think about the slope to the left or the right. Don't think about what's beneath you or how much more you still have to go. Just focus on each step, step by step.

I took my first step and pulled myself up by the cables. Took another step and did the same. Took another step and I was at the first wooden plank. I repeated the process, planting my foot slowly, making sure it was secure on the rock face before using my arms, then pulling myself up to make the next step. Three steps and I had reached the second plank. It seemed easier than yesterday.

Gradually my body relaxed. The tension left my arms and they didn't ache. The fear left my legs and they were more flexible; I was finding secure sole-holds in the rock. I didn't slip, and I was learning to focus my breathing and energy in discrete spurts of arm-pulling.

The trick, I thought, is to restrict the world to the small plot of rock in front of me and the cables on either side, to extend my arm about ten inches up the cable, like this, grab tight hold of it, secure my grip, like this, say, "Okay, now!" and pull—ugh! and up!—and then pause awhile to catch my breath and coil my energy, and then repeat the process, hauling myself up, step by step.

I reached the point where we had stopped the day before and dimly recorded that it had been much easier so far. If I could just focus on each rung.

I kept pulling myself up, foothold then handhold, plank by plank. At one point, with a quick glance up, I realized that Jenny and Jeremy, who seemed to have sprinted up the slope, had disappeared. They were already running freely around the broad summit. Somewhere inside me, I registered the fact that I was going to make it, too.

There were still a few tricky places, where a two-foot fissure appeared between the part of the trail I was on and the spot where the trail continued. Here I had to simultaneously pull myself over the displacement and up the slope, a doubly difficult and slippery task. But by focusing precisely on what I was doing—Plant the foot there, make sure it's secure; okay, now pull yourself up on the cable, move your other foot forward, pull yourself up again—I was able to make it without slipping.

At one particularly steep step, I felt my arms begin to falter and in mid-stride I felt my body begin to sway backward, as if my arms weren't going to be able to pull my body up. Death flickered in my brain and in a millisecond I thought, You've *got* to pull yourself up, and the adrenaline zapped through my arms like lightning and I forced myself—brain and arms pulling together—to the next rung. The prospect of death had glimmered, but it hadn't paralyzed me as the day before.

After about twenty-five minutes I reached the point where the summit begins to taper off and the angle eases. Another ten wooden planks and the end of the ascent was in sight. I almost ran the last few steps, so exhilarated to have made it to the top. Jenny and Jeremy saw me from their post at the peak and came jumping over the summit. We gave each other big bear hugs. "You made it, Dad!" they said.

In another few minutes Kuniko came to the top, grinning widely. We explored the summit, took in the extraordinary 360-degree panorama of snow-capped peaks, piney slopes, glistening waterfalls, and green meadows far below. And we felt on top of the world.

We shared a celebratory chocolate bar I had stuffed in my pocket, and after a half-hour of snapping photos and walking to the extreme compass points of the peak, we heard thunder to the east and saw black clouds massing, moving with deceptive speed our way.

We shared a huge family hug and set off.

Jenny and Jeremy fairly skipped down the slope—or at least that's the way it seemed to me. I slipped and slid—three times I slowly let myself down on the seat of my pants from one rung to the next—but never lost control, and within about a half-hour I was standing on level rock again, tossing my gloves into the heap, my heart pounding wildly and my head splitting-spinning with the triumph.

I had done it! I had overcome all those fear-boulders that we throw up in front of ourselves, that keep us from doing the things we are capable of doing. We had climbed Half Dome, and from now on, whenever we looked at that stunning granite jut from afar, we would have the joyful and astounding knowledge that we had once stood on that very peak, looking down on the whole world around us. We had conquered the slippery slope of Half Dome, and we would have much to celebrate that night.

It seemed symbolic of so many things in life, and I was just beginning to enjoy the light-footed walk back to camp and to feel success suffuse my body from the top of my head to the tips of my fingers and toes, when Jeremy turned to me and said, "Dad, can we do this again next year?"

LOOKING FOR MR. WATSON

Bill Belleville

Just minutes after I leave my home in northeastern Florida to drive down to the Everglades to search for Mr. Watson, I zip past a wood stork. It is standing at the side of the entrance ramp to the busy interstate, looking at once noble and woefully misplaced—like a lonely chess piece on a checkerboard.

The Glades with its vast subtropical wilderness is a good five hours away at the other end of the state. But the stork is here anyway. It is knee-deep in a drainage ditch—cars whizzing by on their way to Disney World without a notion of whatever it can be—and it is doing what wading birds like it have been doing in Florida since before anything like a human or a theme park arrived. It is sweeping its curved beak through the cloudy water, hoping to connect with something alive there.

My friend Terry, an old college pal who will paddle the other end of our canoe, misses the bird altogether, not because he is obtuse but because he lives on the opposite rim of the country and his senses are already saturated with local exotica. It will take a mighty dose of melodrama to jar him.

"Wood stork," I say, pointing with one hand and driving us onto Interstate 4 with the other.

"Is that a rare bird?" asks Terry earnestly, and I tell him that it is. I say I am both heartened to see it and disturbed that it has ranged so far outside its natural home. Not so long ago, this bird with the head that seems fire-charred—this "iron head"—was so integral to the Glades it was considered a barometer of the ecosystem's health. But the Everglades are on the brink, have been for a while now. The wood stork is trying to roll with this change, ranging far outside its historic territory.

Terry is from three decades' worth of my past, a fraternity brother and ex-jock, a reformed party animal like myself seeking redemption in the solitude of distant natural places. Individually, we have struggled to unravel the jumble of civilized threads to get at the nugget of ourselves buried inside. From its discovery, we have come to learn this nature offered solace, living Whitmanesque lessons in the values of singularity and tolerance. So Terry hikes east of Los Angeles, back into places like Death Valley and Borrego Springs, and camps there. I live in Florida and kayak on any wild body of water I can find—the St. Francis Dead River, the Wekiva, the Mosquito Lagoon.

Now we are headed together to the Glades, to canoe deep into its distant western boundary in a hunt for the "Watson Place," a pre-Columbian Calusa midden mound. It is a forty-acre composite of shell and stunted tropical foliage, a thread between us and the time-wronged desperado who once lived there.

Like the Glades and the wood stork, we are on the brink, aging jocks ranging beyond what is safe and known. In this way, we sweep through the experiences that still lie before us, hoping to connect with something alive and essential. All we are sure of is that we have come to appreciate wilderness for the way it lays itself down on the soul.

Unlike other men who seek solace in this way, we don't carry traditional props; we are not hunters or dapper L. L. Bean campers. I carry a set of old binoculars to watch for avifauna, but the truth is, beyond raptors and tropical wading birds, I'm lost unless a species appears clear and unobstructed in the scope. As for our gear, it is jerry-rigged and stuffed into duffels and garbage bags and plastic buckets. Instead of giant foil pouches of official freeze-dried camp food, I have brought noodles-in-a-cup and tins of tuna and chicken. We have granola bars that look and taste like Oreos compressed into little rectangles. I imagine that Jack Kerouac, when he went up on Desolation Peak out west, might have packed like this.

But I do place a lot of significance on a compass and the correct nautical map to lead me in and out of untamed places. Each tiny paper squiggle, each logarithmic degree corresponds to something tangible—an oxbow or bar or tiny islet. Once ground-truthed, these coordinates can sometimes nudge the senses, linking near-meaningless geographic names to remarkable places on the landscape. Ahead in the Glades, my map promises Pavilion and Buzzard keys, Chokoloskee and Rabbit Key passes, Lostman's and Chatham rivers. I have tucked both compass and map inside a waterproof seal-lock bag I will carry on my lap when we finally reach our canoe. Also in the bag is a paperback copy of Peter Matthiessen's novel *Killing Mr. Watson*.

As I drive south on I-95, this odd mix of essential items amuses me, as if the immediacy of the adventure will require me to be ready at any time to understand direction, latitude, and literary metaphor. But *Killing Mr. Watson* and its sequels make up the thread that has relinked Terry and me after all these years, something real our adult selves respond to that goes far beyond the retelling of old locker-room jokes and keg party stories. In *Watson, Lost Man's River,* and *Bone by Bone,* Matthiessen uses the real life and death of renegade cane-grower Ed Watson to re-create a wild place and a maverick culture particular to southwest Florida. But if his books are about a vanished time, they are also about the social evolution of perception, about how the realities of a richly embroidered moment—or a mystifying personality—can be spun down into simple-minded slogans. Time has treated both the Glades and the strong, passionate man who was E. J. Watson this way, turning the Everglades into a swamp and E.J. into "Bloody Watson."

Like me, Terry had read the Matthiessen trilogy on Watson's life and demise. Like me, he felt a kinship with Watson—a complex soul who existed far outside the monotone of local myth. The connection was profound, personal: During our jock-frat era, we were both regarded as bad actors, guys who might do most anything at any time. We fought in bars, we drank to the point of temporary psychosis. We were confused, and when we both quit sports halfway through school, we became chaotic. Terry was fast and good with his fists and seldom lost a fight; I was strong and slow and punched in doors, old hardwood ones. We were considered "dangerous," and when not being dangerous, we were dead drunk.

That was a long time ago, of course, and we had each learned a lot since then—though our old acquaintances, now businessmen and lawyers and doctors, weren't quite convinced. I have been a writer for twenty-five years, choosing subjects that champion the put-upon earth and the people who care for it. Later in life, Terry decided to become a therapist. Now we laugh at the disjunction between our old personas and our current lives—and at the doubting frat brothers with whom we have been out of touch for years—but the truth is that, deep down, the old realities still hurt.

Certainly, Watson had been hurt, too. In *Bone*, which provides an astounding insight into how the wounds of childhood shaped the adult Watson, a young Ed finds himself at an emotional crossroads: "I knew my life had lost its purchase. The future was flying away forever, like a dark bird crossing distant woods. Not knowing which way to turn, with no one to confide in, I hurried onward." Terry and I had hurried onward, too, but we eventually prevailed as adults—not because we were better people than Ed Watson, but because we lived in a different time. We had learned just enough about psychology to understand the grace of forgiving ourselves.

Matthiessen confesses to having "reimagined" Ed Watson's life. But he maintains that the retelling probably "contains much more of the truth of Mr. Watson than the lurid and popularly accepted 'facts.' " If I were honest, I would admit that searching for Mr. Watson was a way of reimagining ourselves; by visiting Watson's still-intact natural world, we might find atonement in the complexities of our own lives.

But searching for Mr. Watson is not a walk in the woods. The Glades are a sprawling subtropical territory larger than the state of Delaware; ranger stations and interpretive boardwalks dot the outer edges, but inside, sawgrass stretches to the east, and mud-rooted mangroves to the west, leaving little dry land between. It is, as Matthiessen has observed, a "labyrinthal wilderness," and its sheer lack of accessibility has been the secret to keeping it so. Or, as Speck Daniel puts it in *Lost Man:* "What the hell kind of tourist would beat his way three to four miles back up a mangrove river to take a picture of some raggedy ol' lonesome place?"

Down we go on the notorious I-95 into Miami, the car-jacking, drug-shuttling, neon-rocker-paneled, middle-finger-in-the-air conduit, finally turning west near the Latino bustle of Calle Ocho. From here, we drive through block after block of urban landscape that barely a half-century ago was freshwater marl prairie, bristling with great fields of sawgrass. Today it is colonized by espresso shops and Santería *botánicas*, 7-Elevens and Texacos hugging every available square inch. "Man," says Terry, shaking his head, "talk about sensory overload." I run this gauntlet for an hour until we are safely west of the city, headed out across the northern boundary of the Glades. Open space and dwarf cypress and sawgrass command the geography now, with great white cumulus billowing overhead, fed by the wet, feral terrain. There may be two more contrary realities this close to each other somewhere else in the world, but I'm not aware of them.

Now we are safely atop the Tamiami Trail (that's "Tampa-to-Miami," condensed). It is the road that split the Glades in two when it was built, water-spitting draglines and dredges crunching through the lime rock in the 1920s. Water-driven, the Glades are at the mercy of the kindness of strangers upstream. And this trail we are driving serves as a massive dam across it. The lazy but deliberate sheet flow of water that once swept down across southern Florida from just below Orlando is now squeezed under us through a series of mechanical gates, giant Erector Set–like devices built for flood control. Man plays God with the upland rainfall and water now, and as gods go, he has proved to be a baleful, selfish sort, a minor deity with more ambition than wisdom.

Soon, we arrive at SR 29, the narrow southerly road that trails past "Panther Crossing" signs and dead-ends six miles south in Everglades City, a fishing village now being transformed into an RV tourist mecca on the far western tip of the park. The fresh water sweeping down from the easterly sawgrass meadows meets the coastal mangrove buffer a few miles inland from here. Everglades City is the jumping-off point for our quest.

Clinging to shards of a hardscrabble pioneer culture still tended by a handful of stone crabbers and mullet fishermen, this little town on the edge of the park now teeters precariously toward a fun-house-mirror version of ecotourism. Anything alive, it seems, is fair game: Airboat rides and canned "safaris" and "jungle boat tours" ("Gators Guaranteed!") are everywhere, as are boutiquelike souvenir shops painted peach and green, with incongruous names like "Jungle Erv's." The natural rhythm—of place and people—has been squeezed and massaged and marketed in a heavy-handed attempt to catch up to the trendiness that has homogenized much of Florida's coast.

As I watch a gaggle of tourists board an air-conditioned Park Service pontoon boat for a guided excursion onto Chokoloskee Bay, my only thought is how white and spanking clean everyone is. The outlaw plume hunters and gator poachers, turtlers and contraband smugglers—the bona fide heirs to the Watson legend and time—have died, trickled away, tried to grow up. *Lost Man*, set in the past, foretells this gentrification: "Beaten flat, [it] would disappear beneath the tar and concrete, the tourist courts and house trailers, the noisy cars of vacationers with their red faces, sun hats, candy-colored clothes."

We are eager to get to Watson's Place, but it is now late in the day. Faced with spending a night in a motel here or paying an outfitter to ferry us and our canoe out to the old Watson mound by motorboat, we choose the latter, planning to use the time saved to more thoroughly explore the creeks and sloughs of the backcountry on our five-day paddle back.

A slight young man named Justin, wearing white rubber fisherman's boots, has brought us to the threshold of the Watson site in his go-fast fiberglass outboard, expertly twisting and turning the wheel behind the center console to deliver us through the lookalike puzzle of mangrove islands and tidal rivers.

Justin's new girlfriend has come along for the ride, and on our trip here, I overhear her asking him who this Watson was. Either Justin has not read the Matthiessen books or he doesn't feel like re-creating the complexities of them. He gives her the shorthand folk version, the one locals have been giving to tourists for years. "He was a guy who lived back up here and grew cane—and when it came time to pay his hired help, he would kill them instead."

The Watson Place is one of several dozen primitive campsites in this odd park; most are docklike "chickees" built where there is simply no dry land to be found. But a few, like this one, are high mounds of shell and bone, constructed first by the Calusas and later colonized by farmers, fishermen, and assorted renegades. It rises from the dark tannin of the Chatham River like a high natural bluff, fringed at one edge with a thick cover of snake plant—a hardy, spiky ornamental that settlers cultivated in their yards in Florida a century and more ago. Snake plant is an odd relief, back here in this mud-driven monoculture of red and black mangrove, an exotic harbinger of other surprises yet to come.

It is four-thirty P.M. and the early spring sun is dipping down toward the top of the tall black mangroves just across the Chatham River; Justin is anxious to get back to the marina at Everglades City before dark. We quickly unload our canoe and supplies on a narrow wooden dock. The ferocious saltwater-marsh mosquitoes—"swamp angels," to the settlers—seem to be marshaling their forces for sundown; their humming from back in the tangle of truncated tropical jungle at the edge of the clearing sounds like low-grade static. It is early April, at the tail end of an El Niño winter in which a few mildly chilly months have barely kept a lid on the hatch of blood-sucking insects. We are as concerned about getting our mosquito-flapped tents set up as Justin is to get home to his warm bed.

As Terry and I sort through our pile of gear, Justin cranks the motor up, eases his boat away from the dock, and disappears in a meringue of froth around the corner of Chatham Bend. I think of Ed Watson's old gasoline launch, the *Brave,* and how he puttered slowly down the Chatham to Chokoloskee Island in it one last time on October 24, 1910, the distinctive *pop-pop-pop* of the ancient motor announcing his arrival to a gathering mob of islanders.

Finally alone now, we establish priorities: First we douse ourselves with repellent; then we hurry to set up camp on the scant half-acre of open, weedy land. An entangled jungle has colonized the rest of the forty-acre mound, slender trunks and boughs of native gumbo-limbo and machineel gridded together like spiderwebs, along with lime and guava and avocado left from the Watson era, all as feral now as a herd of wild hogs.

After I work up a light sweat assembling my tent, I stop and look around, letting the reality of being atop Watson's homestead settle in. The quiet back here is complete, so full it seems to have measurable weight. At the edge of the Chatham River, several large red mangroves, bowlike roots arching into the oyster-shell mud, frame the water. The sun dips down below them to the west. Terry asks, "You think ol' Ed trimmed back those mangroves to give him a good view of the sunset?" I figure he probably did.

The Watson Place is the largest shell mound for miles in any direction. The Calusas shucked oysters and clams here, discarded bones from bear and panther, manatee and deer, for at least two thousand years. Spiritually complex and savvy about nature, they understood its power—especially the water-thrashing energy of tropical hurricanes—and did all they could to (literally) rise above it.

In his time, Ed Watson painstakingly hauled timber in by boat to build a substantial two-story frame farmhouse here, flanking it with flowering red royal poinciana trees. It was said to be the finest house of its type within the great uncivilized wash between Fort Myers and Key West. After Watson's death, the house was used by hunters and fishermen and squatters. Hurricane Donna damaged it in 1960, and the Park Service—looking for any excuse to clear old private structures from public land—razed it soon afterward.

I ask Terry if he's ready to look for Ed's homesite in the jungle; he is. It is Friday night now, a weekend evening in the middle of the Everglades, darkness coming fast. A large, unseen gator bellows a mating call from the edge of the Chatham—or perhaps it is a territorial warning. I can't imagine being in a place more removed from the superficial collegiate atmosphere in which Terry and I met. He must think the same of me, for we both exist far outside the social convention that first bound us.

Off we go on a narrow trail, back into the wall of stunted tropical foliage, ducking under low branches. Terry has on long pants and a T-shirt sporting an E.T.-like extraterrestrial; a large Bowie-type knife is strapped to his belt. I am in jeans and T-shirt, wearing a baseball cap that reads "Jung." The sun barely penetrates the thick canopy back here—by day, it is sepia-tinted; in the early evening, it is downright gloomy. At the edge of the trail lie a skull and skeleton, a small mammal of some sort, maybe one of the wild-eyed raccoons I have been seeing clattering about on the bow roots, dark stripes bleached almost white by salt and sun. We are in the midst of the insect static now, and despite our repellent, the swamp angels blanket us, hanging on for dear life, waiting for the chemical to wear off. Settlers like Watson virtually lived in the black smoke of smudge pots, which they kept burning day and night; when they had window screens, they rubbed crankcase oil on them to keep the insects from clogging the grid.

Just off the trail, I see what look like knee-high concrete boundary markers, scattered haphazardly. I look closer and realize they are the original foundations Watson built his fine house upon, raising it a couple of feet for ventilation. They are made of tabby—crushed lime and shells of the sort the Calusas left behind. From the elegant trunks of the gumbo-limbo trees, tissue-thin patches of red-amber bark curl like the skin of a sunburnt tourist; pineapple-like bromeliads live tucked away in the crooks.

Just when the buzzing seems enough to drive us mad, I notice a mysterious structure peeking out from the thick jungle just ahead. It is made of the same tabby as the foundations, except it is rect-angular, as large as a room-sized funeral vault. The Park Service has built a wooden cap atop it to keep people and animals from falling in. "It's Ed's cistern," I say, "where he gathered rainwater." Weathered by a century of tropical heat and rain, the tabby walls look more like the sides of an ancient Spanish mission. A gumbo-limbo far bigger than any of the others grows from a corner of the cistern, happy for the fresh water still inside. Nearby, Ed and his family slept and dreamed. What of?

The swamp angels, perhaps a mutant breed, are starting to bite now, and we move as fast as we can back to our camp. I fire up my gas lantern and an easy breeze picks up from the Chatham, enough to hold the insects at bay. We concoct a dinner swill over our one-burner stove, and as we eat, the scarlet sky turns gray, then full black. Fireflies, a rarity in Chem-Lawned Florida nowadays, dart at the edge of the jungle with their green-blue light. I look overhead to see Venus hanging just under the sliver of new moon; minutes later, the sky is as full of stars and constellations as any I have ever seen. I turn down the lantern and Terry and I sit in silence, watch-ing meteors streak through the darkness like distant flares, as if to underscore our own sense of awe. From the Chatham, mullet leap and splash, joyous ghosts water-skipping in the night.

The night is warm, so I use my sleeping bag as a mattress. The bright stars burn a soft glow through the thin fabric of my tent. From the river, I hear a deep humanlike exhalation, the sound of a bottlenose dolphin surfacing to blow. From back up the trail, a chuck-will's-widow calls its own name over and over, waiting for an answer that doesn't come. Everywhere, unseen critters rustle and gurgle in the isolation of the Everglades darkness. Instead of distressing me, this has a remarkably calming effect, as if the mound itself is exuding the timeless exhalations of all who have come here before me: the Calusas, the renegades, Ed Watson. And now, into the collective dreams of the mound I also go.

The new morning is fresh, dew on the tent and the wild grass in the clearing. After a quick breakfast, we walk the edge of the jungle, finding what must have been a farm plow in the weeds; its metal wheels are dark with rust. A few yards in is the frame of an old truck, rubber and wood long gone. Terry takes my photograph sitting on it. Out near the shell-encrusted shore of the river, we see the 150-gallon iron kettle where Watson boiled his cane; it's still mounted inside a waist-high concrete-and-brick pedestal. Instead of cane syrup, the kettle holds stagnant rainwater, green with algae, tadpoles swirling back and forth just under the surface. I run my hand on the concrete rimming the kettle; someone once took the trouble to round and smooth the edges, a remarkable act of civilization in such a place.

Watson, as Matthiessen wisely guessed, was ambitious, a person who cared about how the world was ordered around him. He was, after all, the only white man to live on this mound more than a year or two; he farmed it for nearly two decades before he was killed in 1910. I reach down to the ground, pick up a piece of metal, maybe a ladle, iron corroded beyond recognition. Watson's presence here is nearly palpable. I think of him laying down this tool ninety years ago on the smooth concrete rim, going down to Chokoloskee to take care of business, just for the afternoon.

We have spent three days here now, using the Watson mound as a base to explore local waters, feeling our way into tight, canopied creeks, including one that wasn't even on our map. Back there, we paddled for almost a mile, until the tide finally ebbed out from under us, reshaping our path into an impassable slough of foliage and roots. We rested, drank tepid water and ate granola bars, listened to the coon oysters spit, watched the mangrove crabs nervously scuttle over the mud like black mice. Terry, gracious, named the creek Belleville. From there, I watched as my first swallowtail kite of the season, newly arrived from Brazil, joined the frigates soaring overhead like untethered origami. In three days, we have encountered only five other boats, and all were fishermen hunkered down, coming to or going from Florida Bay.

Each night on the mound, the chuck-will's-widow has sung his sweet sad song, a four-note serenade of all he has ever seen and can't fully say, and the stars have fallen, inexorably marking mortal time. One evening, I slept next to the water and Venus rose under a crescent moon, setting down a trail of pale light that connected me to it, a planet too distant to imagine, yet able to touch me in these Everglades.

Now, with our canoe loaded to the gunnels, we are pushing away from the mound one last time for our two-day paddle back to Chokoloskee and Everglades City. Terry began to sketch and paint several years ago, waiting for each image to "push" its way out, allowing his unseen self to become less so on paper, healing old wounds. I try to do much the same with words, a means to remind me of what I have experienced. And now, in our coming back together after all this time, we hold on to the tangible around us, discuss it with great joy, and then let it sink back into ourselves, waiting to see what it will finally reveal.

Upstream we go on this fine river, one eye on the tree line and the sky above, the other on the map and compass. Mangroves surround us. From a distance, they seem like a diminutive northern forest, but seen from up close, the land under them is ephemeral, water and detritus-fueled mud, rich nursery grounds for the same critters— redfish, trout, snook, tarpon—the fishermen hunt. Neither fully land nor fully water, this place has long claimed a hold on the imagination of visitors, spooking them with its mystique.

The early Spanish conquistadors, at once superstitious and brutal, first charted this territory as La Laguna del Espíritu Santo, the Lagoon of the Holy Spirit. As we bear down today against a building wind and an outgoing tide, I think of this place in that way, a terrain with a pulse and a heart, able to breathe. Right now, its breath is sun-warmed mangrove leaves and sea purslane, a dusky perfume of salt and chlorophyll and sap.

Up the Chatham we go, following the more narrow branch that meanders to the west, once almost running aground on a shoal that mysteriously appears in the middle of the river where the chart says eight feet of water should be. Instead of working our way north through Last Huston and Huston bays, we sneak around the lee sides of mangrove islands, crouching as close to shore as we can get to avoid the wind-driven thrash of the waves that pile up in two-foot-high whitecaps. Sometimes the water is so clear we can see blue crabs scuttling across the seagrass bottom, needlefish flashing iridescent at the surface. Other times, it is soil-brown, a moving organic soup. As I paddle, I pay careful attention to direction, to the spin of a little sliver of metal locked inside glass, gauging how the world of mangrove and marl unfolds around us, curious to see how it matches up to my nautical chart.

Suddenly the air is filled with sulfur-wing butterflies fresh from a new spring hatch. We paddle through them for a mile until they vanish as quickly as they appeared, a rain shower of butterflies. Up to the southerly forks of Huston Bay we go, and then down again into an unnamed branch leading to the Huston River. It empties us into House Hammock Bay, named for an old clan that once home-steaded here, collecting buttonwood mangrove for charcoal as Watson did, fishing and hunting.

House Hammock is barely two feet deep; as I dip and draw, my paddle touches mud as often as not. Ospreys are nesting every-where; the chicks are just large enough to rise up and squawk now from their huge beds of twigs. Mother birds fly over us, small mul-let in their talons, headed for home. In the distance, gators, their bodies as black and corrugated as truck tires, thrash in the water and mud to flee this odd apparition, a log with two moving heads.

We spend the night on the wooden dock chickee at Sunday Bay, then surf the rolling breakers back out of the broad lagoon. As we do, we ride an easterly wind beyond Barnes and Crooked creeks and into the lee of the shoal-filled Cross Bays, where we run aground, using our paddles as poles to finally push away. From there, we skim the confluence of Hurddles Creek and the Turner River, an intersection deep enough to hold half-ton manatees up from Florida Bay; they frolic like giant children, tails out of the water, bodies rolling and churning the water in outsized mammalian ecstasy, safe at last from motorboat props. We sit at a distance and watch in quiet reverence, then push on toward Chokoloskee under a bright tropical sun.

Once, just after a flock of white ibis fly low across the mangrove tops, I blunder somewhere off the map, getting lost as thoroughly as I have ever been. When I tell Terry of the mistake, I joke that we must be in such a state before we can ever truly be found, and he smiles and says gently, I know what you mean, bro.

Safely back on track, we finally enter Chokoloskee Bay, windswept and sparkling in the sun; the endgame is in sight now. I wonder what secrets are still hiding from us. But finally I decide it doesn't much matter; this lagoon of the holy spirit and its ghosts will be here, whether I want them to be or not.

But then, there is this: I think one last time of Ed Watson and how Matthiessen treated him more generously than life ever did. And I wish the same for the Glades itself. I wish it in my heart for Terry, for me, for us all.

BEWITCHED ON BALI

Pico Iyer

It was dark when first I set foot on the island, and the jungle all around was chattering. I heard gamelan music through the trees, saw oil lamps flickering along the narrow lanes. The last parties were breaking up along the backstreets of Kuta, and when the taxi dropped me off at an unknown hotel, I was alone in a confounding darkness.

That first night in Bali, still jangled and discombobulated from two days and nights in the air from New York, through Tokyo, to Jakarta, and then here, I wandered out onto the beach in the dead of night, and a figure appeared, smiling, and asked if I'd like "jig-jig" or some carnal services I couldn't follow. I woke up often in the dark, fitful and scratchy, mosquitoes whining all around, and when I went out again at dawn, I found I had landed on a pockmarked lane, with psychedelic paintings hanging from storefronts, and demon masks fringed with human hair, and a few longhairs slumped among the bushes, deadened by the magic they'd eaten or smoked.

I sat on the beach, that first day at sunset, and watched bare-chested boys frolicking among the reddening waves, and snake-armed masseuses packing away their charms, as in some Gauguin fantasy. A girl came over and sat down beside me. "I saw two flowers in my dream last night, and one of them was you," she said. "I put that flower in my hair." She wasn't beautiful, and I could hardly see her face for the sarongs she was carrying on her head, and the night that was falling around us. But I followed her, and followed her down the beach, and into the dark, till I could see nothing but the whites of her eyes and her teeth.

We walked along the buzzing lanes, dogs howling on every side. She took me to a night market, to a movie, and then, again, into the whirring back streets, where, in memory, I can see her eyes burning. I remember her sobbing, I remember her panting, and I remember her laughing when least I expected it.

In the nights that ensued, we went deep into the interior, through magic forests and small towns, into candlelit guesthouses at midnight. We walked on a beach where couples walk under a huge full moon. She laughed as I unbuttoned my shirt, and dug her nails into my arm.

All the best journeys, I have always felt, are like love affairs, not least because they turn you inside out and leave you within a darkness where you can't tell right from left or good from bad. And all love affairs are like journeys deep into a foreign country, where you can't read the signs, and you don't know the language, and you are drawn into a wilderness alive with mystery and possibility, and the knowledge—the certain knowledge—that who you were is irretrievable.

But in Bali, the whole spell is heightened and intensified, as in some charged re-creation of *A Midsummer Night's Dream*, where queens fall in love with asses, and young men lose their heads. In Bali, lovers sit all night with the image of their devotion in a coconut lamp, or catch unwilling souls with moon coins and magic potions made from a serpent's saliva mixed with an infant's tears.

I remember how I would walk through the night—always the night—with Wayan, and she would tell me of the pills she had swallowed once, and of the first boy who'd ever loved her, who died soon after in an industrial accident. She took me into the humming darkness of her culture, its dream messages and *leyak* witches, its singing cremations and unwanted ghosts. Her mind, her being, seldom touched the ground.

Bali is at the best of times a kind of vibrating altered state—a different zone of consciousness, in which dancers are often in trances, and spirits appear at the foot of your bed, and always, at the edge of your mind, you can hear howling dogs and the tinkling gamelan; it is also a province of romance, like some Arcadian forest where bodies fall into couplings by the light of a hundred temples. But I was entering both states at once, with a spirit that didn't seem earthly. Anyone who points out, quite rightly, that Bali is a paradise of angels and Edenic pleasures has to acknowledge that there must be demons there, too, and serpents in the garden.

When Wayan took me to the airport my last day there, she said, "Last night I dreamed I died. I dress all in white and go away." I tried to brush it off, but she was insistent, her gaze intense. I wouldn't see her again, she said; she would be in the realm of her ancestors.

I kept in touch with Wayan from afar and sent her presents for her birthday; I often thought of her trembling form, shaking in the back lanes of Kuta. Yet I realized, too, that it wasn't wise to toy with what I couldn't fathom. The undertow in Bali carries several foreigners to their deaths each year.

The next year, when I returned to Kuta, I didn't tell Wayan when I crept into her village. But she found me, that first night back, in the same lane where she'd held on to me so fiercely I thought she'd draw blood. I heard the sound of her laughter again, saw her rolling eyes. We went back to the full-moon beach, at noon, and walked along its unmagicked sands. I told her I had stumbled into a forest I had not sought and did not trust. She said almost nothing, her dress not flaming scarlet as before, but the blue of daytime skies.

She said almost nothing, and I went back to my hut. For three days after that farewell, I could not move. I lay, feverish and awake, in a room full of insects and crawling bodies. I heard cats yelping outside, and the gamelan incessantly. Dogs, more dogs, howled in the dark, and lizards stood on my walls till I could no longer tell them from the light switches. I couldn't move, I couldn't sleep, I couldn't think—could only hear whispers and rustlings from next door, where a soft-limbed local sprite danced in and out of an Australian's arms.

When finally I could move, I went up into the hills, far away, to a village where I'd been with Wayan a year before. But something in me was lost; I was waterlogged and sluggish, a sleepwalker in a phantom state. It felt as if some guardian spirit had stolen away from me, leaving all the lights turned out.

I finally picked up enough strength to leave the island, and I never heard from Wayan again. But when I returned to New York, I put up on my wall an owl mask I'd bought in her village—and instantly the Manhattan night was so full of chatterings and hauntings that I had to tear the mask down from the wall and stash it away, in a closet, behind a stack of boxes, where I'd never have to lay eyes on it again.

LOST IN THE SAHARA

Jeffrey Tayler

I have seen the Fates stamp like a camel in the dark:
Those they touch, they kill, and those they miss
live to grow old.

—*"The Ode of Zuhayr"*

"He's a thief!" shouted Abdullah. "He has a knife and will slit your throat from ear to ear!" seconded his friend, making a slashing motion across his neck. Both teenagers stood by my car door and pressed their heads excitedly through my window as they described the fate I was delivering myself to by hiring Aziz as my guide for a night excursion into the desert. Aziz had gone to fetch water, tea, and blankets from his house nearby.

I had driven south across Morocco for fifteen straight hours, finally reaching the Drâa Valley and the Sahara as the sun dropped behind the palms. Around nine that evening I was nearing M'Hamid and the end of the tarmac when I stopped in Tagounite at a roadside restaurant.

Aziz approached my table as I sopped up the last juice from a lamb *tagine* with a swatch of unleavened bread, sweat dribbling down my temples, my back aching from the Peugeot's bucket seat. He seemed stunted and looked younger than his professed age of eighteen. But a way he had of lowering his eyes when he talked made him look woebegone, vulnerable even, not criminal, and I felt I could recognize a crook after working for more than two years as a Peace Corps volunteer in thief-infested Marrakech to the north. After a bit of bargaining, we settled on $10 as his fee. The sally into the sands he was offering seemed a manageable outing, involving only a ten-mile drive along a *piste*—a rutted desert track—that branched off the paved road north of M'Hamid, a night on the dunes, and an early return the next day.

Still, the teenagers' words rattled me. Before Aziz returned, I asked about him in the restaurant and at a store nearby. He checked out. But on the way out of town my suspicion got the better of me. I pulled over.

"Those boys say you're a thief, a murderer even."

His eyes bucked as though I had slapped him.

"Give me your national ID card," I said. He pulled it from his back pocket. I got out and examined it in the headlights—it had expired last year, but he was who he said he was. I then hid the card without his seeing where.

"I'm sure there'll be no problem," I said, locking gazes with him back in the car. The darkened desert outside was utterly silent— the Sahara is a domain of silence—there were only our faces in the dashboard light. "You'll get your card back when we return."

We drove on. At a spot marked on the road by a white arrow, we parted with the tarmac and bounced onto *hamada,* the cracked, stony flatland of the Sahara. My headlights illuminated the corrugations, faint ruts of the *piste*. For an hour or so we followed them, until our lights hit dunes. We halted. Aziz scrambled out, lit the lantern, and ignited coals in the sand, on which he perched a teapot.

A flashlight appeared from around the dune. Footsteps edged through the silence.

"*Aaa, Aziz!*"

"Aaa, Ali!"

Ali was Aziz's cousin, a tender of camels from the 'Ariib tribe of M'Hamid. In his immaculate white robes and pointy-toed white slippers, Ali looked as though he might be dressed for a mint tea ceremony in any tiled Moroccan courtyard. His nose was aquiline, his brow broad, his legs and arms sinewy. He sat down cross-legged at the edge of the blanket. After a few minutes, I saw he was no simple Bedouin; his speech resounded with the classical Arabic of the Koran.

As we talked, he revealed that he had studied Arabic literature at the university in Marrakech, but preferred a solitary life on the sands to the bustle of the towns.

"Allah, Allah," he intoned, rising a short while later. "There may be a wind tonight. If need be, come sleep in my tent." He took leave of us and plodded away around the dune, his light a bobbing white orblet on the sand.

Aziz extinguished his kerosene lantern, and I was left momentarily blinded, the image of its yellow flame still flooding my retinas. I lay back on my blanket, settling my elbows and ankles into the sand beneath. A soft crushing sound, a *poosh-poosh-poosh,* came floating through the dark.

A camel, said Aziz. Flat on my back, I gazed upward, and the sky resolved itself into a luminous blue dome, not dark at all, really, not even far away; stars swam as if in holding patterns; infinity extended beyond Polaris, beyond Jupiter and Sirius. I perceived depth in the firmament, or thought I did; it seemed perceptible that the earth was a globe suspended in space. The *poosh-poosh-poosh* of the camel's padded hooves lulled me into reverie. I slipped into sleep, then out again; I felt myself levitating toward the stars, aware of warm breaths of wind, of wafts of warm wind, of blue infinity and wafting warm wind.

I closed my eyes to the starlight.

At midnight, from the *hamada* to the east, a groan arose, a wail, a wind as heavy and cloying as hot breath. I turned my face away. Aziz slumbered on. An hour later, sand was caking on my face no matter what position I assumed. A flashlight-blur of yellow approached from the dune.

"You must come to the tent now," said Ali. "*Sharqi.*" (*Sharqi,* sirocco, derives from the Arabic *sharq,* east, and denotes "a wind from the east.")

The tent flaps whipped and lashed; sand poured in as through a sieve and whirled in eddies around us. Though Ali and Aziz, and another boy, wrapped in black shawls, snored dead to the world, I couldn't sleep with my face covered by my shirt; it suffocated me. I waited and waited for dawn and what I assumed would be the cessation of the wind. Eventually I dozed off.

I awoke at dawn to a dirge of winds, rising and falling and quavering, a cyclonic rhapsody on the sands. I roused Aziz. "We have to go now," I said.

He sprang forth bleary-eyed from his shawl and grabbed his bundle. I clambered to the top of a dune. The sun, the vicious taskmaster of the *sharqi,* drove sand at us in ferocious blasts across the *hamada* that stretched tablelike to the horizon. The wind varied, giving the illusion of abating at times. Gusts broke my balance; blasts of dust would turn the sky and earth into a single whirling gaseous mass. The power of the storm was alarming; I had seen nothing like it before.

We pulled away from the tent at five-thirty in the morning as if into a choppy sea with whitecaps of sand. We bounced, we jolted, the Peugeot rattled and clanked on the cracked earth. Again and again we slowed as Aziz lost the *piste* to the blowing sand.

At a meter-high ledge, we ground to a halt.

"Don't you know the way?" I asked. We were not on the *piste* of the night before.

We backed up and snaked along the edge to a trough. I stopped. If this was a *piste,* it led to a sand patch. Sweat dripped off my brow; the car was turning into an oven with the windows rolled up against the dust.

"Go on!" he said.

We shot over the sand onto more *hamada,* but the wind blasted up a curtain of dust. I slowed; the wheels cut into sand and spun and spun.

Aziz jumped out. "No problem. I'll get Ali and he will drag us free."

He took off at a trot, but the wind manhandled him and he stumbled. I sat vexed at my own shortsightedness; despite all I had read on desert travel, I had entered the Sahara with neither water nor spare fuel, and worst of all, in a car fit for little more than a Saturday jaunt to the mall. I got out and tried to dig myself free; as a result of my exertions, the Peugeot ended up sunk to its axles. I sweated streaks through my shirt and coughed up a gob of sand. Inside the car it was fiendishly hot; outside, the wind harried. I crouched in the doorway and took out Aziz's ID card: How ill-conceived, how urban had been my precautions! A thief? What was a thief alongside the fury of the greatest desert on earth?

An hour later, Aziz came running with a shawl-wrapped waif of a boy, Lahcen, in his mid-teens but wiry, with black, brown, and gray teeth. He and Aziz piled sand around my front wheels and told me to accelerate. I did, and we shot free. We pulled off heading west, away from the sun, with Lahcen in the passenger seat. I followed his left-handed chopping gestures, left . . . left . . . straight on; slow; left.

An hour passed with us trundling this way and that. The *hamada* burned with sand blowing from the east, the direction of the main road. The corrugations of the *piste* faded in and out; we stalled heading west. For a moment we were blinded by a burnt-ocher maelstrom aflame with the sun behind it.

"Stop here!" said Lahcen. He scrambled out. Ahead the brown ghosts of three camels faded in and out with the undulating sheets of sand. Lahcen whistled to them. He seemed not to hear me when I asked him what he was doing. He jumped back in.

"Those are our camels. They will show us the way to our tent."

"Then you don't know the way?"

Aziz whacked Lahcen on the head.

"You don't even know the way!" he shouted.

"But when will they go home? It's not like they go running at mealtimes, is it?" I asked.

"By God, I don't know. But they will go home, sooner or later."

We moved on again, this time in search of a dry riverbed Lahcen said was "just over there."

The sun crept higher; wind tore off the *hamada* in a bellowing rage. We lost visibility to the sands; we regained it, lost and regained it. We rambled ahead, ever bearing left with Lahcen's chopping gestures. I considered the possibilities: If we overshot M'Hamid, nothing would stop us from rolling onward into Saharan barrens extending over a thousand miles to Timbuktu. But we would never reach Timbuktu; our fuel would run out, and without water, death from thirst would arrive within three days. I fought back these thoughts—they led only to a debilitating fear—and focused on the *piste*.

"Are we north of M'Hamid, or west?" I asked Lahcen, to determine what our chances were of overshooting it.

"By God, our tent should be over there," he said.

Black and silvery tents resolved themselves into scrub brush as we approached, dashing hopes over and over again. Mirages. The *piste* itself was either imagined or not; corrugations appeared and disappeared; we were tacking crosswise against the blowing wastes. Left, left, said Lahcen's hand.

"Stop!" said Lahcen.

He opened the door and staggered out. I got out too, and found I had to hunch low or be blown over.

"The camels are over there!" Lahcen shouted.

We proceeded, bouncing over stony *hamada*. But there were no camels over there, and Lahcen's hand returned to chopping the air. I felt panic rising within me, coming out of my gut and passing over my heart. My eyes stung with sweat.

"Maybe we should just wait this out," I wondered aloud. "How long can it last?"

"It could clear this afternoon. Or not."

"But how long does the *sharqi* usually last?"

"Maybe three days, maybe seven. God alone knows."

We had been driving for over four hours; I glanced at the gas tank arrow, which hovered at less than a quarter. We had used up more than a quarter tank.

Hamada. Sand. We swerved. Sand. *Hamada.* Lahcen's hand cut the air. We were circling. I thought to object when, during a blind spell, we slammed into something; I heard a sharp report, steel against stone. Lahcen asked me to stop.

He and Aziz conspired over a baked plate of sand behind the car. I felt panic alternate with despair at the thought of the hours we had spent circling. I didn't show it; there was no one to turn to, no point in a confession. I got out and knelt with them.

"The *piste* ahead leads to M'Hamid!" shouted Lahcen above the gale, pointing south. As I passed around the front of the car, I noticed a wet spot on the sand. I bent down; drops of water, dispersed by the wind, were dripping out from behind the bumper. Our last jolt had punctured the radiator.

I sat back in my seat, speechless with the discovery.

We waited, the horizon having abandoned us to another all-enveloping maelstrom. Sand suffocated us as water would have, had we been fifty fathoms beneath the surface of the sea; it blew in through the ventilators, it entered our lungs as we breathed. I glanced at myself in the rearview mirror; there was my face, tawny with grit and streaked where sweat had poured off my brow and temples. It occurred to me that death as a metaphysical abstraction—a phenomenon of nothingness, of nonexistence, of peace, even—suddenly seemed quite divorced from the bowel-churning ordeal of dying: in our case, dying of thirst, dying roasted by the sun. With the wind and sun and grit between the teeth, there was no way to collect my thoughts and saunter into metaphysics. And I had two people with me; a sense of responsibility as the driver, not to mention elder, prevailed. I turned back to our predicament.

Staying with the car is the key to survival in desert mishaps. How many times had I read that years ago in preparation for a trans-Saharan run across Algeria that never took place? Attempting to walk out means certain death. I rummaged through memories of Wilfred Thesiger's *Arabian Sands,* his account of travels with Arab tribes in Arabia: Bedouins drank the blood of their camels through a straw straight from the jugular; they ate camel vomit; they shampooed in camel urine.

My creaking Peugeot could offer none of these less-than-epicurean survival treats. I rubbed my eyes and found gummy balls of sand on my fists.

By eleven the sun was infusing the maelstrom with a gaseous steely glare; the *piste,* real or imagined, faded and reappeared as we slowly jounced and creaked our way over the *hamada* toward M'Hamid. Or not. But a wash of sand appeared and interrupted the *piste.*

"Don't dunes surround M'Hamid?" I thought aloud. I had been to M'Hamid the year before and seen them! I felt suddenly breathless with the realization that this *piste*—our last hope—would become impassable by the sheer geography of the region. Lahcen stared ahead. I stopped. "Will we make it?"

His head dropped. "In this car, by God I don't know."

"We have only two choices; either we find the tents now or we wait it out." I thought of the water from the radiator leaking into the thirsty earth.

His head remained bowed.

Lahcen got out and knelt, studying the baked earth under his toes. Heat blew in ferocious gales. I fingered the cracked skin on my lips. Lahcen climbed back in and motioned left with his hand. Left again, I thought. We started up. More circling. Baked *hamada* spread under a roiled oncoming wall of dust. A flash of white-brown from a gust of sand blinded us. When it dropped we saw a dune.

Left, chopped Lahcen's hand.

Rage bubbled within me; we were entering the dunes! Left again, he said. Another left, and it appeared we had run into a dead-end of dunes. I laughed out of despair.

"Go on!" said Lahcen. "Go on!" His voice broke.

We reached the end of the dune and turned left. A knee-high piece of scrap metal, a buoylike marker, suddenly stood out black in the white blustering blaze.

The curtain of sand flickered to reveal the tent, battered by the *sharqi*. Ali stepped out as we drove up, his shawl a flailing horizontal mane behind him. He opened my door.

"God be praised. You should not have set out in this *sharqi*. God saved you. Come, have tea."

Lahcen and Aziz kept their heads low. They thought they had failed me, I supposed, though they might have been more worried about the thrashing Ali would give them if I complained or blamed them. I said nothing, seated with my tea amid the eddies of whirling dust in the tent.

I thought about diving headfirst into the cold blue water of a hotel swimming pool; I foretasted the ecstasy of guzzling an entire bottle of Evian; I realized how much a luxury water could be and how ingenious one had to be to survive where it was a rarity, as in the Sahara. Ali's sinew and calm hospitality suddenly commanded new respect from me.

Later, I learned this was one of the worst *sharqis* in years; winds hit ninety miles an hour and bore temperatures of over 125 degrees. That afternoon, the wind briefly abated. After I poured water in my depleted radiator, Ali suggested we make for the main road. The *sharqi* started up again midway, but with his sure guidance it didn't matter. At the whitewashed arrow we bumped and rattled our way to the tarmac, a black runway to salvation.

FEAR, DRUGS, AND SOCCER IN ASIA

Karl Taro Greenfeld

GULF OF SIAM, 1993

I lean the motorcycle on its kickstand, the weight of the 150cc Honda settling onto the spring-loaded metal with a slow groan. It is midday on a coastal macadam road on a small island somewhere in the Gulf of Siam. The sun is bright, and I am sweating through a Singha tank top, the black dye from the shirt running down my cut-off army pants and mingling with the rivulets of blood that now stream from my calf.

I have been in a motorcycle wreck. A mile back, on an elbow of dirt road, the rocks and sand seemed to open up beneath the front tire of my Honda; they sent me sprawling. For a moment I was suspended in air, surprised to be viewing my handlebars from above, and then I was skidding along the hard dirt, ripping up my calf and mingling a streak of dirt, dust, and pebbles with the blood that immediately bubbled up around the strips of dislodged flesh. I remembered the motorcycle wheel, the clutch still engaged, spinning inches from my ear, an evil, buzzing sound like a surgeon's saw cutting through rib cage.

I had been on heroin when I crashed, having sniffed a small dose of whitish powder, plentiful and cheap here in Thailand. I now do not recall how I righted the motorcycle and climbed on for the mile ride to the cluster of bungalows beside the road. I only remember resting the motorcycle on its stand and sitting in the shade, shooing flies away from my wound, while a Thai waiter set down an orange soda in front of me. The air smelled like a combination of chicken shit, dust, and body odor, an earthy smell that implies by its rancidness the infectious agents borne aloft on this hot breeze.

Gingerly rising from the bamboo stool, I stumble over a stone divider and make my way to the deserted beach, where a few French women are sunbathing and reading waterlogged two-month-old copies of *Paris Match*. As I collapse in the sand, I realize I have lost my sunglasses at the scene of the accident. Even through my closed eyes, I can see an outline of the hot ball of sun. I turn over onto my side, my bloody calf pushing painfully into the sand, and I begin to shiver. I have been out here for years, traveling and partying throughout the Far East. Now I feel this has all gone wrong. The drugs. This trip. Now this accident.

"Karl?" A woman's voice asks. I open my eyes. Dina stands above me, her face backlit by the sun. She wears a tie-dye bikini top, a black sarong, and a man's Rolex Daytona. "You've got the shakes, eh?"

She speaks in a British accent, her voice a soothing, warm reminder of a good place, a home—someone's home—far away. Someplace I have never been. Then she sees my leg.

"Bloody hell, what have you done to yourself?"

My eyes adjust to the light and I can make out her small mouth, her pert nose, her almost Chinese eyes.

"Motorcycle accident."

"Get up. Let's scrub that out. It's gonna turn septic on you."

I keep my eyes closed. I am still shivering. "Jesus, Dina, I'm so fucking scared."

She doesn't say anything for a moment, and I can hear the waves breaking and what sounds like wind shimmying through palm fronds and the thwacking sound of someone chopping pineapple on a wooden plank.

"Your fears," she says, "they're like a person you keep seeing over and over again. They follow you until you find a way not to be afraid anymore. Now let's get you cleaned up."

KATHMANDU, 1996

I was stuck in Kathmandu. Waiting for my story to arrive. And hoping that my story would arrive before I found myself standing drunk in one of Tamil's loosely regulated pharmacies, telling the stubbled, turbaned pharmacist that I would like sixty of those blue ten-milligram Valiums, sixty of those Roussel Darvons, and, oh, how about a hundred of those big, thick, white morphine sulphate tablets?

This was my first story in Asia since I had stopped drinking and drugging, my first sober foray back to the fleshpots that had been the site of so many of my most crippling debauches. I had sworn off the sauce and mood-altering substances, and so was facing life for the first time unfiltered. I was making a clean start here at the roof of the world; in Nepalese smog and on Kathmandu turf, this was my new beginning. I had long ago lost the ability to regulate my intake of intoxicants. If I slipped again, up here in the Himalayas, it would be a long, long way down. After six weeks in rehab and a year spent putting my life back together—restoring my family's trust, rebuilding my marriage, relearning how to write—I was, in a sense, making a comeback.

I was in Kathmandu writing a story for *Condé Nast Traveler*. But the story that had begun in Tokyo and gathered momentum in Bangkok was now gasping here in Nepal. I was covering a crowd of kids who lived on what I had come to call the Circuit. They wandered, as I had done for years, between Asian boomtowns and beaches, earning a living as they went and carving out a hedonist, decadent lifestyle. But the last time I had seen Dina and the crew of trendy American and British travelers who personified this sort of cutting-edge, Commes Des Garçons– and Gucci-clad new Asian hand, they were lying in their Koh Tao hammocks smoking joints and typing e-mails on their notebook computers. I had tired of their Ecstasy-driven, rave-y island decadence and, fearing for my always tenuous sobriety, I headed back to Bangkok, making sure I arranged with this stoned gang of Toshiba Tecra–toting, Hang Seng Index–analyzing vagabonds to rendezvous here in Kathmandu. I had been here a week and my fellow travelers were nowhere to be seen. I now wondered who or what they had been e-mailing, because I had been sending them e-mails repeatedly for the last five days without response.

Visible through thick billows of Kathmandu smog, between snow-capped Himalayan gorges, the orange sun cast dim rays that barely broke through the haze. Dotting the foothills around Kathmandu were sprawling villages made up of mud huts and handkerchief-sized vegetable farms. Occasionally, when the wind from the hills blew the smog back up the valleys away from the city, one caught a whiff of manure and nightsoil, earthy smells of the family farms surrounding the city. The odor struck me as obscenely organic in its bouquet, as if nature herself had let out some great, sphincter-relaxing fart.

Wiping the dust from my eyes, I stepped into the crowded Tamil street, hailing a *tuk-tuk* that would take me to Turihil, the gated military parade ground where in the afternoon a few local college students played soccer with some European expatriates and a dozen other Westerners who, like me, for one reason or another, were stranded in Kathmandu.

In almost every city in the world, there are easy-to-access pickup soccer games. I travel with cleats in damp, rainy Europe and turf shoes in dry, dusty Asia. Unlike other travelers, who worry about hotel fitness club hours, tennis court reservations, and golf course tee times, my sport requires nothing more than a swath of grass— or dirt, or pavement, or mud—a ball, and a half-dozen or more players. I have played in pickup games around the world: Bangkok's Lumphini Park, Amsterdam's Vondelpark, Berlin's Reichstag lawn, Barcelona's Ramblas, Tokyo's Yoyogi Park, Paris's Bois de Bologne. I have come to view soccer not only as a way to get to know locals, make friends, and stay fit but also as a vehicle for discovering a culture and its people. A day spent playing *futball* with Moroccans, Chinese, or Italians will tell you more about national character than any number of guidebooks, language courses, or sightseeing excursions. Beware, though: You will fall pray to ethnic stereotypes that are based on how frequently an Arab player passes the ball or how a Mexican plays defense. You will judge a German's character by how he reacts after allowing a goal, and a Japanese man's emotional maturity by his post-goal-scoring celebration. You will quickly realize the fellow American you befriended last night at the bar is actually a selfish, thoughtless ball hog who would rather lose the ball on the dribble than pass it. And you discover that the quiet, balding Greek whom you dismissed as a sociopath is actually a kind soul, one who would sacrifice an easy, ingenuous shot to attempt an ingenious crossing pass.

The game reveals character and intellect and provides a brief glimpse into your soul. If you are frightened—of this new strange city, of returning home, of never returning home, of slipping back into drug addiction—then it will show on the pitch, will be made apparent by how awkwardly you handle a ball. But if you are at peace, resting up from the last journey and readying for the next, then the game will be the pleasant diversion it was meant to be. Your exhausting, relentless running, sidestepping, and backpedaling will be spontaneously choreographed steps subsumed in some massive, ten- or twenty-man dance in which you feel integral. Playing with Nepalese and Thais, Egyptians and Germans, if the game is good and the players are generous and you are at your best, you come to believe you are a part of some *spiritus mundi* of manly good feeling that transcends borders, ethnic groups, religions, and GNPs. You play the game. They play the game.

You belong.

I sat on the pitch, near a white-painted wooden fence, slipping on a pair of Diadora turf shoes while nearby a dozen or so Nepalese and Englishmen kicked around soccer balls, jumped up and down in place, and swung their arms in wild forward and backward gyres. While I stretched, bending so that my nose touched my knee, I took a moment and bowed my head. I often prayed before I took the pitch, especially an unfamiliar field. I didn't know who I was praying to, or why, but I asked that I be allowed to play honestly and to play simply and within myself. That I be patient and let the game come to me. Then we played.

The game enabled me to forget that I was stuck in Kathmandu, that I was waiting for some THC-saturated ex-stockbrokers and nightclub owners and models who were a week overdue, and that the article I had been sent to write was showing signs of miscarrying.

But there were greater issues I played to escape: It is hard work staying sober in a strange town, especially when you have nothing to do but wait for a gang of well-heeled wastrels to blow in from whatever stretch of Asian sand they have laid up on. I fumed as I imagined the clique of Brits and Americans whom I had foolishly let out of my sight, sprawled in some sumptuous bungalow on some pristine Southeast Asian beach while I waited in smoggy, dusty Tamil. The game took me away from my petty worries and my needing a drink, from the temptations of a little legal or illegal sedation to help get through the listless waiting in a town full of inebriated expats.

I could even forget that I was in Kathmandu; instead, I was transported to Soccer Land, a magical country whose boundaries are two goals and whatever one is using as touchlines but whose domain is infinitely vast and encompassing. I had no thoughts outside the game, no wants, no desires. The earthly realm fell away. The surrounding scenery of blooming poplars and sagging bodhi trees, the sacred cows that wandered alongside the pitch, the motorcycles and *tuk-tuks* that rattled past on the narrow road, even the foul smog that we breathed receded into distant, barely perceptible blips on some ignored radar screen. My wants and desires were forgotten. The lures of liquor and drugs, the cravings of the flesh, all vanished.

But after forty-five minutes on the pitch, I felt my concentration begin to break; I stumbled and gasped, taking deep breaths, losing my easy stride. My errant passes went to the other team; my attempts to carry the ball proved feckless. It was like being in one of those dreams where you flee an unknowable evil, yet no matter how hard you try, you find your legs and feet cannot generate any speed. At the same time, I noticed a player whom I had not seen earlier in the game, when we were dividing up our sides. A swarthy man of medium build, he must have come on after the game had started. I could not tell his age or his nationality. Because he was tirelessly in motion, it was hard to catch a clear glimpse of his face, but he had a ruddy complexion and deeply set, black eyes obscured by a shadowy, protruding forehead. He wore a black acrylic jersey, colors of a soccer club whose name was written in an alphabet the characters of which I did not recognize. His most noticeable trait was the almost metallic sheen of his hair. It was not the mottled gray hair of an aging man; it was as if this fellow had had his hair surgically replaced by thick silver filaments.

There was something disconcertingly familiar about the metallic-haired player, like the grown-up version of someone I had known in the first grade, or, more perplexingly, like a vaguely recollected character from a dimly recalled dream, one of those vestigial phosphene images that stays with you for a few moments, burned into your eyelids, before you're fully awake.

He played with ruthless efficiency, a fluid, consistent, creative athlete who made all those who played with him seem better. And he was a physical defender who humiliated me several times, inflicting pain when he slide-tackled me, stripping the ball from me cleanly without committing a foul. On those few occasions when I dared challenge him, he would rake the ball from my feet with such strength that I felt a shiv of pain run up my leg. The other players did not pay particular attention to him. It was obvious to me, however, that he had transformed the character of the game from a friendly afternoon match to a steely, macho test of wills. Even the orange globe of sun had vanished behind thick black clouds of smog, making the sky darken and the late-afternoon city seem more somber. The air now tasted acrid, and each breath of internal combustion effluvium was unspeakably rancid.

I played until this new fellow tackled me near my own goal, pulling the ball back and scoring with a neatly heeled shot while I lay crumpled on the pitch, my nose pressed down into a clod of dried horse manure. As I lay there, all my anxieties and fears returned. What if those hip, swinging travelers never showed up in Nepal? What if I wound up waiting here for months, running up an expense tab that would alienate me from Condé Nast forever? And, more important, what if in the boredom and dissolution of Kathmandu nights I decided I could have just one drink, just a few ten-milligram Valiums? I tried to shake off that thought as I brushed the manure from my nose. The fear had returned.

The game ended. As I slipped off my turf shoes and peeled away a layer of sweaty socks, I looked around for the metallic-haired player, but he had already gone; he must have jumped the white-painted fence immediately after the game and hailed one of the little white Daewoo taxis. I asked some of the other players who he was, what country he came from, but they shook their heads; they had not noticed him.

BANGKOK, 1996

The Bangkok game was different. This regular game of embassy employees and long-term expats took place in Lumphini Park three times a week. Most of the players involved, particularly the half-dozen Thais, had serious skills. I looked forward to the Lumphini game whenever I was in Bangkok. Although I was one of the worst players on the pitch, it was always exhilarating to be part of some first-class soccer.

As I climbed from the taxi on Rama IV, I felt the damp air waft over me and the immediate beginnings of sweat beads along my eyebrows and upper lip. My cleats were slung by their laces over my shoulder. The night before, when I'd arrived from Kathmandu, a hint of a breeze had made its way up the Chao Phraya River, but by day the heat settled over the city like a collective bad memory. Everywhere I went in Asia, I was choked by exhaust, forever wiping

soot particles from my eyes. I had left Kathmandu upon receipt of a
telegram, of all things, from my gang of wandering, trendy Asian
travelers, who had finally made it back to Bangkok and were planning a short stay. They were capriciously peripatetic, these well-
heeled international ravers, but I had also begun to think of them as
a bunch of smug, self-centered, Ecstasy-swallowing morons.

I had arranged to meet two of the fellows, Englishmen named
Trev and Derrek, at the McDonald's near the Robinson's department store at the southwest corner of the park. Trev had been
modeling in Tokyo—and Milan and New York—while Derrek was
a DJ who seemed to be involved with the rock group Oasis in some
capacity. As they had kept me waiting for over a week in
Kathmandu, I was surprised to discover they were here early,
seated at a plastic table near the door, drinking Diet Cokes and
picking at an order of french fries. Both boys were fair-haired, with
cleft chins and absurdly high cheekbones. That Trev was a model
and Derrek was not must have been the result of some arbitrary
selection process a long time ago in London. They were equally
handsome, and in very similar ways, feminine eyes and noses, soft
pink mouths, manly, jutting chins, and slender builds. Wearing
expensive-looking track suits, Adidas running shoes, and the bored
expressions of spoiled lads who almost always get their own way
with whatever they apply themselves to, they merely shrugged
when I greeted them. They slipped on their Oakley shades and
shuffled to their feet.

Despite considerable pregame whining that the match would not
be up to the high standards they were used to back in London, and
despite their boasting about who would score more goals, Trev
and Derrek turned out to be below-average players, plainly not up
to the Lumphini level of play. And part of the fun of this particular
game was that I participated in their humiliation.

Unlike most English players, who are dependable and intelligent
if unflashy ball handlers, Trev and Derrek were lousy footballers. I
have so often struggled in athletic endeavor and known the feeling

of being derided for my on-the-field mistakes that I never thought I would be one of those who vociferously berate other players. Yet I could not help myself. There was something compelling about watching Trev and Derrek come up short on the athletic field, about observing boys who simply were not up to the level of competition and whose every attempt to rectify their inadequacies only compounded their failure.

"Pass the fucking ball!" I shouted at them. "Try passing the fucking ball to your own team!"

I knew a couple of the other players. There were the Nigerians Akemi and Godfrey; Dane, a wire service reporter and veteran of Stanford I-A soccer; and Paolo, a wonderful Italian midfielder. I had played with the Nigerians in Tokyo, at a pitch next to a hospital atop Hiroo Gardens. Paolo and Dane I knew from this game.

"Don't these guys suck?" I shook my head and said to Paolo during a lull in the action. He looked at me strangely, as if he didn't understand what I'd said, and shrugged.

"Everybody sometimes sucks," he said in his Neapolitan accent, and made a run across the bald patch of earth that was the middle of the penalty area. During the next break, he grabbed my shirt when I was telling Trev to get his ass back onside: "Hey, you are talking too much. Just play."

It was then that I realized I had neglected to pray before the game began, neglected to meditate and ask God or Shiva or Buddha or my higher power or whoever to help me enjoy this game, to help me play honestly and authentically within myself, to allow me to be the best player I could be. And that was when I noticed the same metallic-haired player who had totally knocked me off my game back in Kathmandu. I was not terribly surprised—hundreds of people fly between Bangkok and Kathmandu every day—but still, I found his presence disquieting. As soon as I saw him at the far end of the pitch, limbering up and running in place, I lost my concentration.

He stood silhouetted next to the coconut tree that served as the western goal. Clad in the same black jersey, shorts, and black socks he had worn back in Kathmandu, he appeared to be staring at me, his mouth turned down in a slight smirk. Or was I imagining the smirk? Was he just another player of pickup games, a fellow traveler? Was he as surprised to see me as I was to see him? Did he even notice me?

But from the moment he entered the game, I was consumed by self-doubt. Not just about soccer, but about my whole life. Thoughts of the story I had been sent to write returned: I was running out of time and over budget. There was still so much more I wanted to put into the story of the Circuit: the whole decadent culture of these rich kids, the gritty jadedness, the hipper-than-thou vibe. And there were the little details: the relentless backgammon hustling on the Circuit, the way the girls were pretty and young and blond and tattooed in all the right places, the silver Indian bracelets they were all wearing, the camouflage shirts the boys preferred. But I wanted to get something else across; that out here, miles from home in exotic Asian lands, nothing counted. The girls and boys could do what they wanted, to whom they wanted and with whom they wanted, and because it all happened so far from home, it was somehow off the record. Anything went, because no one from home was bearing witness.

But, if that reasoning made sense, then why shouldn't I dabble in some artificial mood-enhancing myself? Here I was in Bangkok, home to some of the best pills and powders and most liberal pharmacies in the world. Why couldn't I partake of the lax morality that pervaded the Circuit? No one was bearing witness. My wife was thousands of miles away. My family was in Los Angeles. None of this counted. So what if I had put together twelve sober months, had stayed off drugs for three hundred and sixty-five long days? What I did out here on the Circuit could stay out here on the Circuit. No one back home would ever know.

By then, I had fallen totally out of the game. The metallic-haired stranger was dominating as usual, gracefully passing to Trev and Derrek, building up a triangular attack and making those two fey Englishmen seem like brilliant players. My perfunctory attempts to break up this new, efficient attack were falling short. And when I received the ball I second-guessed myself instead of doing what came naturally. I was overthinking and then panicking. I was playing in fear.

The player with the metallic hair and black jersey came trotting by me several times. Each time I noticed his smirk had grown wider, as if he had realized some fundamental weakness about my game and my character. It was as if he saw through to some essential defect deep within me, could determine my vulnerabilities and knew how to exploit them, on the pitch and in real life. Here, on this Bangkok soccer field, while traffic whirred by fifty meters away on busy Rama IV Road, while we played between coconut-tree goalposts, I felt that I had been unmasked as a fraud. I was a bad soccer player. I was a bad writer. I was a drug addict. I had traveled to escape those shortcomings, those flaws, and for a time, out here in Asia, I had been able to fend off the knowledge of them.

After all, why do we travel? We travel, in part, to remake ourselves, to reinvent new, better versions of the defective personalities we have become back home. Out here, on the Circuit, we can pretend we are anything we like.

"You're nothing," I thought I heard the metallic-haired player whisper under his breath as he ran past me, "nothing at all."

John Travolta and Uma Thurman were twisting away up on the projection television. The soundtrack was muted and Jimi Hendrix's "Machine Gun" was turned way up so the two stars improvised to the lefty's caterwauling guitar. The bar, a wood-paneled tavern across from Privilege on the illustriously grubby Khao San Road, was crowded with eager-to-get-fucked-up, man-it's-awesome-being-in-Bangkok tourists who hadn't flown thousands of miles on crowded discount Air Pakistan flights to watch a bootleg video of *Pulp Fiction*. The vibe in a Khao San Road bar on Friday night is just about the same as it is any other night of the week. It's all about getting as much as you can as soon as you can and then hoping you don't throw up and then doing it all over again every day for the whole two weeks of your holiday before you're due back in Hamburg or Newcastle.

The gang of swell punks I had been hanging with was here for only one reason: They were supposed to meet a German DJ, Manfred, who had a box of DAT tapes that Derrek needed to DJ a rave at Baddam beach in Goa next week. But Manfred had not showed up and the old Thai lady at his guesthouse said that she had last seen him two weeks ago.

Trev and Derrek had ducked into this bar to stew over the missing DAT tapes of London acetate pressings that would enable Derrek to get over as the DJ he claimed to be. Clad in Versace camouflage shirts, Oakley sunglasses, white Pepe jeans, and green glow-in-the-dark necklaces, they sullenly drank Mekong and Cokes and cursed Manfred for being unreliable. He had assured them at the Breakfast Club back in Tokyo that he would be here, and now where the fuck was he?

As I listened to Trev and Derrek hatch plans and formulate strategy, discuss possible sources for substitute DATs, other raves where the music had been slamming, other venues on the Circuit where the vibes had been trippy, I realized that I had already grown tired of them and the rest of the gang of glamorous expats I had been following. It wasn't that Trev and Derrek were boring; I simply wasn't interested anymore. Their concerns seemed trivial. Some DJ, another rave, a great beach, the flash new spot: None of it seemed to matter. Despite my earnest attempts to rejoin their world, a world I had once known, I was an interloper now, a journalist sent from the outside to steal a little of their energy, fun, and good times. I was five years older than Trev and Derrek; the Circuit was their scene now. It was time to say good-bye to my own decadent past. It was time to leave Thailand, to leave Asia, and return home, to my family and friends, to where I felt safe.

But I was here tonight for Dina, to see her one last time before I got away. She now had Balinese warrior tattoos running up her fleshy, fuzzy arms; her nose was pierced, and her left ear jangled with an array of silver bangles and gold bobbles that she fingered as she sipped Mekong and Coke. In her right ear was a diamond stud, a gaudy rock as big as a dry-roasted peanut. Dina was a rich kid, a refugee from London nightclubs and New York lofts. In her mid-twenties, poshly accented and coolly intelligent, she lent the evening and this crowd of travelers what class they had. Compared to Dina, Trev and Derrek were parvenus—name-droppers and social climbers. Their good looks and connections to swinging London had only gained them toeholds on the sort of life that Dina had come from and took for granted. Dina did not leave her country to find a better or more thrilling life out here on the Circuit. Instead, she possessed the charm and allure of having turned her back on precisely the lifestyle everybody else was seeking: decadent, narcotized freedom was her birthright. Trev and Derrek and the others treated her with appropriate deference. As for the rest of us, she had drifted in and out of our lives. She flew off to Hong Kong fortnightly to see classmates from Cambridge who had been posted there. Or she took off to Tokyo or Delhi, to visit any of a long list of acquaintances, friends, and associates. One had the feeling, as she undertook these voyages, that she was a Mother Teresa of the e-generation, bringing solace and relief to mind-blown ravers throughout the Far East.

I tried to talk to her whenever she was around because she had a way of seeing through to the heart of things, of telling me the truth. And she was beautiful.

I told her I was leaving. I was done with my trip. I had enough for my story. I was worried that if I stayed in Bangkok, in Asia, I would use drugs again. I told her about the metallic-haired soccer player who was following me. I wanted to go home.

I reached down to my calf and felt the scar from the motorcycle accident. It had long ago healed and was now just a rough patch of skin. Did she remember that time on the beach, years ago, the season I met her, when she had found me laid up in the sand after the motorcycle wreck?

She nodded. "Are you still frightened?"

I was.

NEW YORK, 1997

It is a brisk autumn afternoon; the oak trees around the Columbia University campus have turned a feverish red; leaves litter the trodden pathways linking venerable old buildings. I am going to school again, on a journalism fellowship. I play soccer with the Columbia Business School team. Today, we are practicing on campus, on the narrow lawns before the imposing gray Butler Library. I jog across the pitch, gasping for breath, running to take a crossing pass from a Dutch teammate.

The metallic-haired player is nowhere in sight. I have not seen him since I returned from Bangkok. And, for the first time in years, I am not afraid.

MY JUNIOR YEAR ABROAD

Edith Pearlman

Sometimes Nehama got annoyed at me. Fire flashed from her slate-colored eyes. My tenses were mangled, my spelling corrupt, and my penmanship!—a disgrace to civilization.

Most of the time, though, during our twice-a-week Hebrew tutorials, Nehama exercised a quiet vigilance: the very attribute you might expect from a woman who emigrated from Berlin to Palestine as a girl, lived under the British Mandate, endured the Second World War, hailed the partition, and suffered through five further wars. At seventy-eight, retired from the classroom, she still worked privately in her apartment up the hill from the Jerusalem Theater.

And I? A *jeune fille* of sixty, I lived in an apartment down the hill from the theater. I was taking a Junior Year Abroad. People were disconcerted by this airy claim. You've left your husband at home? (This question was accusatory if asked by a man, wistful if by a woman.) He's minding the shop, I'd answer. You're writing a new book? I'm writing letters only. Then you're conducting an inner voyage—you're in Israel to get to know yourself!

I let them think that. But they were wrong: Or, to be as precise as Nehama would wish, they were right only in a general sense.

We all, wherever we are, make daily voyages of self-discovery. I had come here to get to know not myself, but Jerusalem.

I was learning the city by tramping its streets. The map was my syllabus. The local tradespeople were my sociology text—immigrants and their offspring who had been pouring into the country since its beginning. I bought fruit from a Moroccan with a corrugated face and the manners of a correct Parisian. I bought pickles from an energetic Hungarian. A Romanian sold me bread. I got milk and newspapers from the nearby *macolet*, the store that sells everything. Its youthful proprietor had come from Russia a decade ago. This young man also supplied me with wine, a bottle every other day. To polish off a bottle of wine in forty-eight hours is not to have an uncontrollable habit; still, after a few months, I became defensive. "I want you to know," I said while paying for a Tuesday-Wednesday fix, "that I buy a lot of wine because I have a lot of company." He looked at me intently. "I'm so glad," he said, with Chekhovian economy.

I was dispatching the wine myself, as we both knew. I never had a lot of company, and in the beginning I didn't have any at all. I was always out, widening my research. Wearing my customary pants and shirt, I wandered through the humble Katoman neighborhood. Respectfully donning a dress, I glided into the courtyards of God-fearing Mea Sharim. Back in drag, I lounged in hummus stalls on the crumbling Jaffa Road. I entered every shop, exchanged a sentence or two with every shopkeeper—scholars who sold religious books, and scrap ironware dealers, and importers of Italian tiles.

When I wasn't poking my nose into other people's businesses or disturbing the dust of ancient alleys, I sat in gardens, eating figs out of a paper bag. I chose quasi-public gardens—the grounds of the Leper Hospital, for instance—and small private ones, their gates forgetfully ajar, like the fragrant forecourt of the Pontifical Institute.

I rode the buses. With determination learned from Israelis, I joined the bus queue even after threats, even after Incidents. Scores of routes wind through the city. I'd board a bus on a whim and get off if I glimpsed an arbor or a curve of pale stairs, or if my seat-mate happened to mention some unpublicized place—archives open only every other Thursday, say. In this haphazard manner I managed to visit almost every section of Jerusalem. Ramot Polin, where pentagon-walled apartments create a peculiar beehive ef-fect—"We love it here," a kerchiefed woman assured me. Gilo, stiff with neo-Oriental arches. East Jerusalem: unroofed houses and backyard chickens. I took one bus to a convent selling wine and bread; I took another to a mall selling T-shirts and towels. In a café in a suburb I listened to Louis Armstrong on a jukebox. At the uni-versity on Mount Scopus I joined authentic Junior-Year-Abroads at the library. When I tried to withdraw materials, I was asked who I thought I was. But I was grudgingly allowed to read library books in the library, if that suited me.

Meeting people was a snap. Women alone—particularly women of a certain age—arouse interest and invite protection. (Women in pairs, by contrast, seem unapproachable.) Some peo-ple became friends. Some I encountered only once, but unforget-tably. In the Arab quarter of the Old City, a shopkeeper showed me slippers that I ended up not buying. He then invited me to have tea. I said no, thanks. He said: When you don't buy my slippers, you are expressing a preference, but when you refuse my tea you are in-sulting me. I drank his tea and took in his lesson in civility. And in the Armenian quarter one languid afternoon, the cook of a tiny restaurant told me of the rich insular life of Armenians in Jerusalem. He revealed nothing about his own life, leaving me free to invent several unauthorized biographies.

And loneliness too became a friend, a slightly down-in-the-mouth visitor to be pampered with Brie and a detective novel and a refreshing shower of tears.

I telephoned someone whose name I'd been given. She asked me to a party. There I met the eager young organizer of a volun-teer program in an Arab school just outside of the city. "Join us!" And so, most Wednesdays found me in the playground of that underequipped school, getting to know the children and several brisk female teachers and one harsh male, who indicated he'd rather be anywhere but here; did I have connections in New York?

A leftist introduced me to her ardent friends; I marched in demonstrations, learning political science on the hoof. One evening, waiting for a concert to begin, I fell into conversation with a retired diplomat who gave me an impromptu lecture on the importance of water to the Middle East—more important, he told me, his blue eyes looking through me as if I were water, than democracy, than autonomy, than human rights! Then, remembering his diplomatic manners, he invited me to a party, where I met . . . And so it went, until, every so often, in order to return hospitality, I had to buy two bottles of wine at the *macolet.*

It is a Friday afternoon in late spring. I have joined the weekly procession of Franciscan monks along the Via Dolorosa, stopping at each Station of the Cross. We stop also at the intersection of the Via Dolorosa and El Wad Street; we must make way for the crowd of worshippers rushing pell-mell from prayers at the mosque. For a moment I am in the thick of battle, Christianity warring with the Infidel. Then the Muslims—who are only going home for dinner—pass through the square, and the Franciscans advance to the next Station.

I break away and leave the Old City through the Jaffa Gate. In modern West Jerusalem, shops are closing; buses are completing their last runs; people are carrying flowers; a gabardined gentleman with a cellular phone tucked under his earlock is enjoying the final cigarette of the week. The city is closing upon itself. Tomorrow there will be no buses and no entertainment. Shutters of stores will be down. I resent the Orthodox stranglehold on city life; but at the same time I welcome the sweet melancholy that descends every Sabbath.

Meanwhile it is still Friday. I take my usual detour to a leafy cul-de-sac off the Street of the Prophets, where, a plaque says, the poet Rachel once made her home. I'd heard Rachel's name before this year abroad, though I had not read her work; but I had not even heard of Boris Shatz, Benjamin of Tudela, David Elroi. Now I walk on streets that bear the names of these men. I can recite their histories because I searched them out in the library I'm allowed to read in. Benjamin of Tudela was a Spaniard who visited Jerusalem in the twelfth century. David Elroi rebelled against the caliph. Boris Shatz founded the Bezalel Arts Academy.

And Rachel? She came to Palestine in 1909, at nineteen, the age of many college juniors; she died at forty-one of tuberculosis. In her poems she is "alone in a vast land." She, too, has become a kind of friend.

"Your grammar is slightly less muddled," praised Nehama at our last meeting. Her eyes seemed more like velvet than slate.

"I'll miss you," I said, meaning Nehama; meaning Rachel; meaning shopkeepers, monks, gardeners; neighbors, bus-riders, children; Talmudists, secularists, fanatics. They made up a spirited, enlightening faculty. And they didn't spring a single quiz.

EXPATRIATE, WITH OLIVES

Lucy McCauley

I am in southern Spain, walking toward an olive grove. It belongs to Catherine, a poet. She bought it last year when she came to live in the village. The grove has about fifty trees, said Manuel, who knows all those trees better than Catherine does, from years of picking there.

The dog, the small curly-haired one who looks less fierce than he is, barks to announce my arrival. Catherine is there, and Bernhard, the young German, and Manuel. Manuel is seventy-three. Lines carve out his jaw and mouth and deep-set eyes, filmy with cataracts. His clippers are going full speed, a great claw squeaking as the dull blades clutch a branch and pull, strip it of olives, the fruit falling green-purple-black in soft drumbeats on the net below.

Since he was eight years old he's been picking olives. He tells me, "I was even born under an olive tree."

"Is that true, Manuel?" comes Catherine's voice from behind a leafy branch.

"Well, no," he replies, and we laugh. "But almost—in a farmhouse near an olive grove."

Catherine is a Pennsylvanian who is tall and stands perfectly straight, long auburn hair flowing down her back. I have seen her walk for miles uphill, and even then her back is straight. On one of those walks she showed me the rosemary that grows wild near the side of the road in this part of Spain. "She who passes by rosemary and doesn't pick it," she said, reciting a village proverb, "neither has love nor dreams of it." I watched her pick some, bring the pungent leaves to her nose, and drop them in her pocket.

Catherine divorced her husband and came to live in the village near this grove a year ago, after having visited every summer for twenty years. She came to the village, she says, because it is where she feels most at home in the world.

She has had her disappointments. When she first came here she fell in love with a man from a neighboring village. Like many Spanish bachelors, he had lived at home with his mother all his life, but even after she died he could not bring himself to stay with Catherine, of whom his mother had disapproved because of her divorce and her foreignness.

But Catherine has her home in the village, her walls and tables draped in richly woven textiles, colorful clay pots and plates in the cupboards. She has her friendship with Manuel and other villagers who have come to love her.

And she has her olives.

This is Catherine's first time collecting the olives of her trees. Harvesting comes once a year, late fall, and lasts a little over a month. Today at twilight she will take the sacks we have filled to the *molina* in town; even up here in the hills, you can hear it grinding away when the winds blow in a certain direction, making oil from the villagers' olives.

Clip, slide, snap, *whoosh*—we skin olives from branches and they tumble to the ground like rain.

The sun gets hot and bright in southern Spain, even now in late fall. But the breezes from the Mediterranean are refreshing, and dry the sweat beading on my forehead before it can trickle down my face. Bernhard and Manuel use the two pairs of clippers, so

Catherine and I use our hands, better for feeling the round bubbles of meat, smooth and taut, as we gently clasp the branches and pull through silvery-green leaves.

This is a much-needed respite from days at my writing desk in the small house I'm renting in the village. I like the feeling of community that comes of encircling this tree with the others, each with our own group of branches to clear but still working in tandem, accompanying each other with fragments of conversation and the whoosh-whoosh of falling olives.

I had never seen an olive tree up close before I came to this village. I had only driven past groves of them on Spanish highways. Graceful, with small feathery leaves that finger outward optimistically from a bumpy little spine, an olive branch really does look like a symbol of peace.

The sun is in my eyes and light is glinting from the shiny fruit.

First you place the nets on the ground—two nets, side by side, overlapping slightly. Wrap the tree trunk close with them, then spread the nets across the dirt so the olives from every branch have a place to fall.

These are Manuel's directions, which he projects with an edge of impatience to us novice harvesters. Catherine has known Manuel since she began visiting the village two decades ago; she knows the gentle heart beneath his bark, and she laughs at his gruffness. Still, she defers to him in her olive grove, cocking her head when Manuel gives a command, grateful to have this expert midwife for her harvest.

"The strings of the nets *abajo*—down," Manuel says emphatically. The strings tie the downhill part of the nets up, on the branches of a neighboring tree, so that when the olives tumble downhill, they run up the ends of the nets like a soccer ball would, caught in a net-gutter.

After standing in one place for so long, stripping branches of olives, I like bringing the nets to the next tree like an offering, spreading them out to form a perfect chalice. The branches offer themselves, boughs leaning low. We begin taking the olives again, reverently, as if counting prayer beads, thumbs and forefinger moving along branches and over the round pebbles of fruit, pulling through the leaves, olives raining down. Reach, pull, bend, lift; these movements are imprinted on my brain like an archetype, a ritual known to humans since the first tree appeared in the first garden.

I watch Bernhard's dark, bristled hair bob through the high branches where he sits, trying to reach reluctant olives. He is an artist who came from Germany five years ago to live in the countryside, to paint and collect olives by day for cash. His Spanish is fluid, with a German lilt; he flattens vowels long at the ends of words rather than spitting them out as a Spaniard would. He says he paints landscapes; he makes fat, swirling strokes to form clouds and olive groves.

The tree is picked when only the leaves are left shimmering in the sun, no circles of olives spotting the branches dark. Manuel and Catherine lift the net from the upside of the hill to let the straggling fruit roll down; it roars quietly like the ocean in a conch shell. At the downhill part of the net, Bernhard unties the strings. He directs me to hold up one corner, the net heavy with olives, and I'm obliged to keep our work from streaming downhill in a great, bitter river.

By now, almost halfway through the day, this picking is done like a dance. Sometimes we switch roles, but no matter; someone does a job and the others do what's left, get the *cubo*, the bucket used to scoop fruit. It's shining in the sun; then it's in shadow when someone else leans over to pluck the large branches out.

I hold open an enormous burlap sack as Manuel pours in olives from the *cubo* we have filled. The bag grows fuller with each scoop until olives threaten to spill from the top. Bernhard shakes the sack to settle them, then ties the corners together. His face is already beaded with sweat when he hoists the sack to his shoulders in one graceful motion and walks uphill, his broad back one with the sack and the incline.

We lunch under a tree near the edge of the grove, away from our work. I unpack the garlicky green olives I have brought, and veryone groans. But we each take one anyway and nibble in communion. Manuel passes me a *granada*, a lusciously pink pomegranate, seeds spilling like forbidden fruit. He passes a chunk of bread to Bernhard, who has brought oranges, picked from the trees behind his house. They smell sweet as we rip them, the scent mingling with the dirt and olive oil on our palms and under our nails, and the juice is thirst-quenching in the hot Spanish sun.

Catherine has wine that she pours in a mug to share among us. I watch her pour, and I wonder if she gets lonely here in the village, if her nights are long.

When our bellies are full, our bodies growing languid in the heat of the day, Manuel announces it's time to pick the next tree. It feels good to be standing again, pumping my arms like pistons, the branches like udders of a cow that I milk, the olives pelting my tennis shoes and rolling down the net. Manuel bends to find his walking stick and whacks the tree for straggling olives. Bernhard reaches into the high branches. I untie the corners of the net. Catherine lifts the edge and watches her harvest cascade around her feet. She looks at me and her eyes shimmer, pleased at the olives that we have picked from her tree and will load into bags to take to the *molina*.

And whether her love returns or not, at Christmas she will make presents of her olive oil to friends, drop into the bottles long stems of the rosemary she's picked. And throughout the year, until the next harvest, the smell of her oil and the rosemary will waft from her kitchen and wind through the streets of this village that she now calls home.

THE AUSSIE WAY OF WANDERLUST

Tony Wheeler

erminal Wanderlust: It's one of the conditions of today that Douglas Coupland defined in *Generation X:* a state of being so disconnected to anywhere that everywhere is home, or might just as well be. I reckon I'm infected. I was born in Britain, grew up in Pakistan, the Bahamas, and the United States, with short interludes back in Britain, and now live in Australia, although recently there have been year-long interludes in France and the United States. Even when I am at home I'm typically away traveling for six months each year. So nowhere is really home; almost anywhere could be. Perhaps I can blame my personal wanderlust on my peripatetic upbringing—but could a whole nation get this affliction?

I've spent half a lifetime wondering who goes where, and the results of my surveys may be unscientific but they're certainly conclusive: Australians go everywhere. I scan the hotel registers in towns in Africa, I glance back through visitors' books in churches in southern India, I check who has gone scuba diving with a Red Sea dive operator, I add up who has checked into youth hostels along the Pennine Way in England. Everywhere it's the same story: more Australians than there should be. Come on, there are less than twenty million of them. If there's an Australian on the register there should be three Germans, seven Japanese, fifteen Americans. It's never that way.

One night, after the sound and light show at Chichén Itzá in Mexico, a dozen or so of us were left, sprawled on the grass, talking about Mayans, Mexico, and whatever else you talk about when you're in that great Mayan center. And then about where we'd been and where we were going. Mexico is not an Australian destination. Australia is not only a lot farther south of the border; it's also a dateline to the west, and there aren't lots of cheap flights to Mexico from Australia, as there are from Europe. Australia doesn't have a shared history with Mexico or enjoy constant Mexican influences in everyday life (from Taco Bell to Mexican beer to Mexican politics), as America does.

So why should three of the twelve Chichén Itzá travelers be Australians? Okay, twelve people in front of a Mayan pyramid doesn't make a statistically significant survey; this little nationality count really doesn't count. Except it is, it does. In fact, my homespun surveys and gut instinct are more than adequately backed up by hard statistics and clear indicators. On measurements ranging from per capita expenditure on international travel to number of passports held relative to population, Australians are always up toward the top of the charts.

Australia, like America, is a wide and varied land, offering plenty to attract the traveler. So why are Americans perfectly content to see America first, to explore their own country with, comparatively speaking, rarely a thought of setting foot abroad, while Australians seem intent on going everywhere before they give their homeland a second glance?

Perhaps the country's wanderlust dates to its European beginnings. Australia's European settlement, like America's, was relatively recent. It's surprisingly similar in other ways too—a pattern of sailing fleets bringing hardy settlers to a lightly populated country where they displaced the native peoples (often violently) and then did very well for themselves. The people on those sailing ships, however, were aboard for entirely different reasons. The new Americans were fleeing Europe, going in search of a new home with no intention of ever looking back. In contrast, Australia's convict settlers were being flung out from Europe, exiled to Australia against their will, with return home always uppermost in their minds. So perhaps that need to leave, that need to hit the road, to go somewhere, anywhere, everywhere, has been in the Australian psyche from the very start.

Or perhaps it's a more modern affliction, a product of modern media and information. Until the last twenty-five years, when an explosion of Australian movies, books, fashion, and music defined for the first time a real Australian culture, the whole country was said to suffer from "cultural cringe," an overwhelming feeling of being culturally second-rate. To make it meant going abroad, because success achieved in Australia, even if it was exactly the same sort of success as one might find in Europe or America, would inevitably be tainted, second best.

As a result, a whole generation of Australians moved to London, turned that city's Earls Court district into "Kangaroo Valley," and ended up behind the steering wheel, driving half the popular culture of Britain. Just look at Rupert Murdoch and his international media grab; it had its takeoff outside Australia, in Britain, and there were plenty of Aussie foot soldiers ready and waiting in Fleet Street to staff his army when the call to arms came. Today the culinary revolution that has swept through London, leading many food critics to opine that the food's better there than in Paris, has partly been led by Australian chefs, who run the kitchens of many of the city's best restaurants.

Or perhaps it's simple mileage that drives Australians to become the world's premier long-term travelers, the "tyranny of distance," as the Australian historian Geoffrey Blainey has called it. Flying to Europe from Australia takes a solid twenty-four hours; even the most direct flight to the U.S. West Coast involves at least twelve hours aloft. To most overseas destinations from Australia, a flight of at least seven or eight hours is a short hop, a mere kangaroo skip for an outward-bound Aussie. When getting anywhere takes that long, there's clearly an incentive to stay away longer; you don't take a weekend in Europe when it takes the whole weekend just to get there.

Accordingly, a year off between education and employment became an Australian norm, like the gentlemanly European tour of the Victorian era. Grab a representative bunch of Australians and a surprising percentage of them will have spent a year or more abroad at some point. In this activity the Australians may have simply been a bit ahead of the game, for today the expression "gap year" has found its way into the English dictionary, to signify the year between school and university when young Brits set out to see the world. Reportedly, even in America, a "blank" year or two on your CV, once looked upon as a sure sign of unreliability and lack of application, is now starting to be seen as a sign of adventurousness and a wider understanding of the outside world.

Or perhaps Australian wanderlust goes further back than modern travel, back beyond the cultural cringe and the tyranny of distance, even back before Captain Cook, the First Fleet of convicts, and the other pioneering Europeans. After all, the term "walkabout" just puts an English spin onto an Aboriginal concept. Right from the beginning, European observers noted the native Australians' tendency to put down tools and head off somewhere else for an indeterminate period of time for inscrutable reasons. Perhaps from the very beginning the whole island continent was deeply infected with Terminal Wanderlust, waiting to be passed on to the next foolish arrivals.

Or perhaps it's the landscape. When first-time visitors ask me where to go in Australia, I always point toward the Outback. Yes, the cities can be beautiful, but there are other beautiful cities in the world. Yes, the Great Barrier Reef is marvelous, but there are other coral reefs. There's only one Outback, and Australians have a strangely passionate but arm's-length affair with it; it's celebrated in every medium, from songs like "Waltzing Matilda" to movies

like *Crocodile Dundee* to bookshops full of photographic essa
The passion and the celebrations are, however, edged with cau
tion. The Outback is like an exciting but vaguely dangerous lover
who might just roll over and stab you in the back some night.
There's always a distance about it, an alien, vaguely unsettling,
vaguely feral atmosphere. In fact, you don't really love it; the relationship has a touch of love-hate. The green fields and ordered
landscapes of Europe seem infinitely more secure, reliable, and
trustworthy.

Or perhaps linking Terminal Wanderlust with Australia overlooks the most glaring example of all: There's a small country
slightly to the southeast of Australia—human population about
three million, sheep population about twenty times as great—
where they really have Terminal Wanderlust bad.

WHEN WE'RE GOING TO BE THERE

Chris Colin

f I have a son I will not name him Robert Redford and if I have a daughter I will not name her Dolly Parton. These are good names, but they're taken. I will not buy a TV, either, when I have children, though I will also discourage the development of certain "alternative" hobbies, particularly those that could be said to fall under the unfortunate "circus" rubric: juggling, unicycling, balloon-animal tying, and ringside announcing. Pratfalls are fine if realistic/funny.

Also: no spanking, firearms, curfews, honor roll bumper stickers, conspicuous consumption, "European-style" utensil use, gift certificates, bumper stickers that make fun of honor roll bumper stickers, smooth jazz, insensitivity, sensitivity, trench coats, mediocrity, or snack packs. I don't have children or a wife, but one day I might have both. I've taken to planning.

The clearest plan, the elaborate one with the fringed sash, is a car trip. I see it in 3-D, can describe it with the most suggestive of adjectives. The premise is simple: Outside the San Francisco Bay area, we drive and drive. (This trip, I should mention, is just the two kids and me—my wife, tired from performing all that brain

surgery, will stay home for some R&R. We will miss her but
face the road robustly, shiningly.)

We'll leave at dusk. My kids, once they exist, will pack sweat
shirts and toothbrushes and milk jugs full of water. We'll put sandwiches in a bag, and take care not to put the bag under the milk
jugs.

Our drive takes us along Route 80, mostly. It's a brief scratch on
the map east of San Francisco. We'll drive, say, a little past Reno,
then head back. We will head back wiser, better, taller.

It's a boiler when we leave, our own sweaty Oakland sticking all
over itself. We'll put towels on the car seats and keep wiping our
foreheads with our T-shirts. Which we'll soon throw way in the
back. Which will hold not only a spare tire but a flashlight and
flares, because by this point in my life I'll be responsible. Our lives
will be built on a foundation of adventure, uncertainty, and well-
maintained, frequently tested safety devices.

Route 80 pokes out from Oakland like a fuse. Through a wiring
of crisscrossed freeways, wide hot avenues, and great empty
blocks, past metal fabrication plants, skinny hot-dog huts, and
cold-storage facilities, one drives and drives and then one is simply
among fields.

As with the leaving of any city, we'll feel free and a little empty.
We will not be people who don't look back. Our excitement, like
all excitement, will contain a kernel of regret. Where are we
going? Will we ever go back? Why did we leave?

But we'll not stop. Moving east from the Bay Area, past Vallejo,
past Sacramento, brings one to acres of grass. It's flat. Back along
the coast, it's not flat. The feeling that accompanies the drive inland
is that of stepping off a Ferris wheel, this new steady ground just a
little unsettling. Anything can happen when the ground's flat.

Here is something crucial to our outing: These kids come, originally, from the East Coast. It will be arranged in their lives so that the
West is (1) new and (2) seen against the East. To begin in the West and
migrate the other way is like starting with the Concorde and then
moving to the stagecoach. No sense in raising backwards children.

having begun their lives thus, I will point confidently to the wide open of inland California and they'll think, Oooh. It's not the wide open of, say, Nebraska or Arizona. Those places look similar enough, but one understands them differently. They are the in-between; California is the finish. Who, in matters of rope or snakes, cares about the middle? One gathers up the ends. So this is ordinary, pretty wide open, yes, but just beyond is a cliff and then simply sea, at one time gotten to tremendously via horse, starvation, confusion, death, and curiosity.

We'll listen to music and like how it organizes the sights around us. That passing tree makes sense with those violins, etc. We'll note the difference between day and night driving. One is visual, the other moody, both boring after a while. I'll tell them stories about hobos or pioneers. We'll talk about school, friends, pets. (I will also take occasional breaks from warmth and affection just so they don't get too comfortable—they'll thank me later when they realize an occasionally distant father helped them develop a useful rebellious streak.) We'll turn off the music and tell fart jokes.

Did I mention my kids are little? These are no teenagers—this is a trip for youngsters, who still get amazed by streetlights and who are too young to suspect their father of micromanaging their early impressions. I will coordinate their experiences like a tyrant and they will happily chew their sandwiches.

Travel is useful to children. It engages the senses, leaves its little scenes unpackaged, and, most important, shows what the road from Oakland to Nevada looks like. The long gray asphalt line will stick itself in their pea brains, revealing its heart years later when appropriate.

Travel is useful to children, and consequently mine will resist its virtue until they are blue. But it's smooth sailing after that, and then the noticing begins: rabbits on hills, a silo, two brown houses, hay, a person walking, a hat blowing off. Skies with clouds, skies without clouds, skies that have birds that have field mice. Then the inside landscape, just as prominent: the rattle of the steering wheel, the receipt on the floor, the stained seat, the carrot rolling around in the back.

We'll have the hang of the road and travel with rhythm, there's a bag in a tree we'll see if it looks pretty. A fallen bird's nest with orphans, along the road will receive help and whispered tenders. A rodeo in Sacramento? Too late, we already saw the one in Hayward.

"What is it all about?" Child Number 1 will ask. He/she is the precocious one. "What makes the flies fly and the dreams dream?"

At this I will produce a rock from my pocket. Quartz, milky and river-smoothed. They will examine it, hold its clearness up to the sun, lose it in the seat or toss it out the window. The question about life will have been ignored. Suckers. My future children are great suckers, and they are glad.

And this: We are not sissies. We might even shout that, dangerously, when people least expect it. To prove it to ourselves I'll teach them the smashing of bottles after dark, Bad Seed–style, for when the bruisers want to mix it up. I'll tell them about the twist you give as you bring it against the car fender, so that the crack doesn't shoot toward the neck and cut the hand. I'll offer some lines— "Want some of this?" (indicate bottle) or "Hey you! Want some of this?" (bottle)—but let them know they're free to come up with their own.

More driving. Driving and driving. Not always talking. More questions than answers. Depth! Reverence, irreverence. The sun setting, dirtying everything in thick yellows. Then the moon. A shooting star later. Pulling over onto the shoulder, kids peeing in ditches, Dear God please nobody hit our car from behind. Back on the road. Questions about peeing, about ditches.

"What's that?" they'll ask later, before the road to Carson City. They'll be looking at the blinking tower two hundred yards off the freeway. Only it will be too dark to see the tower, so they'll just be looking at the blinking. This is my favorite part of this road. It is reason enough to have kids and take them for a long drive. This tower, in my mind, is somehow about travel.

"I don't know what it is," I'll say, because I don't. We'll watch the white-blue lights pulse—they come on slow and intense, the brightness of lightning with the torpor of cold—and consider their

...sion of the flats. The flats, every three seconds, spread from ...ackness to a glowing sweep, then go black again.

We will appreciate most the lack of coercion so rare in spectacle: This is not commerce—the tower advertises no company, suffers no product association. It is not art—it doesn't beg us to hypothesize, does not claim any creative dominion over the evening. It's a thing to see, if we want.

In Reno we'll stop because it's Reno—flashing of a different kind here. We will be astonished to find a city about luck, and one that appears to have none. At midnight, the grocery stores and gas stations are not empty. They bing and rattle, slot machines on every wall in every retail spot on every block. People who should be tired hunch over the lemons and cherries and sometimes break even. We will witness the occasional win—$200? $400?—and feel the winners' thrill, even though they themselves regard it with the blankness of paper.

Are my kids brats? I hope not, but they're allowed. Late in the drive, they can say, This sucks, we're bored, Mom buys us hot dogs. I'll buy them hot dogs. Someone will sit in mustard by Verdi. In Nixon, forty-five minutes beyond Reno, our course run, we'll most likely turn around. We'll have dangled out aimlessly a while, but now we'll point home decidedly.

Travel is hard. With any luck we'll lead the kind of lives that parlay the meat of travel into the stillest of days: Sitting at home on the radiator watching the guy mow his lawn across the street can be travel. We'll take our hard-earned information home. We'll remember why getting home is good.

Because our wife/mother is a brain surgeon, and because the future is bright and flashing.

A Geographical Index

Index

About the Contributors

ISABEL ALLENDE was born in Peru and raised in Chile, and currently resides in California. Among her books are numerous works of fiction, including *The House of the Spirits*, *The Infinite Plan*, *Of Love and Shadows*, and *Eva Luna*, and the autobiographical family memoir *Paula*. Her most recent book is *Daughter of Fortune*, a novel.

BILL BARICH is the author of seven books, among them *Traveling Light*, *Big Dreams: Into the Heart of California*, *Carson Valley*, and *Crazy for Rivers*.

WENDY BELCHER is a freelance writer who grew up in Ghana and Ethiopia. *Honey from the Lion: An African Journey* won several prizes, including the PEN Martha Albrand finalist for first book of nonfiction and the Washington State Governor's Award. She lives in Los Angeles and teaches at UCLA. She can be reached at wbelcher@ucla.edu.

BILL BELLEVILLE is an award-winning environmental writer and documentary filmmaker who has traveled widely to research projects in the White Sea of Russia, the Amazon, and Australia's Great Barrier Reef. His work has been distributed by The New York Times Syndicate and has also appeared in *Sports Afield* and *Sierra*. His most recent book is *River of Lakes: A Journey on Florida's St. Johns River*. He is currently at

ok about a Discovery Channel oceanographic expedition
avid kayaker, diver, and hiker, he lives in Sanford, Florida.

. BILLINGS is a columnist for the *Saint Paul* (Minnesota) *Pioneer*
. Her writing has also appeared in *The New York Times Magazine,*
utside, Mademoiselle, and *Women's Sports and Fitness,*

Po BRONSON is the author of two novels. His most recent book is a
work of nonfiction, *The Nudist on the Late Shift and Other True Tales of
Silicon Valley*. He is also the screenwriter for two movies in development, *I.P.O.* and *Dotcomarama*. He is a founder of The Grotto, a coop-
erative of writers and filmmakers in San Francisco. More of his work
can be found at www.pobronson.com.

TIM CAHILL is the author of seven books, including *Jaguars Ripped My
Flesh, Pecked to Death by Ducks, Pass the Butterworms,* and *Dolphins*. He is
the coauthor of the Academy Award–nominated short documentary
The Living Sea and the critically acclaimed IMAX movie *Everest*. He
lives in Montana.

CHRIS COLIN lives in Oakland, California, and is an associate editor at
Salon.com.

DOUGLAS CRUICKSHANK is the editor of the People site on Salon.com.

DAVID DOWNIE, Paris correspondent for Salon.com, washed ashore on
the banks of the Seine in 1986. Since then, his articles on European
culture, food, and travel have appeared in leading American and
British magazines and newspapers. His nonfiction books include
Un'Altra Parigi, The Irreverent Guide to Amsterdam, and *Enchanted
Liguria: A Celebration of the Culture, Lifestyle and Food of the Italian
Riviera,* with photography by Alison Harris. In 1999 he published his
first novel, *Towering Folly: La Tour de l'Immonde.*

CARLOS FUENTES is Mexico's greatest novelist and has served as his
country's ambassador to France. His books include *The Old Gringo,
The Death of Artemio Cruz,* and, most recently, *The Years with Laura
Diaz*. He lives in Mexico City and London.

LAURA FRASER is a writer who lives in San Francisco. Her book on her Italian affair, which continued in San Francisco, London, the Aeolian Islands, and Morocco, will be published in 2001.

LAURIE GOUGH is the author of *Kite Strings of the Southern Cross: A Woman's Travel Odyssey*, published in Canada as *Island of the Human Heart*. The book won *Foreword* magazine's silver medal for best travel book of the year in the United States. Gough lives in Ontario, Canada.

KARL TARO GREENFELD is a staff writer for *Time* magazine. He also writes for *GQ, Condé Nast Traveler,* and *Outside,* in addition to Salon.com. His first book, *Speed Tribes: Days and Nights with Japan's Next Generation,* explored the dark side of Japanese youth culture. His essay for this anthology was written as part of his next book, a tour of Asian subcultures and pop cultures.

JEFF GREENWALD is the author of four books, including *Shopping for Buddhas* and *The Size of the World*. He has appeared in a wide range of magazines, from *Details* to *New Scientist,* and as a guest star on *News Radio*. A resident of Oakland, California, Jeff divides his time between Asia and California. He can be reached through his website, www.jeffgreenwald.com.

TARAS GRESCOE has made a specialty of writing about foreign cultures for *The Times* (London), the *Chicago Tribune Magazine, Saveur, Wired,* and *The Independent*. Born in Toronto, he spent four years in Paris in the early nineties. For the past three years he has lived in Montreal, where he is a contributor to *National Geographic Traveler* and *The New York Times*. His first book is *Sacré Blues: An Unsentimental Journey Through Contemporary Quebec*.

SUSAN HACK began traveling at sixteen and has lived in Africa, Europe, and the Middle East. A contributing editor at *Condé Nast Traveler* magazine, she is currently based in Cairo and Paris.

JAMES D. HOUSTON has explored the histories and cultures of the western United States and the Asia/Pacific region in seven novels and several nonfiction works. His books include *Continental Drift, In the Ring of Fire:*

A *Pacific Journey*, and *The Last Paradise*, which received a 1999 American Book Award from the Before Columbus Foundation. His essays about Hawaii have appeared in *The New Yorker*, *The New York Times*, *The Utne Reader*, *Honolulu*, and *Manoa*. He lives in Santa Cruz, California.

PICO IYER is a longtime essayist for *Time* magazine, and the author of six books, including *Video Night in Kathmandu*, *The Lady and the Monk*, and, most recently, *The Global Soul*. He lives in suburban Japan.

AMANDA JONES is a travel writer and photographer. Her work has appeared in *The Sunday Times* (London), the *Los Angeles Times*, *Travel & Leisure* magazine, the *San Francisco Examiner*, *Vogue Entertaining and Travels*, *Expedia*, and various other international publications. A New Zealander by birth, she now lives in the San Francisco Bay Area.

BETH KEPHART's first book, *A Slant of Sun: One Child's Courage*, was a 1998 National Book Award nonfiction finalist, a Salon.com Best Book, and a winner of the Leeway Grant, among other honors. Her second nonfiction book, *Into the Tangle of Friendship: A Memoir of the Things That Matter*, won a 2000 National Endowment for the Arts grant, and she is now at work completing a novel, *Small Damages*, that takes place in Andalusia, her favorite region of the world. Kephart's essays, reviews, and articles are featured frequently in magazines nationwide, and she takes great pleasure from sitting down with her son, his friends, and a pile of books, and reading the classics together.

DAVID KOHN is coordinating producer at CBSNews.com, where he creates Web sites for several news programs. He also works as a freelance writer, covering a variety of topics, from Neanderthals to hot dog-eating champions. He loves eating, traveling, basketball, taking photographs, and his wife, not necessarily in that order.

DAWN MACKEEN is a senior writer for Salon.com.

PETER MAYLE was born in England, and has at various times lived in Barbados, New York, the Bahamas, and Long Island, before settling in Provence, where he plans to stay put. His books include *A Year in Provence*, *Toujours Provence*, *Hotel Pastis*, *Chasing Cezanne*, and *Encore Provence*.

LUCY MCCAULEY is a freelance writer based in Dallas and Boston. Her work has appeared in the anthologies *Travelers' Tales: Spain, Women in the Wild*, and *A Woman's Path*. In addition, her essays have appeared in such publications as *The Atlantic Monthly*, the *Los Angeles Times*, *Harvard Review*, and Salon.com. She has taught travel-writing workshops in Geneva and New York, and is a contributing editor at *Fast Company* magazine.

DON MEREDITH's travel essays have appeared in *Poets & Writers, Image*, Salon.com, the *San Francisco Examiner*, and the *Texas Review*. He lives on Lamu Island, Kenya, and is a contributing editor for *Executive* magazine, which is based in Nairobi. His most recent book is *Where the Tigers Were: Travels through Literary Landscapes*.

LISA MICHAELS is a contributing editor at *The Threepenny Review* and the author of *Split: A Counterculture Childhood*, a *New York Times* Notable Book of the Year. Her first novel, *Grand Ambition*, will be published in 2001.

JAN MORRIS is an Anglo-Welsh writer living in Wales. Her forty-odd books have included works about the rise and decline of the British Empire, and about countries and cities around the world, together with a couple of biographies, some autobiographical books, six books of collected travel essays, and a solitary novel.

Vaquita, a selection of EDITH PEARLMAN's stories, won the 1996 Drue Heinz Prize for Literature. She has published more than one hundred stories in literary journals, anthologies, and national magazines. Her fiction has been included in the *O. Henry Prize Collection* and *Best American Short Stories*; translated into Swedish, Italian, and Japanese; and read on National Public Radio. Her nonfiction has appeared in *The Boston Globe, The Atlantic Monthly, The New York Times*, and *Smithsonian*, among other publications.

ROLF POTTS began writing "Vagabonding," a biweekly backpacker and adventure travel column, for Salon.com in April 1999. His writing has been chosen to appear in *Best American Travel Writing 2000*, and he has been interviewed on NPR. Potts's vagabonding adventures—which meander along an irreverent, postmodern approximation of Marco

Polo's route through Asia, Europe, and the Middle East—can be accessed at www.rolfpotts.com.

ALICIA REBENSDORF has been to East Africa twice, first as a student and later to conduct independent research on pop culture in Nairobi. She is currently a waitress in Oakland, California, and is beginning to pursue freelance writing. This piece was her first published article.

MARY ROACH writes and travels for *Discover, Wired, Outside,* and *Islands.* She is also a columnist for *Health* and lives in San Francisco.

MAXINE ROSE SCHUR is an award-winning author of books for young people as well as a travel essayist. Her essays have appeared in numerous publications, and she has twice won the Lowell Thomas Award for excellence in travel journalism. Her latest book, *Knocking at the Moonlit Door,* is a memoir of her journey around the world.

TANYA SHAFFER is a San Francisco–based writer and actress who has toured over forty cities in the United States and Canada with her solo shows, *Miss America's Daughters* and *Let My Enemy Live Long!,* and her play, *Brigadista.* Her work has also appeared in the anthology *A Woman's Passion for Travel.* She is currently completing *Somebody's Heart Is Burning,* a collection of stories based on her time in West Africa. She can be visited online at www.TanyaShaffer.com.

JEFFREY TAYLER is the author of *Siberian Dawn* and *Facing the Congo.* In addition to his work for Salon.com, he writes for *The Atlantic Monthly.* He lives in Moscow.

SALLIE TISDALE's most recent book is *The Best Thing I Ever Tasted: The Secret of Food.*

LINDSY VAN GELDER is chief writer for *Allure* magazine. She and Pamela Robin Brandt are coauthors of *Are You Two . . . Together? A Gay and Lesbian Guide to Europe* and *The Girls Next Door.*

With more than a little help from his wife, Maureen, TONY WHEELER founded Lonely Planet Publications in the early 1970s. From a kitchen-table guide to the era's "hippie trail" across Asia, Lonely Planet has grown to become one of the world's major travel publishers. Between trips, Wheeler lives in Melbourne, Australia.

SIMON WINCHESTER is the author of a dozen books, including *The Sun Never Sets, Korea, Pacific Rising, The River at the Center of the World,* and *The Professor and the Madman.* A native of England, Winchester has lived in Africa, India and Hong Kong and is currently a resident of New York. He writes for numerous publications and is the Asia-Pacific editor for *Condé Nast Traveler.*

BARRY YEOMAN is a freelance writer in Durham, North Carolina. His work has appeared in *Mother Jones, Redbook, Psychology Today, The Nation,* and many other national magazines.

Essay Credits

About the Editor

DON GEORGE writes Salon.com's weekly travel column, "Wanderlust," and was previously founder and editor of its award-winning travel site. Prior to joining Salon, he was the travel editor at the *San Francisco Examiner*, and then creator and producer of "The Don George Show" for America Online. He has also worked as a translator in Paris, a teacher in Athens, and a television talk-show host in Tokyo. He is cofounder and chairman of the Book Passage Travel Writers Conference, and frequently lectures around the world on travel writing and publishing. In the past quarter century, he has published more than five hundred articles and visited more than fifty countries. He lives with his wife and two children in the San Francisco Bay Area.